D0712303

Diversity
in the Great Unity

Spatial Habitus: Making and Meaning in Asia's Architecture
Edited by Ronald G. Knapp and Xing Ruan

House Home Family: Living and Being Chinese
Edited by Ronald G. Knapp and Kai-Yin Lo

Allegorical Architecture: Living Myth and Architectonics in Southern China
Xing Ruan

Chinese Architecture and the Beaux-Arts
Edited by Jeffrey W. Cody, Nancy S. Steinhardt, and Tony Atkin

Chinese Architecture and Metaphor: Song Culture in the Yingzao Fashi Building Manual
Jiren Feng

Original Copies: Architectural Mimicry in Contemporary China
Bianca Bosker

China's Contested Capital: Architecture, Ritual, and Response in Nanjing
Charles D. Musgrove

Architecture and Urbanism in Modern Korea
Inha Jung

The Hermit's Hut: Architecture and Asceticism in India
Kazi K. Ashraf

Architecturalized Asia: Mapping a Continent through History
Edited by Vimalin Rujivacharakul, H. Hazel Hahn, Ken Tadashi Oshima, and Peter Christensen

Chinese Architecture in an Age of Turmoil, 200–600
Nancy Shatzman Steinhardt

Kyoto: An Urban History of Japan's Premodern Capital
Matthew Stavros

Traces of the Sage: Monument, Materiality, and the First Temple of Confucius
James A. Flath

Modern Kyoto: Building for Ceremony and Commemoration, 1868–1940
Alice Y. Tseng

Diversity in the Great Unity: Regional Yuan Architecture
Lala Zuo

Diversity
in the Great Unity
Regional Yuan Architecture

Lala Zuo

spatial
habitus

University of Hawai'i Press
Honolulu

© 2019 University of Hawai'i Press
All rights reserved
Printed in the United States of America

24 23 22 21 20 19   6 5 4 3 2 1

Library of Congress Cataloging in Publication Data

Names: Zuo, Lala, author.
Title: Diversity in the great unity : regional Yuan architecture / Lala Zuo.
Other titles: Spatial habitus (Series)
Description: Honolulu : University of Hawai'i Press, [2019] | Series: Spatial
    habitus: making and meaning in Asia's architecture | Includes
    bibliographical references and index.
Identifiers: LCCN 2018061664 | ISBN 9780824877316 (cloth ; alk. paper)
Subjects: LCSH: Architecture—China—History—Song-Yuan dynasties, 960-1368.
Classification: LCC NA1543.4 .Z86 2019 | DDC 720.951/0902—dc23
LC record available at https://lccn.loc.gov/2018061664

University of Hawai'i Press books are printed on acid-free paper and meet
the guidelines for permanence and durability of the Council on Library Resources.

Jacket art: Composite drawing of Feilai Hall, Temple of the Eastern Peak.
Illustrations by the author.

Design by Nord Compo

For Jun

CONTENTS

Color plates follow page 150

ACKNOWLEDGMENTS

It is almost a miracle to me that my research is now complete and published as a book. This could not have been done without the help, support, and encouragement of the following people.

Beyond words to express is my deep gratitude to Nancy S. Steinhardt for her patient guidance, enthusiastic encouragement, and critical comments, from the manuscript's early stages to its transformation into a scholarly monograph. It could never have become a reality without her continuous and meticulous critiques of my writing, her handholding whenever the project encountered doubts and difficulties, and the inspiration I received from her lectures and publications as well as our conversations. She has emboldened me to reconsider Chinese architecture in different contexts and from differing perspectives and encouraged me to challenge long-standing ideas and arguments.

I would also like to express my earnest thanks to Sun Hua, Xu Yitao, and Li Zhirong for their decades of mentoring ever since I was an undergraduate at Peking University. The topic of this research was initially suggested by Professor Sun, and he provided me with valuable field-trip connections. My first ever field trip to survey architecture was supervised by Professors Xu and Li. My research journey into Chinese architecture could not have gone this far without their guidance and critiques throughout the years. My great appreciation also goes to my professors in the special program of Heritage Architecture at Peking University: Wang Guixiang, Wang Qiming, Nan Shunxun, Liu Quanyi, and Zhou Hongzhi. The training I received as an archaeologist and a historian at Peking University laid the foundation of my entire career in academia.

Advice given me by my professors at the University of Pennsylvania was a great help in completing this work. I thank Victor H. Mair and Frank L. Chance for reading my manuscript at an early stage and for their insightful comments. Especially, I am thankful to Professor Mair for his valuable suggestions in understanding and translating Buddhist texts. I would also like to thank Paul R. Goldin for his training in working with Chinese historical texts and Julie N. Davis, with her expertise in Japanese art and architecture, for her mentoring.

Special thanks are also due to the anonymous reviewers of this book for their constructive suggestions. In addition, I wish to acknowledge valuable comments of Tracy Miller and Delin Lai. It is always inspiriting and motivating to have discussions and conversations with them on numerous topics for research.

I owe the following people a great deal for their generosity in providing beautiful photos and drawings for this book: Zhang Jianwei, Huang Xiaofan, Zhao Yuanxiang, Cai Yukun, Wu Yunan, Luo Dengke, Gao Feng, and Li Xinjian. Especially, I thank Zhao Yuanxiang and Cai Yukun for sharing their up-to-date research and discoveries with me. I must also acknowledge Huang Shilin, who arranged living accommodations for me during my field trip in Sichuan and personally escorted me (along with his super nice driver) to several sites. Moreover, I am deeply grateful to the local administrators of the sites at Emei, Nanbu, Langzhong, Zitong, Lushan, and Meishan, who granted me unlimited access to those sites and generously shared their relevant records and documents with me. It would have been impossible to work on this project without their help.

As a non-native speaker of English, I would like to give a special thanks to Karen Vellucci and Aurelia Campbell for reading the entire manuscript, correcting my English, and editing at different stages. I also owe Zhao Lu and Kelsey Seymour thanks for their help with translations of classic Chinese.

My great appreciation also goes to my fellow classmates and friends at Peking University with whom I worked in the classroom and during numerous field trips. I could not have accomplished much in my later research without their decades of support and friendship.

My graduate program community at the University of Pennsylvania provided me with support and inspiration. My research and intellectual maturity have benefited from many seminar sessions, graduate student colloquiums, lunch conversations, coffee chats, and e-mail correspondences with them. I am especially grateful to Alexandra Harrer, Aurelia Campbell, Morita Miki, Zhang Jianwei, Zhao Lu, and Ren Sijie, who gave me advice and help for this book. Special thanks go to Tse Wai Kit Wicky, who suggested the book's main title.

I would also like to thank the Provost's Office at Swarthmore College for providing me with research grants to cover expenses while I was working on the manuscript, and my wonderful colleagues there who gave me help and support with my teaching and research. Special thanks go to Alan Berkowitz, who passed away several years ago. His support and friendship will never be forgotten.

I owe my colleagues at the United State Naval Academy appreciation for their support and help in completing this manuscript: my department chairs, Clementine Fujimura and Thomas Wagener; my mentor, Joseph J. Gwara; and my colleagues in the Chinese program, Fangyuan Yuan and Wenze Hu. I also want to extend my gratitude to the Dean's Office for their financial support. I thank Reza Malek-Madani and Karyn Sproles for their guidance in acquiring the publication grant.

I cannot express enough thanks to Ronald G. Knapp and Xing Ruan, editors of the Spatial Habitus series, for being encouraging and patient ever since I first submitted my book proposal. They carefully reviewed my manuscript and offered me invaluable suggestions. I would also like to thank Stephanie Chun, my acquisition editor at the University of Hawaiʻi Press, for her professional advice and her help with the logistics of submitting the manuscript. I also owe Barbara Folsom thanks for her professional editing.

It is a pleasure to thank my friends Rochelle and Eric Mayer for their moral support during difficult times in this journey.

Finally, my deep and sincere gratitude goes to my family for their continuous and unparalleled love, help, and support. I am forever indebted to my parents, who selflessly encouraged me to explore the world and gave me the freedom to choose the profession that I desired. I am grateful to my in-laws for babysitting and helping with a great deal of housework so I can focus on my work. And I owe particular thanks to a very special person, my husband, Jun, for his constant and unfailing love, support, and understanding. This work would not have been possible without his companionship during numerous field trips. He was always around at times when I feared this project was impossible to continue. Last, I thank my little boy, Kai, who was patient enough to wait to enter my life until after most of the manuscript was completed.

INTRODUCTION

This decade-long research journey had an unusual beginning. I conducted my first field trip in Sichuan in 2008 and completed it only days before the Sichuan earthquake (also known as Great Wenchuan earthquake) that hit on May 12, taking more than a hundred thousand lives. It was a narrow escape for me and my husband, Jun, who had thought he was on his honeymoon. I was also lucky, because many of the sites visited during my trip became unreachable for a long time after the earthquake, and some were severely damaged. Although many sites and buildings were eventually restored or rebuilt, I was very fortunate to have been able to document the buildings before then.

The coherence of the Chinese architectural system throughout history is rare and remarkable when compared to other forms of art. From the very beginning of Chinese civilization, timber-framed architecture was dominant in projects of great political and religious significance. As an embodiment of ancient Chinese civilization, it symbolized a hierarchical society ruled by Confucian orthodoxy.

Court-enforced building codes have a history almost as old as this architecture. The *Kaogongji* 考工記 (Records of examination of craftsman), published in the late Zhou (1100–221 BCE) or early Han (206 BCE–220 CE) dynasties, recorded architectural technology, building methods, and principles of imperial city planning.[1] The edict of *Yingshanling* 營繕令 (Rules of construction and repair),[2] enacted in the Tang dynasty (618–907), demonstrated how architecture was hierarchized. During the Northern Song (960–1127), the publication of *Yingzao fashi* 營造法式 (Building standards; hereafter *YZFS*)[3] explained how architecture was completely codified and modularized in almost every detail. Generally speaking, the *Kaogongji, Yingshanling,* and *YZFS* were quite similar in respect to one principle recorded in all three: regulation of the design of architecture based on the social rank of the occupant or the audience. Both the *Kaogongji* and the *YZFS* recorded how the modular system depended on the rank of the building, and in fact the author of the *YZFS* clearly stated that his work was "strictly" and "cautiously" based on the *Kaogongji.*[4]

Throughout history, such regulation of architecture as part of political power made Chinese architecture a highly standardized and modularized system. As Nancy Steinhardt argues, "as every period of disunion has shown,

Chinese architecture . . . is an aspect of civilization, sometimes a rare aspect, that can be counted on to be Chinese."[5] Using examples of Chinese architecture during the tenth century, when China was split during the Five Dynasties and Ten Kingdoms period, and later into Liao (907–1125) and Song, Steinhardt has argued convincingly that architecture made by both Han Chinese and non-Han Chinese during this period of disunion was in fact monocultural.

In contrast to the tenth century when China was multicentered, between 1279 and 1368 China was "unified" by an alien dynasty for the first time. The Mongol conquerors named their dynasty "Yuan" or "Dayuan," meaning "unity" or "great unity," which suggests their intention to rule China as a whole.[6] In terms of architecture, however, the Yuan dynasty is often considered a transitional period that was short-lived and not distinctive in itself.[7] This is largely because when the Mongols conquered and "re-unified" China, the rulers, whose lifestyle was mainly nomadic, showed no intention of creating a dynastic style of their own by regulating the design and construction of architecture. Despite the large-scale palatial structures constructed in their capital of Dadu (modern Beijing),[8] whose design was intentionally based on the Bianliang model of the Northern Song, Yuan architecture outside of Dadu demonstrated regionalism and diversity rather than unity in terms of artistic presentation, technique, and use of material.[9]

The absence of a distinctive dynastic style does not necessarily suggest that Yuan architecture was merely transitional and not significant. On the contrary, the diversity of Yuan architecture that will be discussed here is demonstrated as significant in explaining a major transformation of Chinese architecture from the Song to the Ming-Qing periods. In the 1930s, Liang Sicheng defined the Song dynasty as a period of "elegance" and the Ming-Qing dynasties as a period of "rigidity." These two definitions, from a modern scholar's perspective, suggest a strong transformation in aesthetic values. As I will argue in this book, however, the transformation was in fact a result of changes in structural principles—changes that were caused by the complex social and political transitions from Song to Ming. Yuan architecture, which was diversified and regionalized, is the key to finding out why and how such a transformation happened.[10]

Because of a number of scholarly publications in English concerning the history of construction during the Yuan empire, Western audiences often are familiar with the buildings of Shangdu (Xanadu), an earlier capital of Khubilai Khan, and of Dadu, built by Khubilai Khan and his Chinese advisers.[11] Fu Xinian has tried to reconstruct the imperial palaces in Dadu based on descriptions in historical literature.[12] Fu generalizes that the "architectural style"[13] of the Yuan palaces in Dadu was based on those in Zhongdu, capital of the Jin dynasty (1115–1234), and Bianliang, capital of the Northern Song.[14]

Although no Yuan timber-framed building has been found in modern Beijing, Dening (Virtuous Tranquility) Hall 德寧殿 in the Temple to the Northern

Peak 北嶽廟 complex located in Quyang, Hebei province, about 250 kilometers west of Beijing, serves as "the closest surviving example of what architecture in Kublai Khan's imperial city should have looked like."[15] Dening Hall was built in the late 1260s under the imperial patronage of Khubilai Khan. Therefore, the structural details of the building highlight the standard that was equivalent to the imperial palaces later built in Dadu. Another article by Steinhardt, "Toward the Definition of a Yuan Dynasty Hall," further identifies features that characterize Yuan architecture. In addition to Dening Hall, examples include the architecture at Yongle (Eternal Joy) Palace 永樂宮, Guangsheng (Profound Victory) Monastery 廣勝寺, and several other Yuan buildings in north China (mainly in Shanxi and Hebei provinces). Steinhardt argues that these Yuan structures in north China follow the pre-Yuan system and "are more similar in structural details to earlier architecture ... than to building of the Ming and Qing dynasties." In sum, English-language publications about Yuan architecture or construction projects have focused on the imperial capitals and surviving buildings located in north China.

As for Chinese scholarship on Yuan architecture, a few Chinese scholars have summarized the significance of Yuan (timber-framed) architecture in their publications. In his article published in 1979, Zhang Yuhuan suggested that Yuan timber-framed architecture developed based on Song timber-framed architecture; many of the details directly corresponded with the YZFS. He also admitted, however, that there were some new features in Yuan timber-framed buildings, such as the eliminated-column structure (jianzhuzao 減柱造) and the big-architrave style (da'eshi 大額式); he still acknowledged that the origins of these two features were found in Jin timber-framed architecture. Yuan timber-framed buildings were probably unique only in their building materials—many wooden pieces used in Yuan buildings were unprocessed and retained their natural shapes. Zhang was correct in pointing out these two distinctive features of Yuan timber-framed architecture, but he failed to mention any stylistic diversity among different regions.

In a volume on Yuan-Ming architecture edited by Pan Guxi and others, the differences between Yuan timber-framed architecture in north and south China were explored. According to those authors, both the skill in carpentry and the artistic presentation of this period drastically transformed the architecture, especially in the column-and-beam system and the modular measurement of the bracket components. Artistically, Chinese timber-framed architecture transformed from a luxuriant to a simplistic style during the Yuan dynasty. Such development is symbolized by the decorative members (such as the bracket sets) that originally had some structural function, then became differentiated and separated from the structural members. In general, these scholars believe that Yuan architecture in the north developed out of Jin architecture, whereas Yuan architecture in the south was based on Song architecture. In this statement, we can see that the difference between the south and north has been considered by some scholars. Nevertheless, this does not hold true when we consider Sichuan part of south China. The situation in the south along the Yangzi (Yangtze) River is much more complicated.[16]

There have certainly been changes in Yuan (timber-framed) architecture as a whole over time. Most remarkable is the downgrading of the measurement of bracket sets, which is part of the general trend of the development of Chinese timber-framed architecture. Here, however, the focus is on regional traditions, which can be observed in the Yuan period for the first time.

This book consists of five chapters. The first two discuss Yuan architecture across dynasties and regions. Chapter 1 explores the trans-dynastic transformation of architecture from the Song to the Ming (1368–1644) dynasty. Despite the large-scale construction in the capital Dadu, the Yuan court never had the intention of regulating architecture nationwide as its predecessor, the Song, had done, or as its successor, the Ming, eventually would do. Yet, extant architecture and historical texts have verified that characteristics of the dynastic style of the Song remained in Yuan architecture and aspects of Yuan influenced Ming architecture. This chapter focuses on how the legacy of Song architecture remained in Yuan architecture, and how the diversified Yuan architecture inspired Ming builders and was later incorporated into the Ming dynastic style.

Chapter 2 offers an analysis of Yuan timber-framed architecture in three macro-regions: north China (now Hebei, Shanxi, and Shaanxi provinces), the Upper Yangzi, and the Lower Yangzi. Yuan architecture in north China has been studied comprehensively and surveyed during recent decades. In contrast to the few more than a dozen Yuan timber-framed buildings that have been found in the south, hundreds have been discovered in the north. This chapter will explain how regional traditions were generated under different pre-Yuan regimes and developed independently, without central control, during the Yuan dynasty. In addition to pictures and architectural drawings, statistical tables and charts will be used to analyze the modular system and the scale of architecture geographically and chronologically.

Chapters 3 through 5 present twenty case studies of Yuan architecture along the Yangzi River in south China. Discussions of most of these Yuan buildings have never been published in English. In chapter 3 ten Yuan buildings in the Sichuan basin of the Upper Yangzi are studied. Chapter 4 explores five examples of Yuan architecture in Zhejiang, Jiangsu, and Shanghai Municipality. Chapter 5 examines Yuan architecture that incorporates copper or stone. Based on textual and archaeological evidence as well as my on-site research, the construction history, religious affiliation, and architectural details of each building are examined. Textual evidence is derived predominately from local gazetteers and inscriptions found in or on the buildings, as well as a few travel logs and personal journals. Other evidence includes photographs, drawings, measurements, and so on, many of which were collected on-site by the author.[17] A glossary of Chinese architectural terms widely used in Song and Ming-Qing literature follows the conclusion.

This book is not a survey of Yuan architecture, or of architecture and construction under the Mongols. Its purpose is as a regional study based on on-site surveys from a place and period in China where they were possible. Every building studied here has a firm Yuan date. Admittedly, the twenty buildings studied here are outnumbered by the close to two hundred Yuan buildings in north China; yet their significance should not be underrated. Their representativeness is determined by their broad geographic distribution, which spans the entire reaches of the Yangzi River, as well as by their scarcity. They are the only Yuan buildings remaining in that region.

In addition to in-depth case studies of individual buildings based on fieldwork, this book also attempts to contextualize architecture in the social and political history of the Yuan dynasty. Through examining the diversity of architecture during that time in regions other than the capital, the division of regional traditions, especially those in the south, are shown to have contributed to the transformation of dynastic styles from Song to Ming. I discuss how the traditionally defined "Han-Chinese" architecture, represented by the architecture of a dynasty such as Song and Ming, reacted to the social and political changes of the Yuan. Predominately, the traditional belief that Han-Chinese architecture was coded, uniformed, and controlled by the central government did not occur during the Yuan, when architecture built by the Han-Chinese, not by the Mongol authorities, was regionalized and diversified in terms of both the timber construction system and the building materials. The regional study conducted here will illustrate that "regional traditions" in architecture became more visible in Yuan than in any other period in China's history. Although the primary focus is on the technical evolution of surviving Yuan architecture, I hope that this book may contribute to a reevaluation of Chinese society with regard to the cultural diversity that thrived under the rule of the Mongols.

CHAPTER 1
YUAN ARCHITECTURE
A Transition from the Song to the Ming

In his first English-language survey of Chinese architectural history, Liang Sicheng used the word "elegance" to describe the architecture that was built between 1000 and 1400, including the Song, Jin, and Yuan dynasties. Liang stated that Song builders introduced "a style characterized by elegance and refinement."[1] For the period of the Ming and Qing dynasties, however, he used the word "rigidity" to define their architectural styles. Liang believed that "there appeared, principally in the official architecture of the court, a style of marked departure from the tradition of the Song and Yuan dynasties," and "the change is very abrupt as if some overwhelming force had turned the minds of the builders toward an entirely new sense of proportion."[2]

This critique by Liang in the early twentieth century set the tone for the study of Chinese architectural history for many decades. In a 2002 English-language survey of Chinese architecture, Song architecture is defined as "more artistic, exquisite, elegant, poetic and self-conscious than previous dynasties had aspired to create."[3] As for Ming architecture, although the word "rigidity" now is considered somewhat arbitrary, if not harsh, contemporary scholars often use "simplicity" in addition to "rigidity" to signify the departure from the Song style. On the one hand, Ming emperors tried to revive the Song tradition by institutionalizing architecture; on the other, Ming architecture presents a complete change from Song, at least judging from its artistic presentation. Although in the early twentieth century, Liang thought this transformation had been "very abrupt,"[4] this has proved to be completely unjustified as more and more examples of Yuan architecture have been discovered. Liang's far-reaching labels that emphasize the artistic presentation of Song and Ming architecture involuntarily undervalue the technical aspect of the evolution. To understand Yuan architecture that was diversified in terms of timber construction is the key to understanding the major transition from the Song to Ming architecture beyond the surface details.

This chapter demonstrates how the legacy of Song architecture lived on in Yuan, and how Ming architecture and its architectural institution inherited and reunified the diversified regional styles of the Yuan dynasty. To explain these stylistic changes, this chapter focuses on the differences in principles of design and in details of construction during each dynasty. The first two sections provide brief overviews of Song and Ming architecture respectively; key features in Yuan architecture that were responsible for the Song to Ming transition—plan, columniation, roof framing, and bracket sets—are discussed. In the conclusion, Yuan architecture will be placed in the context of the history of Chinese architecture from 1000 to 1500, which will lead to further discussions in the subsequent chapters.

SONG ARCHITECTURE

The Song dynasty includes the Northern Song (960–1127) and the Southern Song (1127–1276). The Northern Song located their capital in Bianliang, modern Kaifeng, Henan province; and the Southern Song's capital was at Lin'an, modern Hangzhou, Zhejiang province. After the Song-Jin Wars in 1125 and 1127, the Song lost their territories in north China to the Jurchen, who in 1115 had established the Jin dynasty (1115–1234). Those lost territories were mostly north of the Huai River and the Han River, including today's Hebei, Shandong, Henan, Shanxi, and Shaanxi provinces. Therefore, before 1127, Song architecture could be found in both the north and the south; after 1127, however, it was only in the south. Although architecture of the Northern and Southern Song differed according to region and period, the main principles of architecture laid out by both Song courts remained consistent.

According to an article published in 1994 by an official from the Provincial Administration of Cultural Heritage in Shanxi, there are sixty-two extant examples of Song architecture in Shanxi province.[5] In addition, based on my own research in 2007, thirteen Song buildings have been discovered and dated outside of Shanxi province. In 2013, China's Guojia wenwuju 國家文物局 (State Administration of Cultural Heritage, hereafter SACH) announced its seventh list of national cultural heritage sites and included three additional Song buildings in Shanxi.[6] Although the number probably will increase in the future, now there are seventy-eight Song buildings. Of these structures, more than 80 percent are located in Shanxi province, and more than 90 percent are in north China. Therefore, more than 90 percent were built during the Northern Song. Only seven buildings were discovered in south China, in Zhejiang, Jiangsu, Fujian, Guangdong, and Sichuan provinces. Among the remains in the south, four are dated to the Northern Song and three to the Southern Song.[7]

Although there are only a few Song buildings in south China, and buildings dated to the Southern Song are even fewer, the YZFS provides supplementary information that cannot be gleaned from the few extant buildings in the south. The history and background of compiling the YZFS helps to explain the relation between the YZFS and the architecture in south China during the Song dynasty.

The *YZFS*, often translated as "building standards," is the most complete extant textual record of Chinese architecture and building techniques. It was published in 1103 during the second year of the reign of Emperor Huizong 宋徽宗 (r. 1100–1126). The author, Li Jie 李诫, was an official of Jiangzuojian 將作監 (the Department for Palace Construction) of the Northern Song court. Based on his achievement in compiling this book, Li Jie later was promoted to the position of Superintendent of the Department for Palace Construction.[8]

The compilation of the *YZFS* was a time-consuming process that spanned the reigns of three emperors. Before the first official publication of the *YZFS* in 1103, an earlier version was initiated by Emperor Shenzong 宋神宗 (r. 1068–1077). This version was completed in 1091, in the sixth year of the reign of Emperor Zhezong 宋哲宗 (r. 1085–1100). However, Emperor Zhezong was not satisfied with the quality of the work and asked Li Jie to write a new edition in 1097. This version was completed in 1100 but was not published until 1103, during Huizong's reign.[9]

The idea to compile and publish the *YZFS* during the reigns of Emperor Shenzong and Emperor Zhezong was not only "a logical expansion of earlier building codes" but also "the result of the Wang Anshi Reform (1069–1074),"[10] an economic and political reform initiated by Wang Anshi 王安石 (1021–1086), the vice-premier, and supported by Emperor Shenzong. This reform was necessitated by a drop in state revenues, budget deficits accrued over many years, and nationwide inflation due to the long-standing confrontation between the Northern Song and the Liao (916–1125), the Khitan dynasty in the north.[11] It affected Northern Song agriculture, finance, military, education, and personnel selection.

Emperor Shenzong's initiation of the *YZFS* was an immediate reaction to Wang's reform.[12] The word *fashi* 法式 means "law" and "imperative," and was used in other legal documents during the Song dynasty. As Feng states in his monograph on the *YZFS*, "Zhezong's purpose in issuing an effective official building standard was to regulate building practices and prevent graft and waste" and "the central government's insistence on reforming state economic systems, strengthening central financial management, and achieving a strong empire was consistent from Shenzong, through Zhezong to Huizong's patronage of the *YZFS*."[13]

The main purpose of the *YZFS* was not to provide a technical reference but to regulate costs in building materials and manpower. Therefore, it should not be considered an honest documentation of all the architecture built prior to its publication but rather as an adapted version of Northern Song architecture conforming to the reformers' ideal. In his book, Feng also agrees that Li Jie may have made some adjustments in order to "legitimize" some building methods, and the *YZFS* "may have represented, to some extent, an artificial, authoritative ideal of the practical method."[14] Most likely, things that were not effective in terms of cost and that could not be easily regulated might not have been included in the book. These omissions may explain why there is not a single extant building of the Northern Song that was constructed exactly according to the specifications in the *YZFS*.

The *YZFS* was reprinted in Suzhou in 1145, the fifth year of the Shaoxing reign of the Southern Song, making the law easier to enforce during the period of the Southern Song in south China. Indeed, its influence lasted even beyond the Song dynasty in the south.[15] Moreover, many features that existed only in the architecture of the south were included in Li Jie's *YZFS*. This was probably a result of Li Jie's referring to the *Mujing* 木經 (Timberwork manual), a lost classical text on Chinese architecture, which was written by Yu Hao 喻浩, a native of Hangzhou, during the early years of the Northern Song.[16] During the late 900s, he was active in Bianjing, the capital of the Northern Song, as a master carpenter.[17] Therefore, although there were fewer architectural remains in the south, the *YZFS* supplemented the list with additional information about architecture in south China during both the Northern and the Southern Song.

There are two basic sources for Song architecture: the actual seventy-eight extant buildings and the *YZFS*, the latter serving as the primary source for its general features. The discussion here is supplemented by the inclusion of features that are commonly found in extant buildings, as long as they do not conflict with the information in the *YZFS*.

For individual Song buildings, the layout of the plan can be square, rectangular, cross-shaped, I-shaped, T-shaped, or even zigzag.[18] Architecture depicted in Song paintings is usually multistoried with many eaves. The nine-ridged roof, a roof type with the most ridges and slopes, was favored during the Song dynasty. Although most extant Song buildings do not have as much variation as was depicted in contemporary paintings, Moni Hall of Longxing Monastery 龍興寺摩尼殿 in Zhengding, Hebei province, is a good example of the artistic richness in Song architecture, exhibiting a complexity in layout and roof structure (fig. 1.1).[19]

Fig. 1.1. Moni Hall of Longxing Monastery, Zhengding, Hebei, 1052. (Photo courtesy of Wu Yunan.)

Early examples of the *jianzhuzao* 減柱造, "eliminated-column structure," a structural method whereby columns are eliminated to create more interior space, can be found in Song architecture in the north.[20] One of the earliest examples of the eliminated-column structure can be found in a Song dynasty building, the Sage Mother Hall (Shengmudian 聖母殿) of the Jin Shrine (Jinci 晉祠) (fig. 1.2).[21]

Early examples of the "displaced-column structure" (*yizhuzao* 移柱造), a structural method in which columns are relocated away from the original array of the columns, also created more space on the inside of a hall. They can be found in architecture of the Jin dynasty, a dynasty contemporaneous with the Southern Song. These include the Amitābha Hall (Mituodian 彌陀殿) of Chongfu (Venerating Blessing) Monastery 崇福寺 in Shuozhou, Shanxi, and the Mañjuśrī Hall (Wenshudian 文殊殿) in Foguang (Buddha Light) Monastery 佛光寺 on Mount Wutai in Shanxi. The Amitābha Hall is also one of a few Jin buildings that used the eliminated-column structure and the displaced-column structure at the same time (fig. 1.3).[22]

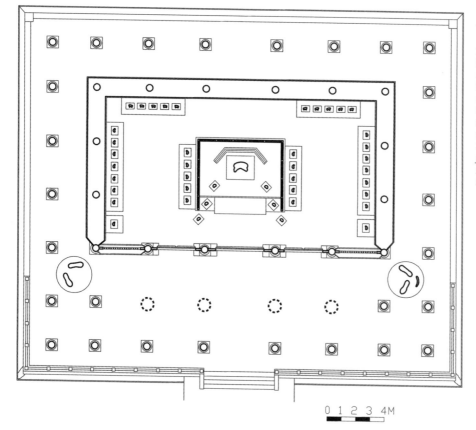

Fig. 1.2. Plan of the Sage Mother Hall of the Jin Shrine, Taiyuan, Shanxi, 1102. The dashed circles indicate where columns have been removed. (Redrawn by author after Chai Zejun, *Taiyuan Jinci Shengmudian xiushan gongcheng baogao*, 125.)

0 1 2 3 4M

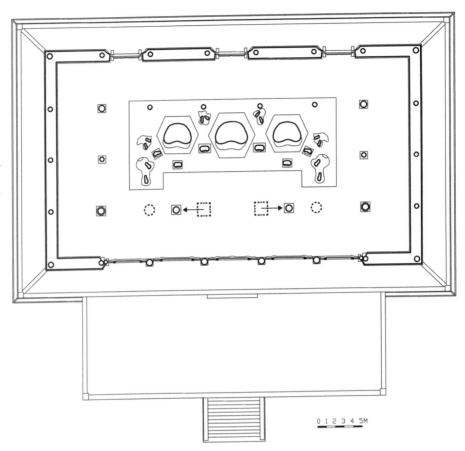

Fig. 1.3. Plan of the Amitābha Hall of Chongfu Monastery, Shuozhou, Shanxi, 1143. The dashed circles indicate the eliminated columns; dashed squares and arrows indicate the relocated columns. (Redrawn by author after Chai Zejun, *Shuozhou Chongfusi*, 140.)

It is important to note that the *YZFS* does not include either the eliminated-column structure or the displaced-column structure; rather, only four types of "trough" (*cao* 槽) are documented in the *YZFS*.[23] In addition, neither of these two column structures was found in any Song building in the south. It is possible, then, that they were not in accordance with the ideal Song style. It can be concluded that the *YZFS* gave less flexibility to column arrangement than actually existed.

Although the manipulation of the columns seems not to have been considered "legitimate" as it was omitted from the *YZFS*, the emergence of the eliminated-column structure and the displaced-column structure during the Song and Jin dynasties *does* indicate an important transformation of the spatial design of the Buddha hall. Most of the space within early extant Buddha halls was occupied by statues.[24] A good example is the Great East Hall of Foguang Monastery 佛光寺, built during the mid-ninth century of the Tang dynasty (618–907 CE) (fig. 1.4). Many examples from the Song and Jin dynasties, however, demonstrate that the Buddha hall became less statue-centered and more worship-centered, meaning more space was allotted for the worshippers and less for the statues. As can be seen in figure 1.3, the Amitābha Hall reveals how the altar shrank in comparison to that in a Tang Buddha hall of similar or even smaller size.[25]

The transformation in the spatial arrangement of the Buddha hall from the ninth to twelfth century likely is related to the "appropriation" of Buddhism in the Song dynasty. Arthur Wright used the word "appropriation" to define Buddhism in Song and post-Song China and noted that there was a gradual withdrawal of upper-class interest and patronage for Buddhism. Eventually, Buddhism was fused into a popular religion almost undifferentiated from Daoism and folk religion.[26] The shift of the popularity of Buddhism from the elite upper class to the lower class with its larger population may have influenced the spatial design of the Buddha hall. The earlier statue-centered Buddha hall, probably a repository of the patronage from the wealthy class, evolved in accordance with the greater attendance by the general public. Similar efforts in Yuan architecture are discussed in later chapters.

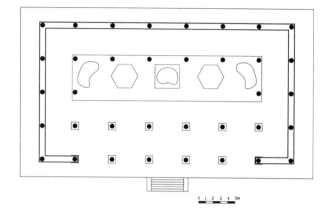

Fig. 1.4. Plan of the Great East Hall of Foguang Monastery, Mount Wutai, Shanxi, 857. (Drawing by author.)

As for the roof framing of Song architecture, three types are recorded in the *YZFS*: the palatial style (*diangeshi* 殿閣式), the mansion style (*tingtangshi* 廳堂式), and the column-and-beam style (*zhuliangshi* 柱梁式). In a palatial-style building, the eave columns and the interior columns are of the same height, and a structural layer of bracket sets can be distinguished easily from the whole roof framing. Sometimes a ceiling is installed in a building of the palatial style. On the other hand, the interior columns in a mansion-style building are higher than the eave columns, and there is no distinct layer of bracket sets. A ceiling usually is not used in mansion-style architecture. Four types of the palatial style, corresponding to the four types of "trough," and sixteen types of the mansion style were documented in the *YZFS*. A hybrid of the palatial style and the mansion style, although existing in real buildings, was not included in the *YZFS*.[27] Lastly, the column-and-beam style means the roof framing consists of only columns (*zhu*) and beams (*liang*) without any bracket set. The column-and-beam style was designed for small and not very important buildings. There are no extant examples of this type.

The *cai-fen* modular system is explained in the *YZFS* in detail. A *cai*, the measurement of the section of a bracket arm, was the major modular unit. The ratio of the height to the width of a *cai* was 3:2. There were eight grades of *cai* that could be used in accordance with the significance of the project and/or social status of the owner. The size of a Grade I *cai* was 9 *cun* x 6 *cun,* and the size of a Grade VIII *cai* was 4.5 *cun* x 3 *cun.*[28] Grade I *cai* were used in the Main Hall of Hualin Monastery in Fuzhou, dated to 964; other extant Song buildings were built with *cai* from Grade III to Grade VII.

A few proportions in the design of Song architecture are noteworthy. As for the slope of the roof, the height of the roof (the distance between the ridge purlin to the level of the eave purlin) was within one-fourth to one-third of the width of the building (the distance between the front and back eave purlins).[29] Therefore, the slope was not too steep. In terms of the bracket sets, the ratio of the height of the bracket set to the height of the eave column was within 25 to 30 percent. Lastly, the height of the column could never be larger than the width of the bay.[30]

As for the bracket sets, the author of the *YZFS* favored the "double-bracket structure" (*chonggong* 重栱) over the "single-bracket structure" (*dangong* 單栱), and the "crisscross projection" (*jixin* 計心) over the "no crisscross projection" (*touxin* 偷心); this means more transversal bracket arms were preferred. In terms of the arrangement of the intercolumnar sets (*bujian puzuo* 補間鋪作), the *YZFS* lists two possibilities: to place two intercolumnar sets in each bay, or two in the central bay and one in the side bays. The distance between each intercolumnar set was not regulated. It also stated that the distribution should be "even," but no further instruction was provided.[31]

Before we conclude this section about the characteristics of Song architecture, it should be noted that Liao and Jin architecture are contemporary with the Song. The exchange of architectural traditions among the Song, Liao, and Jin dynasties was rather complicated. Fu Xinian suggests that architecture dated to the early period of the Liao dynasty still followed the Tang tradition,[32] and Liang Sicheng also grouped and labeled Tang architecture and Liao architecture as "the Period of Vigor."[33] We can argue that, in terms of both the timber-structure technology and the artistic presentation, Yuan architecture had little to do with Liao architecture.[34] As for Jin architecture, the builders certainly were aware of the traditions in the architecture of Liao and the Northern Song, two dynasties conquered by the Jin. Extant buildings dated to the Jin dynasty, however, show more influence from the Song than from the Liao. This probably is because more than 80 percent of extant Jin architecture is located in Shanxi province, most of which was occupied by the Song dynasty from the twelfth to the early thirteenth century.[35]

Moreover, a historical document also proves that the Jin builders were well aware of the *YZFS.* The *Chong jiaozheng di lixinshu* 重校正地理新書 (Re-proof-read new book on geography) published in 1192, the third year of Mingchang 明昌 reign of the Jin dynasty, documented excerpts and illustrations from the *YZFS.* Wang Qiheng argues that citations and discussions of the *YZFS* in this book demonstrated a direct impact of the *YZFS* on the construction activities in the Jin dynasty.[36] Despite the influence from the Northern Song, Jin architecture was also unique due to its splendid, but a bit exaggerated, appearance and adventurous innovation in structure. Jin architecture will not be discussed here in detail because both its remains and its influence on Yuan architecture are regional. More discussion on the relation between Jin and Yuan architecture will be included in chapter 2, on the regional traditions of Yuan architecture.

MING ARCHITECTURE

The Ming dynasty (1368–1644) was the last Han-Chinese dynasty. It was followed by the Qing dynasty (1636–1912), established by the Manchu people. Emperors from both the Ming and Qing dynasties resided in the Forbidden City that was first built by the Ming emperors. The Qing also continued to use other imperial architecture of the Ming dynasty. Liang Sicheng grouped Ming and Qing architecture together and labeled them as "the Period of Rigidity."[37] Although this was not necessarily Liang's original intention, Ming architecture often is bundled with Qing architecture both in academic publications and by common sense. By using the term "Ming-Qing architecture" or "Ming-Qing style," Qing's succession from Ming is overemphasized and Ming's own merit and character overlooked.[38] The concept of "Ming-Qing architecture" is also misleading because it erroneously implies that there was no significant development during the Ming dynasty. Considering the span of more than three hundred years of the Ming, there are a couple of stages in Ming architecture. What was inherited by the Qing dynasty, and is more familiar to people today, does not accurately portray the early stage of Ming architecture, which was related more closely to the transition from the Yuan dynasty.

In order to analyze the architectural development that occurred during the Ming dynasty, Pan Guxi divided Ming architecture into two phases. The first phase ranged from early Ming to mid-Ming of the Jiajing reign (1522–1566). This was when Zhu Yuanzhang 朱元璋 (r. 1368–1398), the first Ming emperor, and his son, Zhu Di 朱棣, Emperor Yongle (r. 1403–1424), respectively, constructed Nanjing and Beijing as imperial capitals of the Jiajing 嘉靖 reign; more imperial architecture was completed or reconstructed in Beijing. Pan summarized the features of this period as "archaistic, simplistic, institutionalized, yet magnificent."[39] Typical examples of this phase include, but are not limited to, the gate tower of Shenwumen (Spiritual and Martial Gate) 神武門城樓 in the Forbidden City, the main hall of Zixiao (Purple Heaven) Palace 紫霄宮大殿 at Mount Wudang, the Longguo (Thriving State) Hall of Qutan (Gautama) Monastery 瞿昙寺隆國殿 in Qinghai province, the complex of Zhihua (Wisdom Attained) Monastery 智化寺 in Beijing, the complex of Bao'en (Repaying Kindness) Monastery 報恩寺 in Pingwu in Sichuan province, and the architectural complex of Changling 長陵 (mausoleum of Emperor Yongle) in Beijing.[40] The second phase, from the post-Jiajing period until the end of the Ming, was characterized by a more "luxuriant, decorative and overelaborate" presentation.[41] Among these are the Bell Tower in Xi'an, Shengji (Sacred Traces) Hall 聖跡殿 of the Temple of Confucius at Qufu 曲阜孔廟, and the Baohe (Preserving Harmony) Hall 保和殿 in the Forbidden City. This phase seems to have been more related to the succeeding Qing architecture.

As most imperial projects were finished during the first phase, the remains of imperial projects from the second phase are relatively few. Nonetheless, plenty of vernacular architecture dated to the second phase has survived. According to Pan, vernacular architecture of the mid- and late Ming were decorated finely with flexible layouts and appropriately designed interior space.[42] In general, the remains of Ming architecture are rich, and the number of extant buildings is probably larger than all pre-Ming buildings combined. Although the majority of remaining Ming architecture is vernacular, many imperial projects have survived and represent the "official style" of Ming architecture.

Guanshi jianzhu 官式建筑, literally translated as "official-style architecture," were projects supervised by *Gongbu* 工部, the Ministry of Works. The so-called official-style architecture primarily consisted of imperial projects in the capital, such as palaces, imperially sponsored shrines, temples, and monasteries, imperial mausoleums, and so on. Moreover, the Ministry of Works would dispatch officials to oversee important projects outside the capital and ensure that the design and construction of the buildings conformed to the laws and regulations of the court.[43] As Klaas Ruitenbeek states, the technical, logistical, and financial aspects of a construction project would be under rigorous top-down control in a bureaucratized environment such as the Ming dynasty.[44] This is also the reason why pre-modern Chinese architecture was codified and often considered uniform.

The idea to exert political authority over architecture by regulating and supervising "official-style architecture" already had had a long history prior to the Ming dynasty. In addition to the Song dynasty's *YZFS*, the compilation and editing of the *Yingshanling* during the early Tang dynasty is one of the earliest examples of such a tradition. Based on excerpts from the original document, the *Yingshanling* indicates "the strict regulation of architectural types, structural measurement, and architectural ornaments in association with the rank of officials."[45] In fact, it is believed that court-enforced building codes were known as early as the fifth century BCE during the Eastern Zhou dynasty.[46]

Although official-style architecture had a long tradition, it was not until the Ming dynasty that we have examples of both official and nonofficial buildings for comparison. In contrast to the official style, "nonofficial" architecture carries little political or religious significance; examples are the dwellings of ordinary people and marketplace buildings. Furthermore, nonofficial architecture received little bureaucratic sponsorship and supervision as long as it did not overstep the owner's social status. Based on the many extant residential buildings of the Ming dynasty, the difference between the official style and nonofficial style is obvious. Compared to the official style, nonofficial architecture usually had simpler bracket sets or none at all. Individual buildings of nonofficial style also tended to be small, and the layout could be more flexible.

Although extant nonofficial architecture of the Ming dynasty outnumbers the official, only the official style is included in the following discussions, due to its significance, influence, and consistency. Of the two phases of Ming architecture defined by Pan Guxi, I shall focus on the first phase, when the most imperial/official projects were undertaken and the phase is more immediately related to the preceding Yuan dynasty.

The most remarkable feature of Ming architecture in comparison to that of earlier dynasties is the downsized bracket sets and the increased number of intercolumnar sets in each bay. The ratio of the heights of the bracket set to the column was less than 15 percent in Ming architecture, proportionally almost half of the Song bracket sets.[47] As for the number of intercolumnar sets in each bay, Ming architecture had six to eight sets in the central bay and one to three in the side bays, almost tripling the standard of the Song dynasty.[48]

Along with the transformation of the bracket sets, the modular system also was simplified and more integrated during the Ming dynasty. First, the *cai-fen* system from the Song dynasty, which was based on the two-dimensional section area of the bracket arm (*gong* 栱), was simplified and replaced by the *doukou* 斗口 system that was based on the one-dimensional *doukou*, the thickness of the bracket arm. Second, the width of a bay in a Ming building also was based on the modular unit *doukou*; while in the Song dynasty, the modular unit was not used to determine the width of the bay. This change suggests that the modular system was fully integrated into the entire building in the Ming dynasty.

In contrast to the downsized bracket set, beams in Ming architecture were proportionally thicker than those of the Song standard.[49] Moreover, more horizontal members were added to the framework to compensate for the loss caused by the smaller bracket sets. At the same time, however, diagonal members, such as the "forking-hand" (*chashou* 叉手) and the "support-footing" (*tuojiao* 托脚), which often were used in Song buildings, were not found during the Ming.[50] The decorative "crescent-moon-shaped beams" (*yueliang* 月梁) also disappeared in Ming architecture.[51] With no diagonal members and no decorative beams, the roof framing of Ming architecture was visually simplistic. As for the slope of the roof, Ming roofs looked steeper than those of Song because the ratio of the height of the roof to the width of the building in Ming was usually larger than 1:3 and larger than most Song buildings.[52]

The three types of roof framing documented in the YZFS—the palatial style, the mansion style, and the column-and-beam style—were also found in the Ming dynasty. The mansion style originally was designed for nonpalatial architecture but also was found in many important buildings in the Forbidden City.[53] It seems that Ming builders appreciated the simple framework of the mansion style and favored it over the palatial style, even when building imperial palaces.

There is one thing about Ming architecture that echoes the theory as presented in the YZFS of the Song dynasty. In terms of the columniation, the eliminated-column structure and the displaced-column structure were, again, omitted. In order to present a plan of order in Ming architecture, every bay, with very few exceptions, had four columns.[54] This was an intentional revival of the Song tradition. In addition, with little flexibility in the array of columns, if more room was wanted the Ming builders had to extend the depth of the building.

Based on this overview of Song and Ming architecture, more details about the two dynastic styles are presented in the next section. Hereafter, "the Song style" will refer to the architectural style documented in the YZFS, and "the Ming style" to the style represented by the imperial/official architecture constructed from the early to mid-Ming. Most important, stylistic and structural details of Yuan architecture will be visited to explain the Song to Ming transition.

SHIFTS OF PLAN AND COLUMNIATION

As stated above, the orderly arrangement of columns, a tradition considered standard in Song architecture, was revived in the Ming dynasty. This suggests that neither the eliminated-column structure nor the displaced-column structure was approved by the building standards of Song and Ming, two Han-Chinese dynasties. As for the Yuan dynasty, the eliminated-column structure and the displaced-column structure commonly were employed in north China as well as in the Upper Yangzi area. Although the earliest known application of the eliminated-column structure to date was discovered in a Song building in Shanxi, both structures were vigorously developed during the Jin dynasty and became a distinguishing feature of Jin architecture. Obviously, the eliminated-column structure and the displaced-column structure were more favored by non-Han Chinese dynasties, such as the Jin and the Yuan.

Although popular in other areas during the Yuan dynasty, the eliminated-column structure and the displaced-column structure never existed in the Lower Yangzi even during the Mongol period. This tradition of using four columns for each bay, also called the "full-house column style" (*mantang-zhu* 滿堂柱), has been preserved in the Lower Yangzi area. Such adherence to the Song tradition in Jiangnan can be explained by the reprinting of the *YZFS* in Suzhou in 1145, the fifteenth year of Shaoxing reign during the Southern Song; this might have reinforced the authority of the book in south China for another century. In the Ming dynasty, the tradition preserved in Jiangnan was picked up again and became an important feature of Ming official style.

In terms of the layout of the building plans, there is other evidence showing that the connection between Ming and Yuan architecture lies in the Lower Yangzi. Due to the lack of flexibility in moving or eliminating the columns in Ming architecture, builders often extended the depth of the bay to provide more room.[55] This practice also was found in Song and Yuan architecture in the Lower Yangzi. Table 1.1 displays the depth of each bay in all three-by-three-bay and squarish building plans of Song-Yuan in the Lower Yangzi. The main halls of Baosheng Monastery and Xuanyuan Palace represent the standard layout; the first/front bay was about the same proportion as the third/rear bay, while the second/middle bay was the widest/deepest. In the other four buildings of the eleventh to fourteenth century, however, it is obvious that the first/front bay was expanded. In the main hall of Zhenru Monastery, the front bay was even wider/deeper than the middle bay. Such a practice was not found in other places where people always could have used the eliminated-column structure and the displaced-column structure to solve the same problem.

Table 1.1. Depth of bay in Song-Yuan buildings in the Lower Yangzi (unit = m)

Building	Date	First bay	Second bay	Third bay	Total
The main hall of Baoguo Monastery[a]	1013 (Song)	4.50	5.80	3.00	13.30
The main hall of Baosheng Monastery[b]	1073 (Song)	3.55	6.10	3.55	13.20
The main hall of Yanfu Monastery	1317 (Yuan)	2.90	3.70	2.00	8.60
The main hall of Tianning Monastery	1318 (Yuan)	4.65	4.93	3.14	12.72
The main hall of Zhenru Monastery	1320 (Yuan)	5.30	5.10	2.60	13.00
The main hall of Xuanyuan Palace	1333–1368 (Yuan-Ming)	2.90	5.60	2.90	11.40

[a] Measurements are from Guo Daiheng, *Donglai diyishan*, 80.
[b] Measurements are from Zhang Shiqing, "Luzhi Baoshengsi," 79.

THE TRANSITION OF ROOF FRAMING

With regard to roof framing, the relation between Yuan architecture and the Song to Ming transition is shown in three aspects. First, the strengthening of architectural members that compose the roof framing is one of the most notable differences between Song and Ming architecture, which, according to some examples of the Yuan dynasty, began during the Yuan. Second, connections between vertical members (columns) and horizontal members (beams) usually was constructed with bracket sets and/or a "camel hump" (*tuofeng* 駝峰)[56] in Song architecture; it became simplified in the Ming dynasty. Such simplification also started in the Yuan dynasty. Last, the disappearance of the crescent-moon-shaped beam in the Ming dynasty also can be traced to the Yuan.

A good example of the strengthening of the roof framing from Song to Ming is the transformation of the architrave (*e* 額) that ran through the upper part of the columns—from the Song dynasty "railing architrave" (*lan'e* 闌額) to the Ming dynasty "big-architrave tie" (*da'efang* 大額枋). The architraves were parallel to the plane of the wall and as long as the width of the bay(s) (*changsuijianguang* 長隨间广). There were four types of architraves listed in the *YZFS*: the railing architrave (*lan'e* 闌額), the eave architrave (*yan'e* 簷額), the associate architrave (*you'e* 由額), and the interior architrave (*wunei'e* 屋內額). In terms of the configurations of the architraves, table 1.2 indicates that there are two types of combinations: a railing architrave plus an associate architrave; and an eave architrave plus a curtain-mounting joist (*chuomufang* 綽幕方). An eave architrave was a larger alternate of a railing architrave and measured differently in a mansion-style or a palatial-style building. In addition to the size, another major difference between a railing architrave and an eave architrave was that the end of an eave architrave protruded from the shaft of the column (*bingchu zhukou* 并出柱口), whereas the end of a railing architrave reached to the center of the column (*zhi zhuxin* 至柱心), meaning it could not go beyond the central axis of the column.

Table 1.2. Configurations of column-top tie beams in the *YZFS*

		Width	Width (mansion-style)	Width (palatial style)
Type I	Railing architrave (*lan'e*)	2C		
	Associate architrave (*you'e*)	[2C+3F] to [2C+2Z+1F]		
Type II	Eave architrave (*yan'e*)		[2C+1Z] to 3C	[3C+1Z] to [3C+3Z]
	Curtain-mounting joist (*chuomufang*)		[1C+1Z+3F] to 2C	[2C+4F] to [2C+2Z]

Key: C = *cai* 材; Z = *zhi* 栔; F = *fen* 份

As for extant architecture dated to the Song dynasty, the railing architrave is the only architrave from the *YZFS* that was commonly used. In a small number of Song buildings, most located south of the Yellow River, the railing architrave was the only member that ran through the top of the columns. In most cases, especially in north China (Shanxi, Hebei, and the part of Henan that is north of the Yellow River), a flat architrave (*pupaifang* 普拍方) that is not considered a

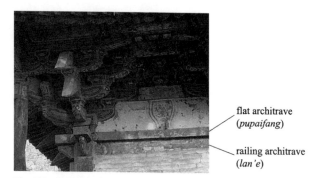

flat architrave
(*pupaifang*)

railing architrave
(*lan'e*)

Fig. 1.5. Railing architrave and flat architrave in the main hall of Longmen (Dragon Gate) Monastery, Pingshun, Shanxi, 1098. (Photo by author.)

standard column-top architrave according to the *YZFS*, was used in addition to the railing architrave (fig. 1.5).[57] A flat architrave was also different from all the other architraves in the *YZFS*, as it was placed on top of the eave columns rather than running through them. In terms of the Ming style, the flat architrave and the railing architrave transformed into and were renamed, respectively, the *pingbanfang* 平板枋 and *da'efang* 大额枋 (fig. 1.6). The Ming version of a flat architrave, *pingbanfang*, probably a little narrower, was not very different from the Song version. The so-called big-architrave tie (*da'efang*) of the Ming was much larger proportionally than the Song railing architrave. The big-architrave tie was wider than the Song railing architrave by 3C and was more than double its width.[58]

In terms of size, the Ming dynasty big-architrave tie seems to be similar to the "big architrave" (*da'e* 大额) found in Yuan architecture in north China. The big architrave, first defined by Zhang Yuhuan in the late 1970s, was a unique large architrave discovered in many Yuan buildings in Shanxi and Shaanxi provinces. The big architrave often was found to have a curtain-mounting joist (*chuomufang* 绰幕方) beneath it. A typical example of the big architrave was

flat architrave
(*pingbanfang*)

big-architrave tie
(*da'efang*)

associate-filler board
(*you'e dianban*)

small-architrave tie
(*xiao'efang*)

Fig. 1.6. Column-top tie beams in Daxiongbao Hall of Bao'en Monastery, Pingwu, Sichuan, 1440–1446. (Photo by author.)

found in the Dacheng (Great Success) Hall 大成殿 of the Confucius Temple 孔廟 in Hancheng, Shaanxi province (fig. 1.7).

In order to contextualize the unique big architrave in pre-Yuan tradition, Zhang Yuhuan speculated that, due to the lack of existing evidence in Song architecture, the big architrave of the Yuan dynasty probably corresponded to the eave architrave in the *YZFS*.[59] The definition of "eave architrave" also puzzled other scholars. Liang Sicheng tried to explain it in his annotations of the *YZFS* by mentioning that the railing architrave found in a Song dynasty pavilion at Jidu Temple 濟瀆廟 (Jiyuan County, Henan) was probably an eave architrave; it was large and had a curtain-mounting joist underneath.[60] The pavilion Liang mentioned as a Song building later was proven to have been rebuilt in the Ming dynasty. Therefore, the editor(s) of his annotation used a photograph of a Yuan building, the Shangdang Gate 上黨門, in Changzhi, Shanxi, to illustrate Liang's point.

Pan Guxi (and his coauthor) disagreed with Liang (and Liang's editors), and argued that the architraves in Liang's examples merely looked like an eave architrave and did not have much structural function. The size of these architraves was not big enough, and they merely were a different type of railing architrave.[61] Following Zhang Yuhuan's lead, Pan also agreed that the Yuan dynasty big architrave found in north China was the eave architrave described in the *YZFS*, and he used the Dacheng Hall of the Confucius Temple in Hancheng as an example.[62]

On the other hand, the Yuan dynasty big architraves found in Shanxi and Shaanxi provinces were not exactly *the* eave architrave described in the *YZFS*. First, unlike the railing architrave that ran through the columns, the big architrave mostly sits on top of the columns, resembling a flat architrave. The eave architrave, however, should be similar to the railing architrave in this respect. As the eave architrave was recorded as a subentry of the railing architrave in the *YZFS*, only the differences between the two types of architrave were noted, not the similarities. If the positioning of the railing architrave and eave architrave were that much different, it would have been mentioned. Moreover, the end of an eave architrave was described as "protruding from the shaft of the column" (*bingchu zhukou* 并出柱口) in the *YZFS*. It would have been pointless to note this if the eave architrave was hung over the columns. Therefore, big architraves found in north China during the Yuan more likely were created based on a flat architrave, which was also popular in the north during the Song dynasty but seems to have been replaced by the big architrave.

For the same reasons, the big architrave was also less likely to be a precedent for the big-architrave tie of the Ming dynasty. The latter also ran through the columns like the eave architrave in the *YZFS*. The eave architrave in the *YZFS* was a possible prototype of the big-architrave tie of the Ming. More important, there are eave architraves in extant Song monuments that have been overlooked for a long time.

As mentioned previously, there are two types of configurations of architraves recorded in the *YZFS*. The main hall of Baoguo (Protecting State) Monastery (dated to 1013, Ningbo, Zhejiang) exemplifies both types in the same building: under the frontal eave are the eave architrave plus curtain-mounting joist; on other sides of the building, the railing architrave was found with an associate architrave underneath (fig. 1.8). Although the frontal architrave has never been called an eave architrave in previous publications, I have two reasons to use that term. First, the frontal architrave is 45 cm wide (*guang* 广), which equals 2C+1Z, and the architrave on other sides measures 35 cm, equal to 2C.[63] These measurements match exactly with the regulation in the *YZFS*. Moreover, given that the frontal architrave also was supported by a curtain-mounting joist, the main hall of Baoguo Monastery presents the most accurate example of an eave architrave up to this

Fig. 1.8. The main hall of Baoguo Monastery, Ningbo, Zhejiang: (*left*) eave architrave under the frontal eave; (*right*) railing architrave and associate architrave in the side bay. (Photo by author)

point. The different but coexisting designs of the eave architrave and the railing architrave in the main hall of Baoguo Monastery further reveal an implicit logic of the railing-architrave entry in the *YZFS*: the larger eave architrave (*yan'e*) was supposed to be used on the facade of the building, while the slenderer railing architrave (*lan'e*) was designed for the sides.

Remarkably, the main hall of Baoguo Monastery is not the only physical example of the eave architrave's usage in the Song dynasty. The combination of eave architrave and curtain-mounting joist, although not discovered in any other Song timber-framed building so far, was found carved in stone in the tomb of the An Bing family of the Southern Song. The tomb, completed around 1222–1223, is located in Huaying, Sichuan province. Features of timber architecture replicated in this tomb include a sloped eave, bracket sets, columns, and an architrave (fig. 1.9). The measurement of the *cai* based on the bracket sets is 6 cm, and the width of the architrave is 14 cm, very close to 2C1Z (14.4 cm), the measurement of the eave architrave in the *YZFS*.[64] With the curtain-mounting joist underneath, this architrave clearly is another good example of eave architrave.

During the Yuan dynasty, the usage of the eave architrave continued in the Sichuan area. In the Feilai (Flying-hither) Hall 飛來殿 of the Temple of the Eastern Peak (Dongyuemiao 東嶽廟), a Yuan building dated to 1327, eave architraves with curtain-mounting joist were used on the facade. The width measured 60 cm, equal to 2C2Z. On other sides of the building, the column-top tie beams were much slenderer and should be considered a railing architrave. Eave architrave and railing architrave, again, coexisted here as in the Northern Song Main Hall of Baoguo Monastery.

Fig. 1.9. Timber architectural features replicated in M1 Tomb of An Bing, Huaying, Sichuan, 1222–1223. (Photo courtesy of Cai Yukun.)

Fig. 1.10.
Guanwang Temple,
Dingxiang, Shanxi,
built in 1123,
repaired in 1346.
(Photo courtesy of
Wu Yunan.)

Nevertheless, there are still a few differences among Feilai Hall, the Main Hall of Baoguo Monastery, and the *YZFS*. First, the eave architrave of Feilai Hall was built with a flat architrave that is found neither in Baoguo Monastery nor in the *YZFS*. Second, the eave architrave in the central bay of Feilai Hall obviously was curved upward, which was also found in the An Bing family tomb. Last, the eave architrave on the side bays of Feilai Hall was placed a little lower, leaving a space for a filler board (*dianban* 墊板) between the eave architrave and flat architrave. These three features were all commonly found in other Yuan buildings in Sichuan and may be considered local features.[65]

The eave architrave, or a variety of architrave similar to it, was often found in Yuan buildings in Sichuan. Even in north China where the big architraves were more dominant, there was still a big architrave that differs from others. In the Guanwang (King Guan) Temple 關王廟 in Dingxiang, Shanxi, the big architrave in the central bay on the facade was a later addition in the Yuan dynasty, dating to 1346; the rest of the building was built during the Song or Jin periods.[66] Figure 1.10 indicates the huge frontal architrave, a perfect example of an eave architrave, given its larger size compared to the railing architrave right next to it and its positioning between the columns.

Based on the above examples in Sichuan and Shanxi, the type of eave architrave recorded in the *YZFS* continued to be used in some regions during the Yuan dynasty. Moreover, those Yuan dynasty eave architraves found in Sichuan and Shanxi all had a flat architrave placed on top. The two examples from the Song dynasty, the Main Hall of Baoguo Monastery and the An Bing family tombs, however, did not include a flat architrave. The combination of a flat architrave, eave architrave, and curtain-mounting joist in Yuan architecture perfectly corresponds to the later Ming standard that has a combination of a flat architrave (*pingbanfang*), a big-architrave tie (*da'efang*), and a sparrow brace (*queti* 雀替). The eave architrave found in Yuan buildings shows a transitional stage understandable in the context of the Song tradition and also anticipating the Ming style.

Besides the strengthened roof framing with thicker and more lateral beams, the framework of Ming architecture was more simplistic compared to the Song style. The interface between the beams and columns in a Song building usually involved bracket arms, capital blocks, or a camel hump (fig. 1.11). On the contrary, there was almost no transitional structure between the beams and columns/posts in Ming buildings, and both the beams and columns/posts were proportionally stronger than those of the Song (fig. 1.12). Therefore, bracket arms, camel humps, or capital blocks no longer fit in this new structure of the Ming. The beams and columns/posts simply were mortised together. Only a pair of *heta* 合踏 (foot bearer), two plain blocks that support the king post, were used.

A transitional stage in the simplification of the interface between beams and columns also existed in Yuan architecture. Although the interface of the Song style was preserved in Yuan buildings in the Lower Yangzi, buildings in the Upper Yangzi already had a simplified interface between the columns and beams. Except for Feilai Hall, rafter beams of most buildings in the Upper Yangzi simply were inserted into the shaft of interior columns without any transitional member. It seems that the simplification of the roof frame in Sichuan was later absorbed into the Ming official style, regardless of the continuity of the Song style in the Lower Yangzi.

Fig. 1.11.
Structural details in the main hall of Longmen Monastery, Pingshun, Shanxi, 1098: (*left*) bracket set used between an interior column and a crossbeam; (*right*) camel hump with a capital block on top. (Photo by author.)

The last aspect that represents simplicity in Ming architecture is the disappearance of the crescent-moon-shaped beam. In architecture dated to early Ming, the surface and corner of the exposed crossbeams still were curved slightly, reminiscent of the Song style. After mid-Ming, however, exposed beams all were made completely straight.[67] Back in the Yuan dynasty, the crescent-moon-shaped beam was a regional feature of the Lower Yangzi, but they were rarely found in the north. In Sichuan, the railing or eave architraves were sometimes shaped like the crescent moon,

Fig. 1.12. Roof frame of Huangqian Hall, Temple of Heaven, Beijing, 1538. (Photo by author.)

but the crossbeams were never treated the same way. Therefore, the disappearance of the crescent-moon-shaped beam was another connection between Ming official style and Yuan regional traditions in Sichuan and north China.

Although Ming official style shared more common features with the Lower Yangzi tradition in terms of plan and array of columns, the simplistic roof framing of the Ming dynasty was clearly an inheritance from the Upper Yangzi tradition and the northern tradition of the Yuan dynasty. Furthermore, the transformation of roof framing from the "elegant" Song style to the simplistic Ming style was accompanied by the transformation of the bracket sets.

THE TRANSFORMATION OF BRACKET SETS

As stated above, another noticeable difference between Song and Ming architecture was "the sudden change" in the proportion of the bracket sets.[68] The ratio of the height of the bracket set to the height of the column was between 25 and 30 percent in the Song dynasty, but decreased to less than 15 percent in the Ming dynasty. The downsized bracket sets in the Ming dynasty were a result of the strengthening and simplification of the roof framing. The bracket sets were no longer as essential as before to the roof support system and became more decorative. It can be observed in Yuan architecture that the "sudden change" in the proportion of the bracket sets from Song to Ming was not in fact "sudden."

Table 1.3 displays the available data regarding the proportion of bracket sets in Yuan architecture in the three regions—the Upper Yangzi, the Lower Yangzi, and north China. It is obvious that the proportion of most Yuan buildings falls

Table 1.3. Proportions of bracket sets in Yuan buildings

Region	Building	Date	BS/EC[a]	Number of intercolumnar sets[b]	Note
Upper Yangzi	Main Hall of Lifeng Temple	1307	17%	1	Eave architrave
	Feilai Hall	1327	23%	2	Eave architrave
	Main Hall of Bao'en Monastery	1327	15%	3	Eave architrave
	Main Hall of Yong'an Monastery	1333	17%	2	Eave architrave
	Wenchang Hall	1343	22%	1	
	Main Hall of Qinglong Monastery	Yuan	21%	3	Eave architrave
	Yong'an Temple	Yuan	14%	1	Eave architrave
	Pantuoshi Hall	Yuan	19%	1	Eave architrave
Lower Yangzi	Main Hall of Yanfu Monastery	1317	25%	3	Conventional style
	Main Hall of Tianning Monastery	1318	24%	3	Conventional style
North China	Sanqing Hall of Yongle Palace[c]	1262	29%	2	Conventional style
	Middle Hall of Qinglong Monastery[d]	1289	26%	n/a	Conventional style
	Main Hall of Sansheng Monastery[e]	1346	23%	1	Conventional style
	Main Hall of Longtian Temple[f]	Yuan	25%	1	Conventional style
	Theater of Niuwang Temple[g]	1321	20%	n/a	Big-architrave style
	Transit Hall of Jieyi Temple[h]	Yuan	20%	n/a	Big-architrave style
	Grand Hall of Jiangzhou[i]	Yuan	16%	4	Big-architrave style

[a] BS/EC = the height of the bracket sets/the height of the eave column
[b] Number of intercolumnar sets in the central bay of the facade
[c] Calculation is based on the measurements in Du Xianzhou, "Yonglegong de jianzhu," 16.
[d] Calculation is based on the measurements in Zhang Yuhuan, "Shanxi Yuandai diantang de damu jiegou," 74.
[e] Calculation is based on the measurements in Zhang Yuhuan, "Shanxi Yuandai diantang de damu jiegou," 74.
[f] Calculation is based on the measurements in Zhang Yuhuan, "Shanxi Yuandai diantang de damu jiegou," 75.
[g] Calculation is based on the measurements in Chai Zejun, *Chai Zejun wenji*, 277.
[h] Calculation is based on the measurements in Zhang Yuhuan, "Shanxi Yuandai diantang de damu jiegou," 75.
[i] There are two extra pillars built in the central bay of the facade. Calculation is based on the measurements in Zhang Yuhuan, "Shanxi Yuandai diantang de damu jiegou," 75.
n/a = not applicable

between 25 and 15 percent, filling the gap between the Song standard (25–30 percent) and the Ming standard (15 percent and less). Early Yuan examples in north China, such as the Sanqing Hall of Yongle Palace 永樂宮三清殿 dated to 1262, were still in accordance with the Song style. For other Yuan architecture labeled as "conventional-style" in both in north China and the Lower Yangzi, the proportion of the bracket sets to the eave columns was still around 25 percent, the lower limit of the Song standard. To be discussed with more detail in the next chapter, the conventional style proved to be a continuity of the Song style. As for buildings labeled as the "big-architrave-style" in north China, the proportion decreased to 20 percent and below, which suggests the relation between the thickening of the lateral beams and the downsizing of the bracket sets.[69] Concerning the Yuan buildings in Sichuan, the proportion ranged from 23 to 14 percent and seems to have less regularity. The Ming standard of less than 15 percent was reached for the first time in Sichuan. Due to the lack of uniformity in Yuan architecture, the proportion of the bracket sets was not regulated and became quite diverse in different regions. The Ming standard, whose bracket sets were shorter than 15 percent of the eave columns, was preceded by examples in the Yuan dynasty.

In addition to the size of bracket sets being reduced by half from the Song to the Ming, the number of the intercolumnar sets in each bay tripled in the Ming standard. According to the *YZFS*, the central bay of a building could have a maximum of two intercolumnar sets. This number increased to four during the early Ming (fig. 1.13). Precedents of the increase also can be found in Yuan architecture. Many Yuan buildings in the Upper Yangzi, the Lower Yangzi, and north China were built with three or more intercolumnar sets in the central bay.

In addition to the changing size and number of bracket sets as a whole, there are a few more noteworthy details related to the Song–Ming transition. First, the oblique arm (*xiegong* 斜栱), a projecting bracket of 45°, 30°, 60° angle, although occasionally used in some official and nonofficial buildings outside the capital, almost disappeared from imperial projects of the Ming in Beijing and Nanjing.[70] This is similar to what happened in the Song dynasty. Although the oblique arm very likely was created during the Song dynasty and has been found in many important extant Song buildings (fig. 1.14), it was never mentioned in the *YZFS*. Moreover, it was not found in the Lower Yangzi area, the heartland of the Song court and the Han-Chinese culture. The elimination of the oblique arm in imperial projects of the Ming court is another sign of the revival of the Song tradition.[71]

Fig. 1.13. Intercolumnar sets in Daxiongbao Hall of Bao'en Monastery, Pingwu, Sichuan, 1440–1446. (Photo by author.)

Fig. 1.14. Oblique arms in Moni Hall of Longxing Monastery, Zhengding, Hebei, 1052. (Photo by author.)

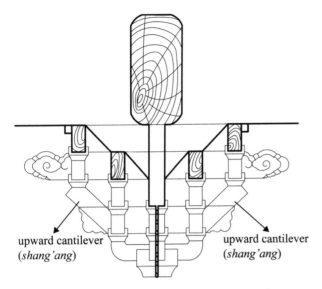

upward cantilever (*shang'ang*)   upward cantilever (*shang'ang*)

Fig. 1.15. Upward cantilevers inscribed in the bracket sets of Ling'en Hall at Changling Mausoleum, Changping, Beijing, 1415. (Redrawn by author after Guo Huayu, *Mingdai guanshi jianzhu damuzuo*, 165.)

First, the oldest extant oblique arm is from the middle hall (*zhongdian*) of South Jixiang (Auspicious) Monastery 南吉祥寺 dated to 1023–1031, in Linchuan, Shanxi province. Another Northern Song example of the oblique arm is at Moni Hall of Longxing Monastery in Zhengding, Hebei, dated to 1052. Oblique arms became popular during the Jin dynasty in its territory of today's Shanxi and Hebei provinces. Due to its popularity during the Jin dynasty, the oblique arm also is considered a signature of Jin architecture.

Second, the wing-shaped bracket (*yixinggong* 翼形栱) that was found in the architecture of the Upper Yangzi and north China during the Yuan, but neither in the Lower Yangzi nor in the *YZFS*, became part of the Ming official style. The wing-shaped bracket was renamed "three-breadth cloud" (*sanfuyun* 三幅雲) in the Ming dynasty and was always placed on interior projections of the bracket sets.[72] In the Yuan dynasty, however, the wing-shaped bracket could be placed on both outward and inward projections.

Last, the upward cantilever (*shang'an* 上昂), a strut used in the inner part of a bracket set to adjust the angle of the cantilever, is documented in the *YZFS* but found only in the Lower Yangzi during the Yuan dynasty. In the Ming dynasty, the upward cantilever was no longer a structural part but merely a decorative emblem. The shape of the upward cantilever often was inscribed on horizontal boards as a reminder of the Song tradition (fig. 1.15).

THE LOSS AND REVIVAL OF THE SONG TRADITION

The diversity of Yuan architecture played an important role during the Song–Ming transition. On the one hand, Yuan architecture in the Lower Yangzi retained many traditions from the *YZFS*; on the other, new features and techniques had been created in the Upper Yangzi and north China. Through the comparison between the extant Yuan architecture and the official style of Ming architecture, it is clear that the establishment of the Ming official style, with its regular and orderly design of the building plan and the array of columns, was a continuation from the Song tradition that had been retained in the Lower

Yangzi. The seemingly "sudden" change of downsizing and de-functioning of the bracket sets in the Ming dynasty was a result of the revolution of roof framing that was initiated in north China, very likely since the Yuan. The so-called elegance of Song architecture was retained partially in the Yuan but was somewhat compromised by the simplification of the roof framing. The diversity of Yuan architecture was further simplified and became the source of the simplistic and more uniform architectural style of the Ming dynasty.

The diverse architectural legacy of the Yuan was absorbed by the new Ming style through two large-scale national projects. The Ming style initially was developed in the construction of Nanjing during the reign of Zhu Yuanzhang. Later, it was further regulated when Emperor Yongle constructed Beijing. Hundreds of thousands of craftsmen across the country were summoned to the new capitals, bringing with them their skills and experience.[73] These two undertakings, one in the south (Nanjing) and one in the north (Beijing), were probably the first opportunities since the early twelfth-century compiling of the *YZFS* to bring together craftsmen and integrate architectural styles from south and north. This was not the case when Khubilai Khan built Dadu. As he had not yet conquered the Southern Song, he merely employed craftsmen he had captured in the north and had them try to imitate the palaces in the Northern Song Bianliang. The builders of Ming dynasty Nanjing and Beijing were aware of the different features that remained in various regions during the Yuan dynasty, but they did not and could not utilize them all. The regional features had been carefully selected to be included in the Ming official style to serve political as well as practical needs.

There were clearly two policies advocated by the early Ming emperors. First, the Song/Han-Chinese tradition should be revived, but at the same time expenses on construction projects should be minimized. To ensure the revival of the earlier style, the Lower Yangzi tradition and the conventional style in the north were adopted in order to re-create the regulated "order" in Chinese architecture. To control costs, the Upper Yangzi tradition and the nonconventional big-architrave style in the north were applied when the artistic presentation and refinement of architecture were compromised to save resources. Elaborate features of the Song style had to be sacrificed for financial reasons. At the same time, the flexibility often seen in Yuan architecture had to be eliminated as it was not in accordance with the Chinese ideal. Ming builders seemed to have no choice but to further simplify the timber frame by reducing the number of members but increasing the size of each.

Evidence of these two policies regarding architecture/construction can be detected in the historic record, for example the *Mingshi* (History of the Ming) complied by Zhang Tingyu under the sponsorship and supervision of the Qing imperial court. As for the revival of the Song/Chinese tradition, "the Song system" (*Songzhi* 宋制) often was referred to when conducting the imperial rites during the early Ming. In the chapter about the rites in the *Mingshi,* the reference to "the Song system" concerns mortuary ceremonies of the empress and other members of the imperial family.[74] In the chapter on "vehicles and trappings" (*yufu* 與服), the "Song system" is again mentioned in the entry for plowing and seal making for imperial family members. Although architecture is not mentioned in the *Mingshi,* it can be speculated that, as an indispensable part of the system of the imperial rites, it should have followed the same as the other rites. In terms of specific issues regarding architecture/construction, simplicity was also discussed. When Zhu Yuanzhang was advised to use an expensive kind of marble for the flooring in his palace, he replied: "[I] advocate thrift and simplicity. I am still afraid this is too luxurious. Are you advising me to be more extravagant?"[75]

In theory, the Ming emperor tried to revive the Song/Han-Chinese tradition by regulating and institutionalizing architecture along with other aspects of the imperial rites. In reality, the first Ming emperor, Zhu Yuanzhuang, explicitly advocated thriftiness and simplicity when constructing his palaces in Nanjing, and his decision set the tone for the entire Ming dynasty. Therefore, the so-called elegance of the Song style was compromised and economized into the Ming style that is seemingly "rigidity/simplistic," by removing transitional members in the framework, and de-functioning and downsizing the bracket sets. The successful adaptation of the elegant Song style into the simplistic Ming style without sacrificing much Chineseness was based on selection from the divided legacy of Yuan architecture.

CHAPTER 2

REGIONAL TRADITIONS
An Age of Division

In 2001, a comprehensive volume dedicated to Yuan and Ming architecture was published as part of a multivolume book project on the history of Chinese traditional architecture—a project in which more than a dozen eminent Chinese scholars in the field collaborated. In this volume, Pan Guxi presents a summary of the architecture in north China (the Yellow River reaches) and south China (the Yangzi River reaches) that was further differentiated in the Yuan dynasty. He suggests that architecture drastically transformed during the Yuan dynasty in both form and structure. Structural changes can be found in the modular system, columniations, and beams. In terms of the form, Yuan architecture appears to be less elaborate and luxuriant. One indication is the decorative members that began to be separated from structural members. Pan believes that Yuan architecture of the north developed on the basis of Jin architecture, while in the south, Yuan architecture was based on the earlier Song architecture.[1] During the tenth through twelfth centuries, prior to the arrival of the Yuan rulers, the division of Yuan architecture in the north and south followed that between Jin architecture in the north and Song architecture in the south.

Although Pan's argument for the difference between the north and south is convincing and groundbreaking, he simplified the problem in the south and did not explore the issue of regionalization. Therefore, following his lead, this chapter will provide an overview of Yuan (timber-framed) architecture, focusing on discussions of regional features and characteristics in three areas. As shown in plate 1, these three regions are north China (now Hebei, Shanxi, and Shaanxi provinces); the Upper Yangzi[2] (now Sichuan province and Chongqing): and the Lower Yangzi[3] (now Zhejiang and Jiangsu provinces and Shanghai).

Extant Yuan buildings in each region will be analyzed and compared based on their plans, columniation, bracket sets, roof framing, and decorative details. Bracket sets will be emphasized, as they usually are the most complicated yet significant feature of Chinese timber-framed architecture. Bracket sets, composed of blocks (*dou* 斗) and bracket arms (*gong* 栱), play an essential role in transferring the load from horizontal members (beams) to vertical members (columns). They also provide considerable information about stylistic issues as well as the modular system of the building. Relevant content in the Song dynasty *YZFS* is cited frequently in this chapter. The *YZFS* serves as a reference to compare these three Yuan regional traditions with the Song standard. Terminology used throughout the remainder of this volume is based on the *YZFS* unless otherwise noted.

The choice of these three regions is based on the distribution of extant Yuan buildings: more than 95 percent of extant Yuan timber architecture in China is in these three areas. Moreover, the Yuan buildings in each region show common regional features and characteristics. An examination of how timber-framed architecture was built in each area demonstrates the diversity of Yuan architecture in terms of the timber construction system. This chapter also explains how these varied regional traditions were generated under different pre-Yuan regimes and how they developed autonomously during the Yuan without top-down regulations from a central authority.

THE NORTHERN TRADITION

The majority of Yuan architecture is in north China. More than two hundred Yuan timber-framed buildings have been discovered in the provinces along the Yellow River. The rich remains of Yuan architecture in the north include various types of buildings—ranging from monasteries, temples, and municipal halls to stages. Moreover, in addition to individual buildings, two Yuan monastic complexes (first mentioned in the introduction) have been preserved in Shanxi: a Daoist monastery, Yongle Palace 永樂宮;[4] and a Buddhist temple, Guangsheng Monastery 廣勝寺.[5] In contrast to Yuan architecture in south China, which did not receive scholarly attention until recently, since the 1930s Yuan architecture in the north has been surveyed and studied extensively when the *Zhongguo Yingzao Xueshe* 中國營造學社 (Society for Research in Chinese Architecture, hereafter the Society) became active.[6]

Chinese architectural historian Zhang Yuhuan published an article in 1979 examining Yuan timber-framed architecture in Shanxi province. He argued that a large number of Yuan buildings were reconstructed based on remains of Song and Jin buildings.[7] According to the style of the roof framing, he categorizes Yuan timber-framed architecture into two types: "the conventional style" (*chuantongshi* 傳統式) and "the big-architrave style" (*da'eshi* 大額式). Zhang emphasizes that the big-architrave style, usually considered unique to Yuan architecture in Shanxi, originally was created during the Jin dynasty.[8]

Zhang's theories in the 1970s paved the way for later research on Yuan architecture. But there has been no more recent study since Zhang's article that covers a similar scope of regional traditions of Yuan architecture.[9] Given new discoveries of Yuan buildings and information about Yuan history, however, the big picture always is changing. Therefore, based on previous scholarship and my own observations, it is important to revisit the features that demonstrate the flexibility and innovation existent in the northern tradition of Yuan architecture.

Yuan architecture in north China includes buildings with both squarish and rectangular plans.[10] Contrary to the examples in the Upper and Lower Yangzi regions, where squarish plans are found only in small main halls three bays wide, squarish plans in the north can be either five-by-five bays, such as Ming-yingwang (King of Bright Response) Hall 明應王殿 of Shuishen (Water God) Temple 水神廟 of the Lower Guangsheng Monastery; or three-by-three bays, such as the main hall of Erlang Temple 二郎廟 and the main hall of Longtian (Dragon Heaven) Temple 龍天廟 (fig. 2.1).[11] Buildings with rectangular plans can be as wide as five bays or seven bays. Figure 2.2 shows three examples: Chunyang Hall 純陽殿 in Yongle Palace, the main hall of Lower Guangsheng Monastery, and the main hall of Guangji (Profound Salvation) Monastery 廣濟寺大殿.[12]

In terms of the columniation, both the eliminated-column structure (*jian-zhuzao* 減柱造) and the displaced-column structure (*yizhuzao* 移柱造) are prevalent in Yuan architecture.[13] As discussed in chapter 1, the eliminated-column structure and the displaced-column structure already had been used in north China prior to the Yuan dynasty. It is not until the Yuan dynasty, however, that both were developed fully and widely used in north China. The main hall of Lower Guangsheng Monastery and the Mañjuśrī Hall (Wenshudian 文殊殿) of Yanshan (Rocky Mountain) Monastery 岩山寺 are examples of the coexistence of the eliminated-column structure and the displaced-column structure.[14] In the main hall of Lower Guangsheng Monastery, half of the interior columns

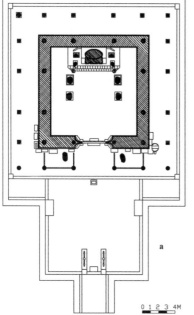

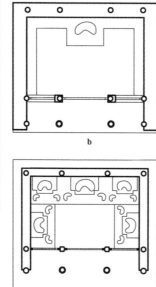

Fig. 2.1. Yuan buildings with squarish plan in north China: (a) plan of Mingyingwang Hall, Shuishen Temple, Hongdong, Shanxi, 1315 (redrawn by author after Chai Zejun, *Hongdong Guangshengsi*, 201); (b) plan of the main hall of Erlang Temple, Pingyao, Shanxi, Yuan (redrawn by author after Zhang Yuhuan, "Shanxi Yuandai diantang de damu jiegou," 88); (c) plan of the main hall of Longtian Temple, Jiexiu, Shanxi, Yuan (redrawn by author after Zhang Yuhuan, "Shanxi Yuandai diantang de damu jiegou," 88).

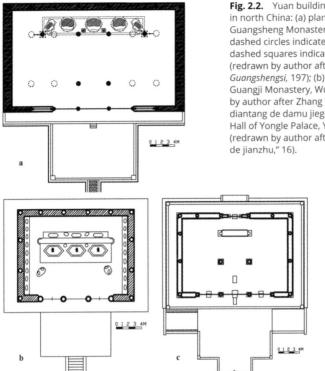

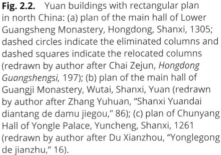

Fig. 2.2. Yuan buildings with rectangular plan in north China: (a) plan of the main hall of Lower Guangsheng Monastery, Hongdong, Shanxi, 1305; dashed circles indicate the eliminated columns and dashed squares indicate the relocated columns (redrawn by author after Chai Zejun, *Hongdong Guangshengsi*, 197); (b) plan of the main hall of Guangji Monastery, Wutai, Shanxi, Yuan (redrawn by author after Zhang Yuhuan, "Shanxi Yuandai diantang de damu jiegou," 86); (c) plan of Chunyang Hall of Yongle Palace, Yuncheng, Shanxi, 1261 (redrawn by author after Du Xianzhou, "Yonglegong de jianzhu," 16).

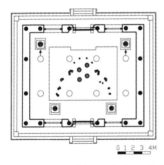

Fig. 2.3. Plan of the Mañjuśrī Hall of Yanshan Monastery, Fanshi, Shanxi, 1158. Dashed circles indicate the eliminated columns and dashed squares indicate the relocated columns. (Redrawn by author after Chai Zejun, *Fanshi yanshansi*, 37.)

were eliminated, and two interior columns were displaced (fig. 2.2). In the Mañjuśrī Hall, except for the four displaced columns, all other interior columns were removed (fig. 2.3). These two structures confirm that builders were already skilled in the eliminated-column structure and the displaced-column structure and were able to arrange the columns freely to provide more flexibility in the interior space.

BRACKET SETS

Three types of bracket sets are featured in Yuan architecture in north China: the oblique arm (*xiegong* 斜栱); the press-projection (*ya-tiao* 壓跳, a variety of projecting bracket in a capital set whose inner part is made quasi-trapezoidal to support a beam); and the wing-shaped bracket (*yixinggong* 翼形栱).

As discussed in chapter 1, the oblique arm usually is considered a signature of Jin dynasty architecture, and yet it was still quite prevalent in north China during the Yuan. One example can be found in the Mingyingwang Hall of Shuishen Temple in Shanxi province (fig. 2.4).

The press-projection was prevalent in the Yuan buildings in the north. Examples can be found in the Mingyingwang Hall of Shuishen Temple and Chuanfa Zhengzong (Dharma Transmission Orthodoxy) Hall 傳法正宗殿 of Yong'an (Eternal Peace) Monastery 永安寺 (fig. 2.5).[15] In both cases, the press-projection was put on top of a projecting bracket that projects toward the interior and supports a four-rafter beam (sichuanfu 四椽栿).

The wing-shaped bracket was frequently used in Yuan buildings in north China. Zhang Yuhuan

Fig. 2.4. Oblique arms in Mingyingwang Hall of Shuishen Temple, Hongdong, Shanxi, 1315. (Photo courtesy of Wu Yunan.)

argues that these wing-shaped arms, usually crossing the projecting bracket on both the interior and exterior tiers, first became popular in the Yuan dynasty, especially in southern Shanxi.[16] Examples of wing-shaped brackets can be found in the stage of Niuwang (Bull King) Temple 牛王廟戲臺, the main hall of Lower Guangsheng Monastery, and the Grand Hall of Jiangzhou 絳州大堂.

ROOF FRAMING

As mentioned above, according to the manner in which the roof structure was framed, Zhang Yuhuan divides Yuan architecture in Shanxi into two types: "the conventional style" and "the big-architrave-style." His categorization especially concerns beams or architraves in the framework.[17]

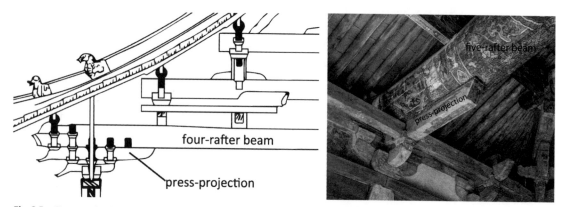

Fig. 2.5. Press-projection (yatiao) in North China: (a) press-projection in Mingyingwang Hall, Shuishen Temple, Hongdong, Shanxi, 1315 (redrawn by author after Chai Zejun, *Hongdong Guangshengsi*, 202); (b) Press-projection in Sanqing Hall of Qingmeng Daoist Temple, Gaoping, Shanxi, 1261. (Photo courtesy of Wu Yunan.)

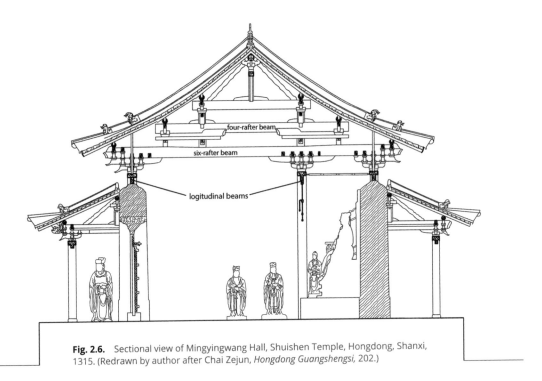

four-rafter beam

six-rafter beam

logitudinal beams

Fig. 2.6. Sectional view of Mingyingwang Hall, Shuishen Temple, Hongdong, Shanxi, 1315. (Redrawn by author after Chai Zejun, *Hongdong Guangshengsi*, 202.)

The so-called conventional style was inherited from the "convention" prior to the Yuan dynasty. According to Zhang's definition, in a conventional-style building, the transversal beams (*fu* 栿) are perpendicular to the facade of the building. The transversal beams are usually the thickest horizontal members in a building. This way of roof framing had been a longtime tradition in timber-framed architecture during the Song, Liao and Jin dynasties. Mingyingwang Hall exemplifies the conventional style (fig. 2.6), and it has no longitudinal beam that is thicker and stronger than the transversal beams, such as the six-rafter beam (*liuchuanfu* 六椽栿) and the four-rafter beam. The transversal beams carry the main load of the building.

The second type, "the big-architrave style," on the other hand, is notable for its longitudinal beams, usually called *e* 额, the architraves that are parallel to the facade of the building. In a Yuan building of the big-architrave style, it is the longitudinal beams, such as the big architraves (*da'e* 大额), instead of the transversal beams (*fu* 栿), that carry the main load of the roof structure. In this case, these architraves became much thicker and were even stronger than the transversal beams. The main hall of Shousheng (Sage of Longevity) Monastery 壽聖寺 exemplifies the big-architrave style. In this building, a big architrave was placed on top of the interior columns, and it is much thicker than any transversal beam, such as the four-rafter beam and three-rafter beam (*sanchuanfu* 三椽栿) (fig. 2.7). Such a big architrave placed on interior columns is also called an "interior architrave" (*wunei'e* 屋內額).

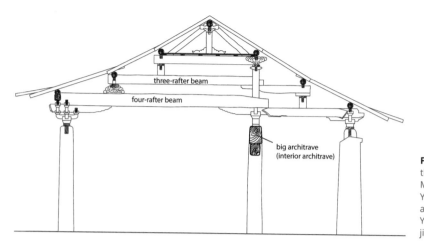

three-rafter beam

four-rafter beam

big architrave
(interior architrave)

Fig. 2.7. Sectional view of the main hall of Shousheng Monastery, Xinjiang, Shanxi, Yuan. (Redrawn by author after Zhang Yuhuan, "Shanxi Yuandai diantang de damu jiegou," 85.)

Municipal Hall of Huo Prefecture 霍州大堂 is another example of the big-architrave style.[18] This building featured a huge frontal beam, a typical "big architrave," lying on top of the eave columns (fig. 2.8). This big architrave is the most striking element on the facade; it replaced the flat architrave (*pupai-fang* 普拍方)[19] and overshadowed the railing architrave (*lan'e* 闌額), which ran

between the eave columns and was the major architrave in the conventional style. In other more revolutionary examples, such as the stage of Niuwang Temple, the railing architrave and the flat architrave both were omitted, and the big architrave was the only architrave on top of the eave columns (fig. 2.9).

Fu Xinian points out that the longitudinal frame (beams) carried the main load in timber architecture of early China; the transversal frame (beams) did not become load-bearing and more important until the Northern and Southern dynasties.[20] Therefore, the popularity of the big-architrave style in the Yuan dynasty is actually a revival of an ancient tradition. Occasionally found in Jin architecture, the big-architrave style was in general unique to the Yuan period and disappeared along with the fall of the Yuan dynasty. As discussed in chapter 1, the

Fig. 2.8. The Municipal Hall of Huo Prefecture, Huo County, Shanxi, 1304. (Photo courtesy of Zhao Yuanxiang.)

Fig. 2.9. Stage of Niuwang Temple, Linfen, Shanxi, 1283–1321. (Photo courtesy of Wu Yunan.)

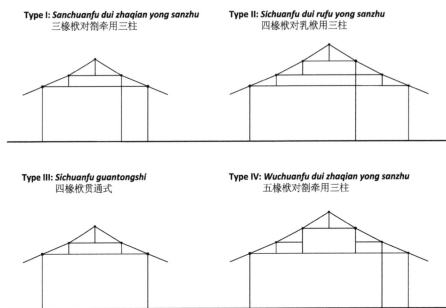

Fig. 2.10. Four types of the conventional style in north China defined by Zhang Yuhuan. (Drawing by author.)

Type I: *Sanchuanfu dui zhaqian yong sanzhu*
三椽栿对劄牵用三柱

Type II: *Sichuanfu dui rufu yong sanzhu*
四椽栿对乳栿用三柱

Type III: *Sichuanfu guantongshi*
四椽栿贯通式

Type IV: *Wuchuanfu dui zhaqian yong sanzhu*
五椽栿对劄牵用三柱

disappearance of the big-architrave style was related to the Ming regulations on architecture and the Ming revival of the Song tradition.

In addition to the beams, there are other features related to the big-architrave style. According to Zhang Yuhuan, the development of the big-architrave style in the Yuan dynasty was a result of the development of the eliminated-column structure and the displaced-column structure contemporaneously.[21] Architraves were thickened to compensate for the loss of load support due to the elimination and/or displacement of the columns. Therefore, the big-architrave style often is found with eliminated-column structure and/or displaced-column structure. Moreover, a wing-shaped bracket and a curtain-mounting joist (*chuomufang* 綽幕方) are also often found in Yuan buildings of the big-architrave style in north China. The curtain-mounting joist usually is used to compensate for the loss of the railing architrave that ceased to be used with the appearance of the big architrave.

In terms of the conventional style, Zhang Yuhuan further divides Yuan buildings into four subcategories based on the configuration of the (transversal) rafter beams (fig. 2.10). Type I is called *sanchuanfu dui zhaqian yong sanzhu* 三椽栿對劄牽用三柱; the building is spanned mainly by a three-rafter beam and a one-rafter beam with three columns (two eave columns and one interior column). In Type II, *sichuanfu dui rufu yong sanzhu* 四椽栿對乳栿用三柱, the building is crossed by one four-rafter beam and one two-rafter eave beam with three columns (two eave columns and one interior column). Type III, *sichuanfu tongguanshi* 四椽栿通貫式, has a master four-rafter beam spanning the whole section of the building, and no interior column was installed. Type IV is called *wuchuanfu dui zhaqian yong sanzhu* 五椽栿對劄牽用三柱, suggesting that the building was crossed by a five-rafter beam and a one-rafter beam with three columns.

Buildings of the big-architrave style were arranged in five subcategories (fig. 2.11), Type I, *sichuanfu guantong yong erzhu* 四椽栿貫通用二柱, has a master four-rafter beam spanning the whole section of the building with two eave columns; Type II is called *sanchuanfu dui zhaqian yong sanzhu* 三椽栿對劄牽用三柱, meaning the building is spanned mainly by a three-rafter beam and a one-rafter beam with three columns (two eave columns and one interior column); Type III is named *sichuanfu qianhou dui zhaqian yong sizhu* 四椽栿前後對劄牽用四柱, indicating that the building is crossed by one four-rafter beam and two one-rafter beams (on each side of the four-rafter beam) with four columns (two eave columns and two interior columns). In Type IV, *sichuanfu dui rufu yong sanzhu* 四椽栿對乳栿用三柱, the building is crossed by one four-rafter beam and one two-rafter beam with three columns (two eave columns and one interior column). Finally, Type V, *liuchuanfu dui rufu yong sanzhu* 六椽栿對乳栿用三柱, suggests that the building is crossed by a six-rafter beam and a two-rafter beam with three columns.[22]

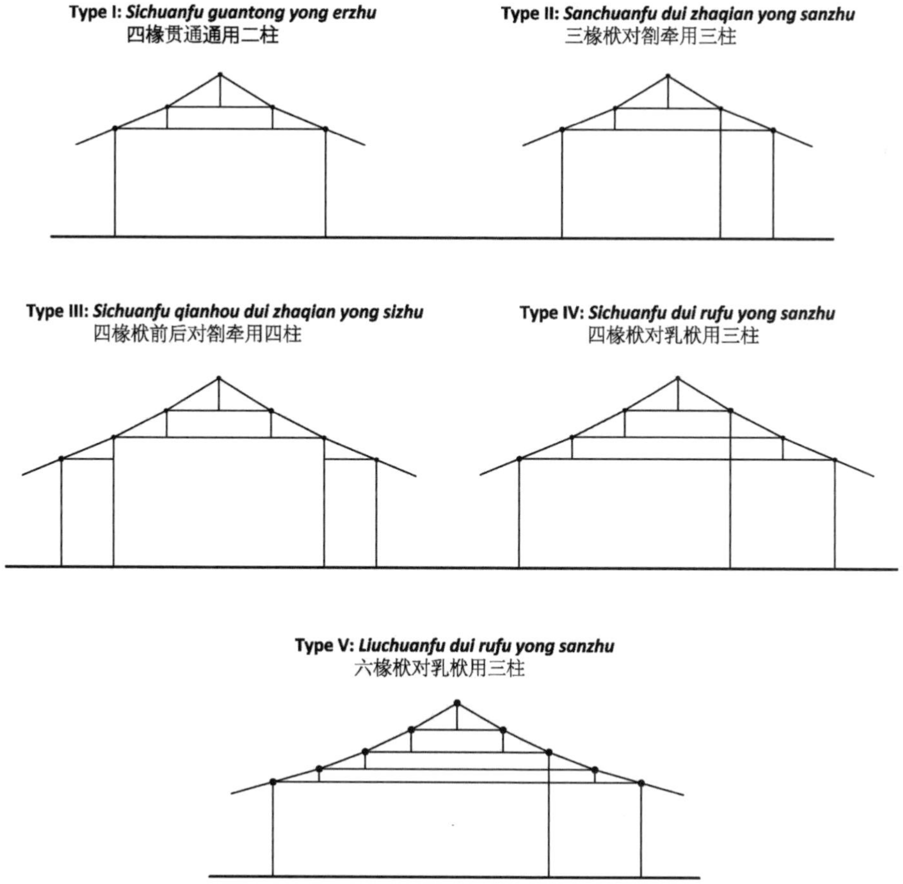

Type I: *Sichuanfu guantong yong erzhu*
四椽贯通通用二柱

Type II: *Sanchuanfu dui zhaqian yong sanzhu*
三椽栿对劄牵用三柱

Type III: *Sichuanfu qianhou dui zhaqian yong sizhu*
四椽栿前后对劄牵用四柱

Type IV: *Sichuanfu dui rufu yong sanzhu*
四椽栿对乳栿用三柱

Type V: *Liuchuanfu dui rufu yong sanzhu*
六椽栿对乳栿用三柱

Fig. 2.11. Five types of the big-architrave style in north China defined by Zhang Yuhuan. (Drawing by author.)

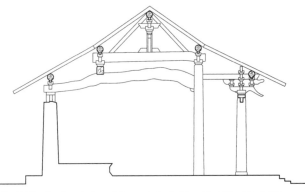

Fig. 2.12. Sectional view of the main hall of Longtian Temple, Jiexiu, Shanxi, Yuan. (Redrawn by author after Zhang Yuhuan, "Shanxi Yuandai diantang de damu jiegou," 82.)

The coexistence of the conventional style and the big-architrave style with their many variations in north China obviously indicates the builders' flexibility and creativity when constructing the roof frame. In addition to the configuration of the roof frame, there are a few more noteworthy details. First of all, the finishings of some Yuan buildings in north China are not as refined as those of the Song and Jin dynasties. Sometimes the joinery of the timber frame is not decorated. For example, beams in the main hall of Shousheng Monastery are connected directly to the posts and columns without any bracket sets or camel humps built into the joints of the timber members (fig. 2.7).[23] Besides the non-finished joinery, Yuan buildings in the north also feature the usage of rough logs. For instance, the three-rafter beam in the main hall of Longtian Temple that spans from the eave column to the interior column is made of a non-processed curved log (fig. 2.12). Crescent-moon-shaped beams (*yueliang* 月梁), a structural and decorative member documented in the *YZFS*, also were rare in north China during the Yuan dynasty.

To summarize characteristics of the northern tradition, there seems to have been a great deal of flexibility in the arrangement of columns as well as in the configuration of the roof framing. Yuan architecture of the north is noted for a more advanced and adventurous employment of the eliminated-column structure and the displaced-column structure compared to that of the Song and Jin periods. Moreover, the new method of roof framing, the big-architrave style, demonstrates the creativity and innovation of the local builders and a compromise in the decorativeness of the architectural members.

THE UPPER YANGZI TRADITION

As already discussed, only a dozen examples of Yuan architecture have been found in the Upper Yangzi. Although the number of extant buildings is just a small percentage of those in north China, it is still possible to generalize a regional tradition based on these structures. The following analyses are based on the ten examples in the Upper Yangzi that were surveyed by the author in person. A case study of each building in this section can be found in chapter 3.

The ten buildings in the Upper Yangzi all face roughly south. Two have rectangular plans, and the other eight have a small squarish plan. The eight squarish buildings can be further divided into two types: five buildings have a three-by-three-bay plan with four columns on every side of the building;[24] three have a three-by-four-bay plan with five columns, instead of four, on the sides. The three-by-three-bay type displays a proper proportion of the bays: the central bay on the facade is twice or one-and-a-half times wider than the side bays, which are almost as wide as both the front and rear bays on the side. As for the buildings belonging to the three-by-four-bay type, the main hall of Bao'en Monastery (fig. 3.14) and the main hall of Qinglong Monastery (fig. 3.33) both have one additional column on the midpoint of the side, perhaps to provide extra support on the side. The main hall of Yong'an Monastery has a different design: its side elevation is noticeably wider than the facade (fig. 3.21). In addition, Feilai Hall of the Temple of the Eastern Peak (fig. 3.8) and Pingxiang Pavilion (fig. 3.43) have rectangular plans. Given their five-bay-wide facade and four-bay-wide side, they both may be considered large-sized buildings. In the Upper Yangzi, a rectangular plan was chosen for a larger building although a squarish building also could be large.

The eliminated-column structure and the displaced-column structure, considered the most typical features of Yuan architecture in north China, are also used in some buildings in the Upper Yangzi. The eliminated-column structure is found in three Yuan buildings in the Upper Yangzi that are relatively near to each other: the main hall of Lifeng Temple (fig. 3.1), Pantuoshi Hall (fig. 3.46), and Yong'an Temple (fig. 3.56). They all have a squarish three-by-three-bay plan, suggesting that they were supposed to have sixteen columns to compose a three-by-three plan. Nevertheless, in order to provide a spacious worship room with fewer columns, two interior columns of Yong'an Temple and two front eave columns of the main hall of Lifeng Temple were removed. Furthermore, both front eave columns and interior columns were removed in Pantuoshi Hall; due to the hall's small size, its structural stability seems to not have been compromised by this elimination of four columns.

In terms of the displaced-column structure, the main hall of Bao'en Monastery is the only example in the Upper Yangzi: two interior columns and two side eave columns of the same row were relocated a little farther back, thus enlarging the central bay (figs. 3.14 and 3.19). Feilai Hall, the largest known Yuan building in the Upper Yangzi, is the only structure in which both the eliminated-column structure and the displaced-column structure are used (fig. 3.8). It is an excellent example of how the eliminated-column structure and the displaced-column structure were combined to create a spacious entrance with the fewest columns. The number of bays on the facade was reduced from five to three, making it possible to expand the width of the front entrance from less than five to more than eight meters.

BRACKET SETS

The first important factor related to the bracket sets is the layout of intercolumnar bracket sets. Unlike capital sets that sit on top of a column, intercolumnar sets are built in between the columns and usually sit atop horizontal architraves. In regard to Yuan architecture in the Upper Yangzi, there are four layout types for intercolumnar sets (fig. 2.13). Type A includes buildings in which only one intercolumnar bracket set was installed in the central bay (*dangxinjian* 當心間) on the facade.[25] The main halls of Yong'an and Qinglong Monasteries belong to

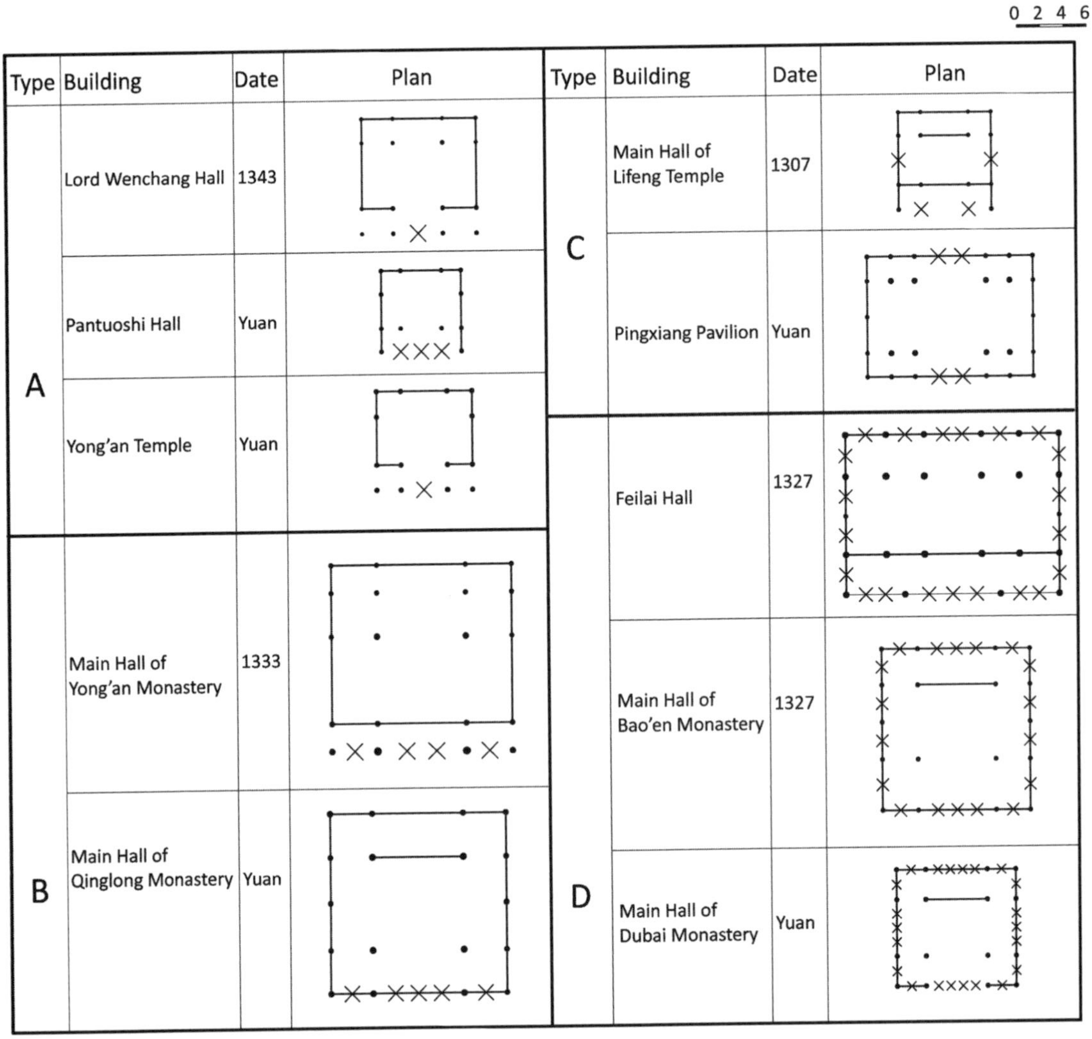

0 2 4 6

Type	Building	Date	Plan	Type	Building	Date	Plan
A	Lord Wenchang Hall	1343		C	Main Hall of Lifeng Temple	1307	
	Pantuoshi Hall	Yuan			Pingxiang Pavilion	Yuan	
	Yong'an Temple	Yuan		D	Feilai Hall	1327	
B	Main Hall of Yong'an Monastery	1333			Main Hall of Bao'en Monastery	1327	
	Main Hall of Qinglong Monastery	Yuan			Main Hall of Dubai Monastery	Yuan	

Fig. 2.13. Four layout types for intercolumnar sets in the Upper Yangzi. (Drawing by author.)

Type B; their intercolumnar sets were placed on each bay of the facade but not on any other side of the building. There are two intercolumnar sets in the central bay of the main hall of Yong'an Monastery, whereas at Qinglong Monastery there was only one. Type C includes buildings with intercolumnar sets installed on the side elevations in addition to the facade. In the main hall of Lifeng Temple, intercolumnar sets were built in the middle bay on the side elevation. In the Pingxiang Pavilion, intercolumnar sets were constructed in the middle of the rear side of the building. In buildings of Type D, intercolumnar sets were installed in every bay around all sides of the building.

As for the number of intercolumnar sets in a single bay, some buildings have one, some two, and others three. It seems that the craftsmen could choose either to build or not to build intercolumnar sets in any bay, and they also had several options of how many to have. In addition, the facades of buildings of Type A and Type B received special treatment, as intercolumnar sets were installed only on the facade and not on any other side.

As introduced in chapter 1, *cai* 材 is the major modular unit of a building, and *zhi* 栔 is a sub-unit. The sizes of *cai* and *zhi* usually are indicated by the bracket sets. The cross-section of a bracket arm is one *cai*, and the distance between two bracket arms, which are vertically stacked one above the other, is one *zhi*. Table 2.1 displays some measurements of Yuan architecture in the Upper Yangzi, with a reference to the standard in the *YZFS*.

According to Table 2.1, the modular system of Yuan architecture in the Upper Yangzi seems to be very different from the standard in the *YZFS*. The modular unit *cai* in the Upper Yangzi ranges from Grade IV to even smaller than Grade VIII. *Cai* can be as big as 21.5 cm and as small as 13 cm wide. The grade of the *cai* is not in proportion to the width of the central bay, nor does it change regularly

Table 2.1. Measurement of the modular unit in Yuan buildings of the Upper Yangzi (unit = cm)

Building	Date	CB[a]	Grade	WC	TC	WC/TC (%)	WZ	WC/WZ
Standard in the *YZFS*	1103					1.5		2.5
Main Hall of Lifeng Temple	1307	405	VII–VI	17.5	12.5	1.40 (−6.7%)	9.0	1.94 (−22.4%)
Feilai Hall (outer-eave bracket sets)	1327	490	V–IV	21.5	14.0	1.53 (2%)	9.5	2.26 (−9.6%)
Feilai Hall (interior trough bracket sets)	1327		VI	18.0	11.0	1.64 (9.3%)	6.5	2.77 (10.8%)
Feilai Hall (small-scale carpentry)	1327		<VIII	13.0	8.5	1.53 (2%)	5.5	2.36 (−5.6%)
Lord Wenchang Hall	1343	430	<VIII	13.0			9.0	1.44 (−42.4%)
Main Hall of Qinglong Monastery	NA	777	VI	18.0	12.0	1.50 (0%)	7.5	2.40 (−4%)
Pantuoshi Hall	NA	355	VII–VI	17.0	12.0	1.41 (−6%)	7.0	2.43 (−2.8%)

Note: In this table, CB = width of the central bay, WC = width of *cai*; TC = thickness of *cai*; WZ = width of *zhi*.

[a] The width of the central bay does not count those that are widened because of the eliminated-column structure or the displaced-column structure. The width of the central bay in this table is the measurement of the original condition.

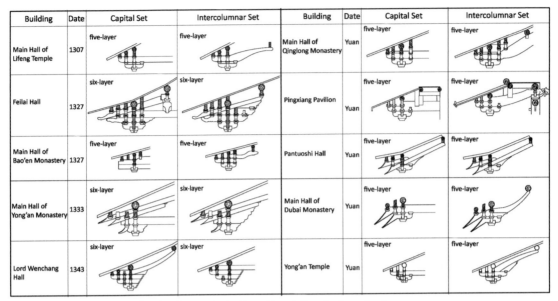

Building	Date	Capital Set	Intercolumnar Set	Building	Date	Capital Set	Intercolumnar Set
Main Hall of Lifeng Temple	1307	five-layer	five-layer	Main Hall of Qinglong Monastery	Yuan	five-layer	five-layer
Feilai Hall	1327	six-layer	six-layer	Pingxiang Pavilion	Yuan	five-layer	five-layer
Main Hall of Bao'en Monastery	1327	five-layer	five-layer	Pantuoshi Hall	Yuan	five-layer	five-layer
Main Hall of Yong'an Monastery	1333	six-layer	six-layer	Main Hall of Dubai Monastery	Yuan	five-layer	five-layer
Lord Wenchang Hall	1343	six-layer	six-layer	Yong'an Temple	Yuan	five-layer	five-layer

Fig. 2.14. Number of layers of the bracket sets in the Upper Yangzi. (Drawing by author.)

over time. The ratio of the *cai*'s width to its thickness (WC/TC) also varies. In the Upper Yangzi, three buildings are close to the standard of *YZFS* with less than 5 percent deviation; these vary from 6.7 percent to 9 percent larger or smaller than the standard of *YZFS*. No regulations have been shown to be related to the date or size of the building. Moreover, ratios of the width of *cai* to *zhi* (WC/WZ) differ significantly from the standard of *YZFS*. Only one building deviates within 5 percent from the standard of *YZFS*. Most of the buildings are smaller than the standard in this aspect. In Wenchang Hall, the ratio is only 1:1.44, which is more than 40 percent smaller than the standard. Feilai Hall is the only example whose ratio of WC/WZ is bigger than the standard of *YZFS*.

When using the modular unit *cai* and sub-unit *zhi* to construct bracket sets, there are two kinds of projecting bracket (*huagong* 華栱): the "single-unit" (*dancai* 單材), meaning the measurement of the section of the projecting bracket is one *cai*; and the "full-unit" (*zucai* 足材), meaning that the size of the section of the projecting bracket is one *cai* plus one *zhi*. According to the *YZFS*, the projecting bracket in a capital set was a full-unit; however, that of an intercolumnar set was a single-unit. This rule, again, is not applied in the Upper Yangzi. There, all Yuan buildings in without exception were built with a full-unit projecting bracket on both the capital and intercolumnar sets.

A "step" (*tiao* 跳) is any projection in a bracket set, either a bracket arm (*gong* 栱) or an inclined cantilever (*ang* 昂), that transversally projects from the capital block (*ludou* 櫨斗). According to the *YZFS*, the bracket sets (*puzuo* 鋪作) are "numbered" according to the number of "steps." A bracket set with one step is considered as four-layer (*sipuzuo* 四鋪作), two as five-layer (*wupuzuo* 五鋪作), and so on. The number of layers in Yuan architecture in the Upper Yangzi are mostly five or six, regardless of the date or the size of the building (fig. 2.14). Among the ten extant examples surveyed in the Upper Yangzi, seven have five-layer bracket sets. Most of them project either two tiers of projecting bracket, such as Yong'an Temple, Pingxiang Pavilion, and the main halls of Lifeng Temple, Bao'en Monastery, and Qinglong Monastery, or two tiers of inclined cantilever, such as Pantuoshi Hall and the main hall of Dubai Monastery. Three buildings have six-layer bracket sets: Feilai Hall, the main hall of Yong'an Monastery, and Wenchang Hall. Except for Feilai Hall, whose plan is evidently larger, there is nothing extraordinary about the other two buildings with six-layer bracket sets.

The number of the steps is important in configuring a bracket set. Further, the way in which a step was constructed also matters. There are two common methods to make a step: the "stolen-heart structure" (*touxinzao* 偷心造) and the "crisscross-heart structure" (*jixinzao* 計心造). The stolen-heart structure is a successive transverse projection; no bracket arm parallel to the elevation of the building is built on the step. The crisscross-heart structure, however, has such a bracket arm. In the Upper Yangzi, most exterior steps (*waitiao* 外跳, the steps of a bracket set that projects toward the outside of the building) were constructed as the crisscross-heart structure. As for the interior steps (*litiao* 裡跳, steps of a bracket set that projects toward the inside of the building), both crisscross-heart and stolen-heart structures can be found. Table 2.2 shows no pattern in terms of choosing the stolen-heart structure over the crisscross-heart structure or vice versa. It is related neither to chronology nor to the number of the layers in the bracket sets.

If a step is constructed as the crisscross-heart structure, it can have two kinds of bracket arm parallel to the plane of the wall: a single bracket (*dangong* 單栱) or a double bracket (*chonggong* 重栱). Table 2.3 shows that the single bracket was used more often than the double bracket. Among the ten examples in the Upper Yangzi, six use only single brackets and four use both kinds.

Table 2.2. Interior steps of the buildings in the Upper Yangzi

Building	Date	Number of layers	Interior step
Main Hall of Lifeng Temple	1307	5	Stolen heart
Feilai Hall	1327	6	Crisscross heart
Main Hall of Bao'en Monastery	1327	5	Crisscross heart
Main Hall of Yong'an Monastery	1333	6	Stolen heart
Lord Wenchang Hall	1343	6	Stolen heart
Main Hall of Qinglong Monastery	Yuan	5	Crisscross heart
Pantuoshi Hall	Yuan	5	Stolen heart
Yong'an Temple	Yuan	5	Stolen heart
Main Hall of Dubai Monastery	Yuan	5	Stolen heart
Pingxiang Pavilion	n/a	5	Crisscross heart

Table 2.3. Single bracket and double bracket in the Upper Yangzi

Building	Date	Single bracket	Double bracket
Main Hall of Lifeng Temple	1307	X	
Feilai Hall	1327	X	X
Main Hall of Bao'en Monastery	1327	X	X
Main Hall of Yong'an Monastery	1333	X	
Lord Wenchang Hall of Wulong Temple	1343	X	X
Main Hall of Qinglong Monastery	Yuan	X	X
Pantuoshi Hall	Yuan	X	
Yong'an Temple	Yuan	X	
Main Hall of Dubai Monastery	Yuan	X	
Pingxiang Pavilion	NA	X	

The double bracket was used not only on the projections of bracket sets but is found more frequently on the axis of the eave columns as part of the configuration of the buttress-bracket (*fubigong* 扶壁栱). The buttress-bracket, called "shadow-bracket" (*yinggong* 影栱) in the *YZFS*, is a multipiece frame parallel to the wall and sitting directly above the row of eave columns. A set of buttress-brackets is composed of a plain beam having a one-*cai* section (*sufang* 素方), a single bracket or a double bracket, and blocks (*dou* 斗). The buttress-bracket can have various configurations. According to the *YZFS*, the arrangement of the buttress-bracket is part of the configuration of the entire bracket sets. It may differ depending on whether the bracket set has a projecting bracket built as a stolen-heart structure (*touxin huagong* 偷心華栱) or as a crisscross-heart structure (*jixin huagong* 計心華栱), or whether it has a crisscross-heart double bracket (*chonggong jixin* 重栱計心) or a crisscross-heart single bracket (*dangong jixin* 單栱計心), and the number of layers.[26]

Five types of buttress-bracket are listed in the *YZFS*, and each type is related to a specific type of bracket set (fig. 2.15). Type A and Type B are related to bracket sets with the crisscross-heart structure. Type A consists of one layer of double bracket and one layer of plain beam, and is used in bracket sets that have double brackets on the exterior steps. Type B consists of one layer of single bracket with two plain beams on top and is designated for four-layer bracket sets or those with single brackets on its exterior steps. Type C through Type E are related to bracket sets whose first step is constructed as a stolen-heart structure. Type C is used in five-layer bracket sets and consists of, from bottom to top, one layer of double bracket, one layer of plain beam, one layer of single bracket, and another layer of plain beam. Type D and Type E are both used in six- or seven-layer bracket sets. Two single brackets and two plain beams alternately top the capital block in Type D. Type E has one double bracket on the capital block with two plain beams on top.

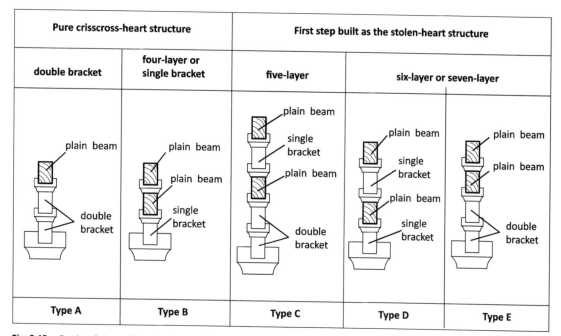

Pure crisscross-heart structure		First step built as the stolen-heart structure		
double bracket	four-layer or single bracket	five-layer	six-layer or seven-layer	
Type A	Type B	Type C	Type D	Type E

Fig. 2.15. Sectional views of the five types of buttress-bracket listed in the *YZFS*. (Drawing by author.)

The configuration of the buttress-bracket in the *YZFS* is specified strictly. The actual buildings, however, do not always follow the *YZFS*. In Table 2.4 it is shown that only four Yuan buildings in the Upper Yangzi follow the *YZFS* in this aspect. The other six were built like Type A as opposed to Type B. In these six examples, all single brackets, as supposed in the *YZFS*, were converted into double brackets in the actual buildings. Although Table 2.3 indicates that the single bracket was favored on the projections of the bracket sets in the Upper Yangzi, Table 2.4 shows that the double bracket was preferred in the buttress-bracket here.

Table 2.4. Comparison of buttress-bracket in the Upper Yangzi and in the *YZFS*

Building in the Upper Yangzi	Date	Type of buttress-bracket	As in the *YZFS*
Main Hall of Lifeng Temple	1307	A	B
Feilai Hall	1327	A	A
Main Hall of Bao'en Monastery	1327	B	B
Main Hall of Yong'an Monastery	1333	A	B
Lord Wenchang Hall	1343	A	A
Main Hall of Qinglong Monastery	Yuan	A	B
Pantuoshi Hall	Yuan	B	B
Yong'an Temple	Yuan	A	B
Main Hall of Dubai Monastery	Yuan	A	B
Pingxiang Pavilion	n/a	A	B

n/a = not applicable

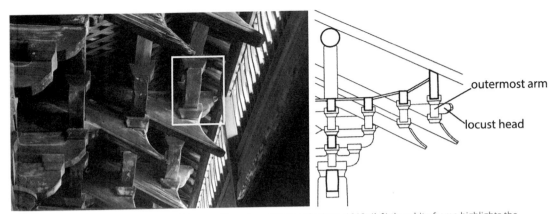

Fig. 2.16. Bracket set in the main hall of Baoguo Monastery, Ningbo, Zhejiang, 1013: (*left*) the white frame highlights the outermost bracket and the locust head (photo by author); (*right*) drawing (redrawn by author after Guo Daiheng, *Donglai diyishan: Baoguosi*, 88).

As mentioned previously, the oblique arm was not recorded in the *YZFS*, but can be found in Song, Jin, and Yuan architecture in north China. In the Upper Yangzi, four Yuan buildings have oblique arms at a 45° angle. The main halls of Bao'en and Qinglong Monasteries have oblique arms built on intercolumnar sets (figs. 3.18 and 3.36). For the other two buildings, Lord Wenchang Hall and Yong'an Temple, an oblique arm is used on both the capital and intercolumnar sets (figs. 3.28, 3.29, and 3.58). The presence of an oblique arm in the Upper Yangzi may suggest influence from the north, which will be further discussed below.

The outermost bracket (*linggong* 令栱) in a bracket set is parallel to the plane of the wall and usually is crossed by a locust head (*shuatou* 耍頭), an overhanging bracket-end and the topmost member parallel to and above the projecting bracket and the inclined cantilever (*ang* 昂; fig. 2.16). It is surprising that the outermost bracket is not found anywhere in Yuan architecture in the Upper Yangzi, let alone the locust head. All the topmost projecting brackets were made to support directly the square eave purlin (*liaoyanfang* 撩檐方) without a set of the outermost bracket, locust head and small blocks (fig. 2.14). The lack of both the outermost bracket and the locust head is unique to Yuan architecture in the Upper Yangzi.

Different from the capital set that was built to connect columns with rafter beams, the intercolumnar bracket set was made to transfer the load of the lower purlin to the architraves through an inclined cantilever, or more precisely, a downward cantilever (*xia'ang* 下昂). Usually there were two ways to design a downward cantilever. One is called *angwei tiaowo* 昂尾挑斡, which means the inner end of the downward cantilever inclines upward to carry a lower purlin, and at the same time it also projects toward the outside of the building. The other one, called *angting tiaowo* 昂桯挑斡, was composed in the same way at its inner end but had no projections toward the outside.[27]

Based on extant examples, the *angting tiaowo* was more popular than the *angwei tiaowo* in the Yuan dynasty in the Upper Yangzi: seven out of ten buildings had their intercolumnar sets built as *angting tiaowo* (fig. 2.17). The downward cantilever of these buildings varies in shape, dimension, and position. Some are curved upward, some are curved downward, and others are straight. Some look slender and as thick as one unit of a *cai*, while others are thicker with irregular shapes. In some buildings, such as Wenchang Hall, Yong'an Temple, and the main hall of

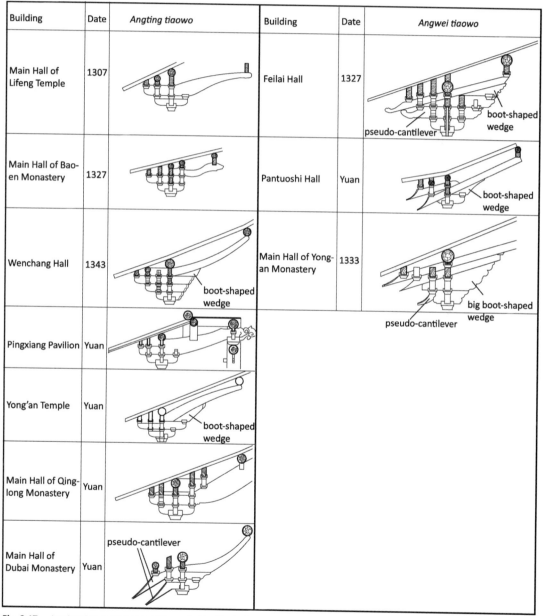

Fig. 2.17. *Angting tiaowo* and *angwei tiaowo* in the Upper Yangzi. (Drawing by author.)

Dubai Monastery, the downward cantilever connects the eave purlin directly to the lower purlin; others, however, connect members that are parallel to the purlins.

In terms of the other type, *angwei tiaowo*, there are three examples found in the Upper Yangzi: Feilai Hall, Yong'an Monastery, and Pantuoshi Hall. It is interesting that each building has a unique downward cantilever: Feilai Hall has only one, and the other two buildings have two. Pantuoshi Hall has two non-parallel downward cantilevers, while the main hall of Yong'an Monastery has two downward cantilevers that are parallel to each other. It is noticeable that the top downward cantilever in Pantuoshi Hall is unusually short, ends right above the end of the first inner projecting bracket, and is much shorter than the bottom one. This short downward cantilever may be evidence of the transition from a real cantilever to a pseudo-cantilever.

A pseudo-cantilever (*jia'ang* 假昂, a variation of projecting bracket but disguised as a downward cantilever) is found in three buildings, and was built in both the capital set and the intercolumnar set in all three. Lastly, a boot-shaped wedge (*xuexie* 靴楔) that was used to adjust the level of the downward cantilever is found in the bracket sets of five Yuan buildings. It is noteworthy that the boot-shaped wedge in the intercolumnar sets of the main hall of Yong'an Monastery can be considered a great boot-shaped wedge (*daxuexie* 大靴楔) due to its size and its similar function as an upward cantilever, which will be introduced later.

ROOF FRAMING

As discussed in chapter 1, there are three types of roof framing recorded in the *YZFS*: the palatial style (*diangeshi* 殿閣式), the mansion style (*tingtangshi* 廳堂式), and the column-and-beam style (*zhuliangshi* 柱梁式). Most Yuan buildings in the Upper Yangzi were constructed in the mansion style. In a few buildings, however, features of the palatial style were mixed with the mansion style. For instance, the middle bays of the main hall of Lifeng Temple (fig. 3.6) and Yong'an Temple (fig. 3.61) are spanned by a two-rafter beam along with a layer of bracket sets built on the interior columns. In Feilai Hall (fig. 3.10), bracket sets are installed on two rows of interior columns that partially resemble those of a palatial-style building.

A mansion-style building with three bays along its side is listed in the *YZFS* that has a roof structure, from the sectional view, crossed by eight rafters with two two-rafter eaves beams (*rufu* 乳栿) spanning the front and rear bays, and four columns. In the *YZFS*, it is called *bajia chuanwu qianhou rufu yong sizhu* 八架椽屋前後乳栿用四柱; fig. 2.18).

Compared to the *YZFS*, configurations of rafters and beams of actual Yuan buildings in the Upper Yangzi have more varieties. The first type, represented by Feilai Hall (fig. 3.10) and the main hall of Qinglong Monastery (fig. 3.40),

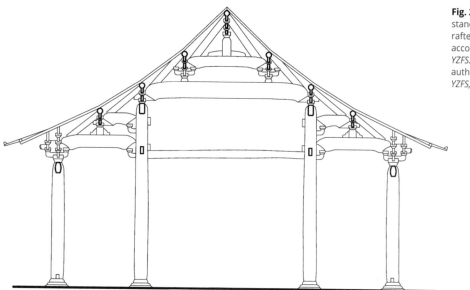

Fig. 2.18. A standard eight-rafter building according to the *YZFS*. (Redrawn by author after the *YZFS, juan* 31.)

was designed exactly like the standard eight-rafter hall in the *YZFS*. The interior space is divided into three parts. The front and rear parts are crossed by a two-rafter eaves-beam, and the middle part is crossed by four-rafter beams. The second type, as shown in the main hall of Lifeng Temple (fig. 3.6) and Wenchang Hall (fig. 3.31), looks basically like the standard in the *YZFS* except that it has four or six rafters rather than eight. The third type, such as Pantuoshi Hall (fig. 3.50) and Yong'an Temple (fig. 3.61), also has three bays along the side but is only crossed by four rafters in total. The third type is different from a four-rafter building of the second type because the former has one interior column removed and the interior space is spanned by a one-rafter beam (*zhaqian* 劄牽) and a three-rafter beam. Last, a few examples in the Upper Yangzi are irregular. The main hall of Bao'en Monastery is crossed by ten rafters that are divided by two interior columns as 3–5–2—three in the front bay, five in the middle, and two in the rear (fig. 3.19). The main hall of Yong'an Monastery is an eight-rafter building with three interior columns (fig. 3.24). In summary, the number of rafters in these Yuan buildings varies from four to ten, and the front bay in most Upper Yangzi buildings is one rafter or two rafters wide.

In a mansion-style building, the major crossbeam, usually known as the two-rafter eaves-beam, the T-beam (*dingfu* 丁栿), or the three-rafter beam, is used to connect the eave columns and the interior columns. At one end, the beam is supported by the interior part of a capital bracket set; while at the other end, the beam is inserted into the shaft of the interior column. In terms of the beam-bearing method, some beams are supported by one tier of projecting brackets (fig. 2.19a), some by none (fig. 2.19b), and some by a press-projection (fig. 2.19c). Both the projecting brackets on the interior steps (*litiao huagong* 裡跳華栱) and the press-projection (*yatiao* 壓跳) are mentioned in *juan* 4 of the *YZFS* as methods to support the major beams from the eave columns.[28] As for the other end of the beam, crossbeams of all but one the Yuan buildings in the Upper Yangzi simply are inserted into the shaft of the interior columns without any transitional member (fig. 2.19). The exception is Feilai Hall, which has a press-projection-like member supporting its two-rafter beam from the interior column.

The crescent-moon-shaped beam is a type of artistically crafted beam with both its top and bottom profiles curved slightly downward. The method of making curved profiles is illustrated in *juan* 5 of the *YZFS*. Regardless of the length of the crescent-moon-shaped beam, the middle part of its body is straight, but both its ends are curved downward and are symmetrical from left to right (fig. 2.20). Moreover, according to the definition of the palatial style in the *YZFS*, the exposed beams (*mingfu* 明栿, a visible main beam that was below the ceiling) usually are processed into a crescent-moon shape as a decorative part of the building. The rough beams (*caofu* 草栿, the beam above the ceiling and invisible in the room), on the other hand, are not processed into any decorative shape and are known as straight beams (*zhiliang* 直梁). Based on Liang Sicheng's commentary on this issue, if a beam is shaped like a crescent moon, it is merely decorative and does not help to carry the load of the roof structure.[29] This is not the case in a mansion-style building where all the beams are exposed. The crescent-moon-shaped beam could be both a decorative and structural member.

All buildings in the Upper Yangzi were built in the mansion style, and all their beams were exposed. The beams in the Upper Yangzi, however, were not carved into the crescent-moon-shaped beam, nor were they absolutely "straight." They were merely unshaped timber pieces without much of a decorative profile. Thus, Yuan architecture in the Upper Yangzi did not follow the rules in the *YZFS* in this detail.

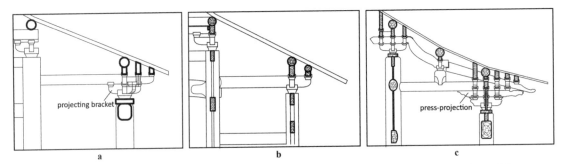

Fig. 2.19. Beams supported by one tier of projecting bracket in the Upper Yangzi: (a) Yong'an Temple, Langzhong, Sichuan, 1333; (b) the main hall of Lifeng Temple, Nanbu, Sichuan, 1307; (c) Feilai Hall of the Temple of the Eastern Peak, Emei, Sichuan, 1327. (Drawings by author.)

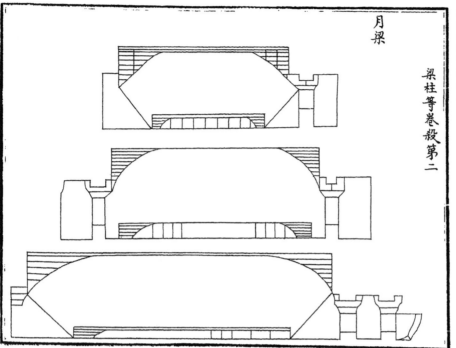

月梁

梁柱等卷殺第二

Fig. 2.20.
Illustration of the crescent-moon-shaped beam in the *YZFS, juan* 30. (From https://archive.org/details/06051724.cn.)

Table 2.5 shows various members used atop eave columns in Yuan buildings of the Upper Yangzi. The flat architrave, a flat beam that rests directly on a railing architrave or an eave architrave (*yan'e* 檐额), seems to have been popular in the Upper Yangzi. A filler board (*dianban* 垫板) is used in the Upper Yangzi to fill the space between the flat architrave and the eave architrave/railing architrave. The associate architrave (*you'e* 由额) is used in three buildings there. It usually is installed at a proper height under the railing architrave or the eave architrave. It is noteworthy that many railing architraves or eave architraves are curved downward and can be considered as a crescent-moon style (*yueliangzao* 月梁造). It is quite unique that the transversal beams (*fu* 栿) are not crescent-shaped in the Upper Yangzi, but the longitudinal beams, such as the architraves (*e* 额), are, which is the opposite of the *YZFS*. This is an important sign of the shifting focus in the design.

Last but not least, based on the information in Table 2.5, the eave architrave, instead of railing architrave, seems to have been quite popular in the Upper Yangzi. As already discussed, the size of an eave architrave was usually much larger than a railing architrave, which somewhat resembles the buildings of the big-architrave style in north China. The eave architrave of these Upper Yangzi buildings, however, was not exactly like the big architrave in north China: the former still is built between the eave columns, while the latter was placed on top of the eave columns. Nevertheless, these buildings can still be defined as a sub-type of the big-architrave style because huge interior architraves, another

Table 2.5. Members atop eave columns in buildings of the Upper Yangzi

Building	Date	Railing architrave	Eave architrave	Curtain-mounting joist	Flat architrave	Filler board	Dwarf pillar	Associate architrave	Crescent-moon-shaped beam	Fig. no.
Main Hall of Lifeng Temple	1307	X		X	X	X			X	3.20
Feilai Hall	1327		X	X	X	X			X	3.90
Main Hall of Bao'en Monastery	1327		X		X	X		X		3.15
Main Hall of Yong'an Monastery	1333	X		X	X	X			X	3.22
Lord Wenchang Hall	1343		X		X	X			X	3.27
Main Hall of Qinglong Monastery	Yuan		X		X	X	X		X	3.34
Pingxiang Pavilion	Yuan	X			X		X		X	3.44
Pantuoshi Hall	Yuan		X						X	3.47
Main Hall of Dubai Monastery	Yuan	X			X			X		3.51
Yong'an Temple	Yuan		X		X			X	X	3.57

feature defining big-architrave style, were also found in buildings in the Upper Yangzi. Examples are the main halls of Yong'an, Bao'en, and Qinglong Monasteries.

Although the Yuan buildings in the Upper Yangzi are not exactly like those big-architrave-style buildings in the north, they share many important features of that style, which suggests a connection between the Upper Yangzi buildings and the techniques of the big-architrave style in the north. Such a connection is important, as it suggests a departure from the *YZFS*, the idealistic Song style.

The last feature found uniquely in the Upper Yangzi is the simplification or complete lack of the column base (*zhuchu* 柱础). According to the *YZFS*, a column base is composed basically of four parts: the plinth (the square base underneath the ground); the overturned bowl (*fupen* 覆盆, usually carved with decoration and above the ground); the lip of the bowl (*penchun* 盆唇, the thin layer above the overturned bowl); and the column foot (*zhuzhi* 柱櫍,

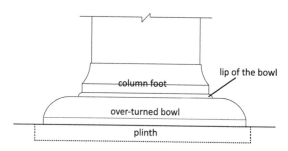

Fig. 2.21. Column base in the *YZFS*. (Drawing by author.)

the top part right under the wooden column) (fig. 2.21). It is unique that a few buildings in the Upper Yangzi simply do not have column bases: for example, in Pantuoshi Hall and the main halls of Lifeng Temple and Dubai Monastery the columns were built directly into the ground. For the rest, there are three types of column base (fig. 2.22). Type I, found in Feilai Hall, Yong'an Monastery, and Qinglong Monastery, merely has a plain overturned bowl above the plinth with neither the lip nor the foot; Type II, found in Pantuoshi Hall, Wenchang Hall, and Bao'en Monastery, has an overturned bowl with lip on top, but still no column foot was installed; Type III, found in Yong'an Temple, still has no column foot, but the plinth was elevated about ten cm above the ground.

To summarize, in the Upper Yangzi tradition of Yuan architecture there is flexibility in the designs of the plan and in the arrangement of columns. There were both squarish and rectangular plans, and both the displaced-column structure and the eliminated-column structure were used. In terms of the design of the bracket sets in the Upper Yangzi, a few patterns could be discerned. First, bracket sets of five or six layers seem to have been the most common types. All bracket arms were built full-unit instead of single-unit. Furthermore, it is very unique that the outermost bracket and the locust head never existed in the Upper Yangzi during the Yuan. In some other aspects, the designs of the buildings are seen to be flexible: the distribution of intercolumnar sets seems to be varied, the crisscross-heart structure coexists with the stolen-heart structure, and *angting tiaowo* coexists with *angwei tiaowo*.

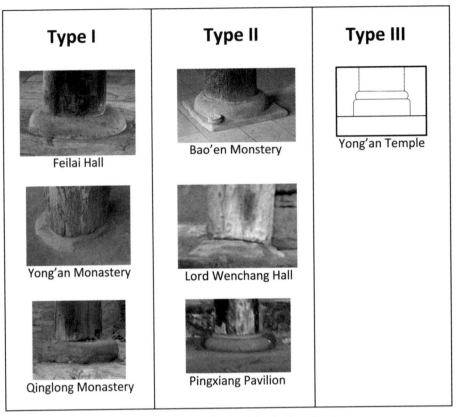

Type I	Type II	Type III
Feilai Hall	Bao'en Monstery	Yong'an Temple
Yong'an Monastery	Lord Wenchang Hall	
Qinglong Monastery	Pingxiang Pavilion	

Fig. 2.22. Column bases in the Upper Yangzi. (Photos and drawing by author.)

It is interesting that the single bracket was more favored than the double bracket on the projections of the bracket sets, while the double bracket was more popular than the single bracket on the central axis of the bracket sets. The latter differs from the *YZFS*. Also deviating from the *YZFS* designations were the use of oblique arms and the various modular units. The usage of an oblique arm is also a connection between the Upper Yangzi tradition and the northern tradition.

Moreover, the Upper Yangzi tradition is also unique in terms of the roof framing. First of all, most Yuan buildings are mansion style, and some had a mixture of the mansion style and the palatial style. Second, exposed rafter beams were not made in a crescent-moon shape—which is, again, against the rule in the *YZFS*. The configurations of rafter beams and columns also differed from the *YZFS*. Finally, there are many more longitudinal beams than cross/rafter beams, and it is also rare to find an eave architrave replacing a railing architrave. The big-eave architrave found in the Upper Yangzi, though not exactly the same as the big-eave architrave in the north, does seem like a connection to the big-architrave style in north China. The eave architrave is often made in a crescent-moon shape, which is rarely seen elsewhere.

THE LOWER YANGZI TRADITION

This section concerns the five extant Yuan timber-framed buildings in the Lower Yangzi, the area customarily called "Jiangnan." It is still possible to identify a regional tradition based on the relative consistency of these five examples. Case studies of each building are presented in chapter 4.

PLAN AND COLUMNIATION

Similar to north China and the Upper Yangzi, there are two types of plan found in the Yuan buildings of the Lower Yangzi: the squarish three-by-three-bay plan and the rectangular two-by-three-bay plan. The main halls of Yanfu Monastery (fig. 4.2), Tianning Monastery (fig. 4.7), Zhenru Monastery (fig. 4.12), and Xuanyuan Palace (fig. 4.23) belong to the first type. Their layouts and columniations are similar: sixteen columns are arranged into two rings that compose three bays on each side; no column is removed or relocated. Except for the main hall of Xuanyuan Palace, the ratios of the bays are quite analogous: on the facade, the central bay is about twice as wide as the side bay (*cijian* 次間); on the side elevation, the front bay is about the same size as the middle bays that are nearly twice the size of the rear bays. By minimizing the size of the side bay on the facade and the rear bay on the side elevation, the central bay on the facade and the front bay on the side become more spacious to accommodate a large number of worshippers, and there is also enough room for an altar in the central bay. The altar in the main hall of Yanfu Monastery is worth additional attention. The shape of the altar is not a rectangle but a U-shape, which provides more space for the worshippers in the central bay (fig. 4.2).

The only building in the Lower Yangzi that has a rectangular plan is the Second Gatehouse of Yunyan Monastery. A gatehouse in a Buddhist monastery is often known as the Hall of the Heavenly Kings (*Tianwangdian* 天王殿), as it is supposed to enshrine the statues of the four Heavenly Kings. In a three-bay-wide Hall of the Heavenly Kings, each side bay usually enshrines statues of two of the four kings, while the central bay serves as a hallway. The Second Gatehouse has a two-by-three-bay rectangular plan and is a typical building of this kind (fig. 4.17). The differences in the plans between this building and other squarish Yuan buildings, mostly Buddha halls, are due to their different functions.

BRACKET SETS

Table 2.6 displays measurements of the modular unit (*cai* 材) according to the bracket sets in the main halls of Yanfu and Tianning Monasteries.[30] The *cai*

Table 2.6. Measurement of the modular unit of Yuan buildings in the Lower Yangzi (unit = cm)

Building	Date	WCB	Grade	WC	TC	WC/TC	WZ	WC/WZ
YZFS	1103					1.50 (3:2)		2.50 (5:2)
Yanfu Monastery	1317	460	VIII–VII	15.5	10.0	1.55 (+3%)	6	2.58 (+3%)
Tianning Monastery	1318	616	VII–VI	17.0	10.5	1.62 (+8%)	6	2.83 (+13.2%)

Note: In this table, WC = width of *cai;* TC = thickness of *cai;* WCB = width of the central bay; WZ = width of *zhi.*

measured from Yanfu Monastery is smaller, between Grade VIII and Grade VII. In Tianning Monastery, the *cai* is 2 cm larger and falls between Grade VII and Grade VI; the grade of *cai* in Tianning Monastery is higher because that building is proportionally larger than the main hall of Yanfu Monastery. The proportion of the *cai* of these two Yuan buildings also differs. According to the *YZFS,* the ratio of the width to the thickness of a *cai* is 1.5 (3:2), and the ratio of the width of *a cai* to a *zhi* was 2.5 (5:2). Therefore, as shown in Table 2.6, the values of the main hall of Yanfu Monastery deviate only 3 percent from the *YZFS* standard. Tianning Monastery, however, has a ratio of the width to the thickness of *cai* of 8 percent more than the *YZFS* standard, and the ratio of the width of the *cai* to the *zhi* was 13 percent more than the *YZFS.* Although the two monasteries are located close to each other and were built at around the same time, the modular unit used in each building was different.

One thing that is consistent about Yuan bracket sets in the Lower Yangzi is that intercolumnar sets are built in every bay of each extant building (fig. 2.23). As for the usage of the single-unit and full-unit sets, it is specified in the *YZFS* that the full-unit should be used in capital sets while the single-unit is for the intercolumnar set. There is no extant Yuan building in the Upper Yangzi that follows this tradition. However, in the Lower Yangzi, this rule is applied in the main hall of Yanfu Monastery and the Second Gatehouse. The main hall of Tianning Monastery is slightly different; there the projecting bracket on both the capital and intercolumnar sets is measured as wide as full-unit (fig. 2.24).

Main Hall of Yanfu Monastery (1317)

Main Hall of Tianning Monastery (1318)

Second Gate House of Yunyan Monastery (1338)

Fig. 2.23. Layout of intercolumnar sets in the Lower Yangzi. "X" stands for one intercolumnar set. (Drawing by author.)

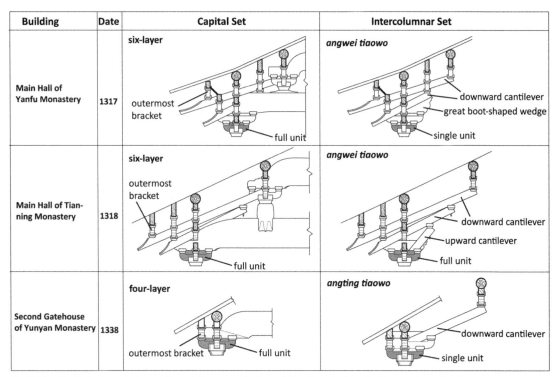

Building	Date	Capital Set	Intercolumnar Set
Main Hall of Yanfu Monastery	1317	six-layer / outermost bracket / full unit	*angwei tiaowo* / downward cantilever / great boot-shaped wedge / single unit
Main Hall of Tianning Monastery	1318	six-layer / outermost bracket / full unit	*angwei tiaowo* / downward cantilever / upward cantilever / full unit
Second Gatehouse of Yunyan Monastery	1338	four-layer / outermost bracket / full unit	*angting tiaowo* / downward cantilever / single unit

Fig. 2.24. Bracket sets in the Lower Yangzi. Gray areas indicate full-unit or single-unit. (Drawing by author.)

In terms of the number of layers of the bracket sets, the main halls of Yanfu and Tianning Monasteries have six-layer bracket sets: they both have one projecting bracket and two downward-inclined cantilevers. Due to the different function of the Second Gatehouse, however, its bracket sets only have one projecting bracket and are considered four-layer, the lowest grade of bracket sets according to the *YZFS* .

According to the *YZFS*, an outermost bracket can be constructed with or without a locust head.[31] It seems that the locust head completely disappeared from the bracket sets that were built in the Yuan dynasty in the Lower Yangzi. None of these three buildings has a locust head accompanying the outermost bracket.

All the interior steps were built as a stolen-heart structure in the Lower Yangzi. With regard to the exterior steps, there are two kinds of composition: crisscross-heart structure and stolen-heart structure. The bracket sets in Yanfu and Tianning Monasteries belong to the first type, with the first tier of projecting bracket built as the stolen-heart structure and the rest as the crisscross-heart structure. The bracket sets of the Second Gatehouse belong to the second type, where the only step was built as a crisscross-heart structure. Since the bracket sets in the Second Gatehouse are four-layer, it is reasonable for a four-layer bracket set to have had a bracket arm cross its only projecting bracket.

In terms of the ways to design the inclined cantilever (*ang* 昂), the main halls of Yanfu and Tianning Monasteries use an *angwei tiaowo;* and the Second Gatehouse has an *angting tiaowo.* The intercolumnar sets in Yanfu Monastery and Tianning Monastery have two downward cantilevers, both constructed as *angwei tiaowo.* The intercolumnar set of the Second Gatehouse exemplifies a typical *angting tiaowo* that was installed with one projecting bracket but no cantilever projecting toward the outside.

The buttress-bracket in Yanfu and Tianning Monasteries was configured similarly to that of the *YZFS,* except that one additional single bracket and one additional plain beam were placed on top to support the purlin in Yanfu and Tianning Monasteries (fig. 2.25). In regard to the four-layer bracket set in the Second Gatehouse, the regulation in the *YZFS* was not followed, and the single bracket was replaced by a double bracket. Such a practice also is found in the Upper Yangzi, and even can occur with bracket sets of five or six layers.

Several miscellaneous details concerning the bracket sets of the Yuan buildings in the Lower Yangzi are also worth attention. An upward cantilever (*shang'ang* 上昂) is a transverse arm in a bracket set that projects from the

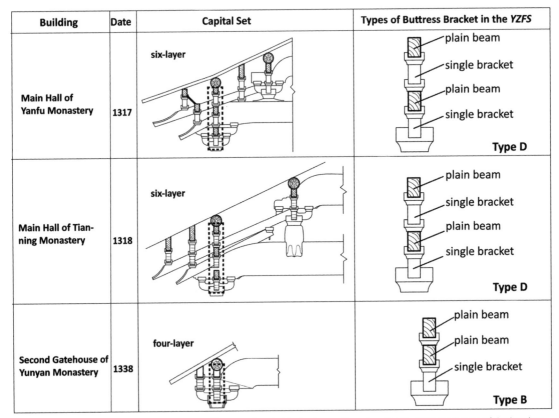

Fig. 2.25. Comparison of buttress-bracket in the Lower Yangzi and in the *YZFS.* Each type of the bracket set in the Lower Yangzi is given a corresponding type of the buttress-bracket listed the *YZFS* that is previously illustrated in fig. 2.15. (Drawing by author.)

first step of the inner projection with its head raised to adjust the height of the bracket set. As described in the *YZFS*, the upward cantilever is found only in the Lower Yangzi. It is one of the most remarkable features of the Lower Yangzi buildings dated to the Song, Yuan, and Ming. There are two types of the upward cantilever in the Lower Yangzi. The first type, as described in the *YZFS*, is built as a projection to support an outermost bracket by itself with a boot-shaped wedge right beneath it. The second type, found in the main hall of Tianning Monastery, is not recorded in the *YZFS*. The upward cantilever is installed under a downward cantilever to adjust the gradient of the cantilever with a boot-shaped wedge. A boot-shaped wedge, however, is not always built with an upward cantilever as recorded in the *YZFS*. It also appears subjacent to the downward cantilever in the Lower Yangzi, such as in the main hall of Yanfu Monastery (fig. 2.24). This boot-shaped wedge is big enough to function similarly to an upward cantilever to adjust the gradient of the downward cantilever. Thus, it can be considered a big boot-shaped wedge (*daxuexie* 大鞾楔).[32] Last but not least, a rounded-off block (*e'jiaodou* 訛角斗), a capital block with its angles rounded off, is also unique to the Lower Yangzi. It is found in the Second Gatehouse (fig. 4.20). With a convex profile on its corners, it looks more decorative than a normal block. This type of capital block has been found only in the Lower Yangzi.

ROOF FRAMING

According to the definition of the palatial style and the mansion style, all the extant Yuan buildings in the Lower Yangzi basically belong to the mansion style. Their interior columns are higher than the eave columns, and they have no distinct layer of bracket sets throughout the entire building. The main hall of Zhenru Monastery, however, is an exception. This building is essentially a mansion-style building, but mixed with a small part of palatial style as a ceiling with a layer of bracket sets covers part of its front bay (fig. 4.13).

According to the *YZFS*, in a mansion-style building of three bays depth, two two-rafter eaves beams and four columns (two interior columns and two eave columns) should have been used. Therefore, using two interior columns instead of one or none, as is done in the Lower Yangzi, is in accordance with the *YZFS*.

In terms of the number and size of rafter beams, however, most Yuan buildings in the Lower Yangzi do not conform to the *YZFS*. Comparing the standard in the *YZFS* (fig. 2.18), it is clear that instead of two two-rafter eaves beams and one four-rafter beam, Yanfu and Tianning Monasteries have two three-rafter beams crossing the front and middle bays, and one two-rafter eaves beam crossing the rear bay (figs. 4.5 and 4.11). In Zhenru Monastery, the expansion of the front bay is even more exaggerated (fig. 4.13); both the front bay and the middle bay of the main hall have four rafters, and the rear bay has two rafters, which make the building a

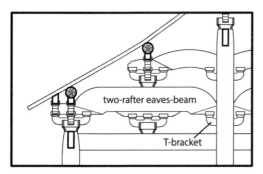

Fig. 2.26. Detail of the roof frame in the Second Gatehouse of Yunyan Monastery, Suzhou, Jiangsu, 1338. (Drawing by author.)

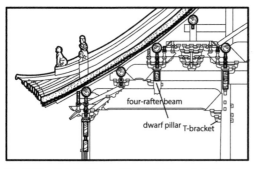

Fig. 2.27. Detail of the roof frame in the main hall of Zhenru Monastery, Shanghai, 1320. (Drawing by author.)

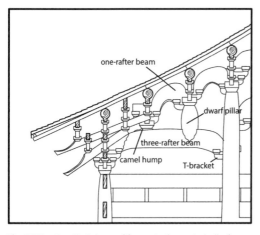

Fig. 2.28. Detail of the roof frame in the main hall of Yanfu Monastery, Jinhua, Zhejiang, 1317. (Drawing by author.)

ten-rafter hall. Xuanyuan Palace is the only one that follows the exact model of an eight-rafter building in the *YZFS* (fig. 4.27).

As previously stated, the *YZFS* specifies that crossbeams in a mansion-style building are exposed and should be shaped like a crescent moon. Yuan buildings in the Lower Yangzi all follow the *YZFS* in this aspect. The crescent-moon-shaped beams are not all alike. The bottom line of the two-rafter crescent-moon-shaped beam in the Second Gatehouse is not curved downward (fig. 2.26). The four-rafter crescent-moon-shaped beam in Zhenru Monastery seems quite rigid and not so curved (fig. 2.27). It can be defined as a crescent-moon-shaped beam only because of the curved profiles on both ends. The one-rafter beam in Yanfu Monastery is a special crescent-moon-shaped beam (fig. 2.28). Instead of being treated as a normal beam that usually is horizontal, it is not only curved downward but slanted upward as well. Such a diagonal one-rafter beam has not been used elsewhere in this area.

Although the shape of the crescent-moon-shaped beam in the Lower Yangzi varies, beam-bearing structures supporting crescent-moon-shaped beams are quite unified. All rafter beams in the Yuan buildings of the Lower Yangzi are supported by one or two layers of projecting brackets on the interior steps (*litiao huagong* 裡跳華栱) from the eave columns, and one or two layers of T-bracket (*dingtougong* 丁头栱, a half-projecting bracket with its tenon at the rear mortised into a column) from the interior columns (figs. 2.26–2.29).

Table 2.7 shows various members atop eave columns used in the Lower Yangzi. The railing architrave seems to be the most important architrave atop eave columns. Three buildings have extra tie member(s) in addition to the railing architrave. The main hall of Yanfu Monastery has an associate architrave, and the main hall of Xuanyuan Palace has a flat architrave. The main hall of Zhenru Monastery has most members built atop its eave columns: in addition to a railing architrave, there are a flat architrave, an associate architrave, and a filler board (*dianban* 墊板) to fill the space between railing architrave and the associate architrave.

The railing architrave still seems to be the major architrave on top of the eave columns in the Lower Yangzi. Therefore, all Yuan buildings in the Lower Yangzi are more similar to the conventional style than to the big-architrave style of the northern tradition. If considering the usage of the rafter beams and interior columns, however, none of the four types of conventional style in north China (fig. 2.10)

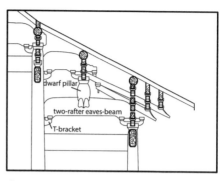

Fig. 2.29. Detail of the roof frame in the main hall of Tianning Monastery, Jinhua, Zhejiang, 1318. (Drawing by author.)

can be found in any Yuan building in the Lower Yangzi. Except for the Second Gatehouse, all Yuan timber-framed buildings have three rafter beams across the building with two interior columns; whereas in north China, most buildings of the conventional style have one or two rafter beams, and one interior column or none at all.

The dwarf pillar (*shuzhu* 蜀柱) and the camel hump (*tuofeng* 駝峰) are architectural members usually placed above a beam to receive the end of a higher-level beam or to support a purlin. A capital block (*ludou* 櫨枓) with a bracket set usually was placed on top of the dwarf pillar or camel hump. In the Lower Yangzi, the dwarf pillar and camel hump are both used in the main halls of Yanfu (fig. 2.28) and Tianning (figs. 2.29–2.30) Monasteries. Both buildings were built between 1310

Table 2.7. Members atop eave columns in buildings of the Lower Yangzi

Building	Date	Railing architrave	Eave architrave	Curtain-mounting joist	Flat architrave	Filler board	Dwarf pillar	Associate architrave	Fig. no.
Main Hall of Yanfu Monastery	1317	X					X		4.6
Main Hall of Tianning Monastery	1318	X							4.11
Main Hall of Zhenru Monastery	1320	X			X	X		X	4.14
Second Gatehouse of Yunyan Monastery	1338	X							4.21
Main Hall of Xuanyuan Palace	Yuan	X			X				4.27

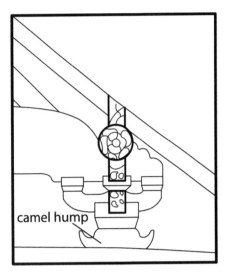

Fig. 2.30. Camel hump in the main hall of Tianning Monastery, Jinhua, Zhejiang, 1318. (Drawing by author.)

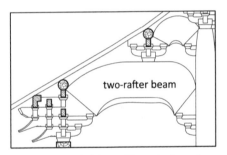

Fig. 2.31. Detail of the roof frame in the main hall of Xuanyuan Palace, Suzhou, Jiangsu, Yuan to Ming. (Drawing by author.)

and 1320. For buildings of later times, such as the Second Gatehouse (1338) and the main hall of Xuanyuan Palace (late Yuan or early Ming), there is neither a dwarf pillar nor a camel hump. Instead, a capital block holding a bracket set sat directly on the two-rafter beam to support a high-level beam and a purlin (fig. 2.31).

The *YZFS* also regulated the shape of a column. Both ends of a column should be tapered, with a slightly convex curving profile in order to make the top end of the column as wide as the bottom of the capital block. The bottom of the column should also have a convex and less curving profile.[33] Such a column is known as a shuttle-shaped column (*suozhu* 梭柱). Almost all columns in a Song, Yuan, or Ming dynasty building are tapered at the top; but columns tapered at both ends, as those described in the *YZFS*, are only found in the Lower Yangzi. Shuttle-shaped columns are found in the main halls of Yanfu Monastery, Tianning Monastery, and Xuanyuan Palace.

In terms of the column base, there are four types in Yuan architecture in the Lower Yangzi (fig. 2.32). Type I, found in the main halls of Yanfu and Zhenru Monasteries, looks similar to that in the *YZFS* (fig. 2.21); it consists of a plinth, a decorated or plain overturned bowl, and a stone column foot. Type II, on the other hand, does not have an overturned bowl, but rather a stone column foot installed directly on the plinth. Comparing Types I and II, the cylindrical part of the column foot in Type II is taller than that in Type I. In Type III, however, the cylindrical part is even taller than that of Type II. The column base in the main hall of Xuanyuan Palace, categorized as Type IV, is unique. It is the only one that had a wooden column foot, which, according to *juan* 1 of the *YZFS*, already had been replaced by stone when the book was written in the Song dynasty.[34] Although there are various types of column bases in the Lower Yangzi, they all share one common feature: they all have a column foot of either stone or wood.

In the Lower Yangzi tradition, there were many influences from the *YZFS*, with a few unique and local features. First, in terms of the columniation, Yuan architecture in the Lower Yangzi still retained the principle taken from the *YZFS*, which is not to remove or relocate any column on the grid plan, although the distance between the first row and the second row of columns had been widened in most cases. Second, bracket sets of the Lower Yangzi buildings

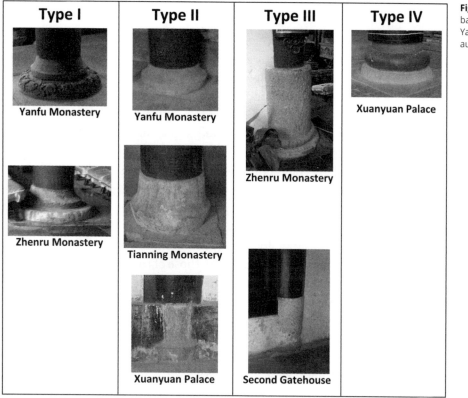

Type I	Type II	Type III	Type IV
Yanfu Monastery	Yanfu Monastery		Xuanyuan Palace
Zhenru Monastery	Tianning Monastery	Zhenru Monastery	
	Xuanyuan Palace	Second Gatehouse	

Fig. 2.32. Column bases in the Lower Yangzi. (Photo by author.)

in general recall some rules set forth in the *YZFS*, such as the proper way to use single-unit and full-unit, the configurations of the buttress-bracket, and the usage of upward cantilever. Moreover, in this architecture intercolumnar bracket sets were regular: they were used in every bay in every building. The capital block that has its angles rounded off is unique to the Lower Yangzi tradition and is not found in the *YZFS*. Third, in terms of the tie beams atop the eave columns, as regulated in the *YZFS*, the railing architrave is still the major member, and the eave architrave or the big architrave never existed in the Lower Yangzi. Therefore, transversal crossbeams, rather than longitudinal architraves or tie beams, were still the major load-bearing members in the Lower Yangzi, which is in accordance with the conventional style in north China. As for the usage of interior columns and crossbeams in the roof framing, similarly to the *YZFS* there are always two interior columns. In regard to the crossbeams, however, both two-rafter beams and four-rafter beams could be replaced by three-rafter beams. Again in accordance to the *YZFS*, all exposed beams were made like crescent-moon beams. The wooden or stone column foot and the shuttle-shaped columns, which are not seen elsewhere, are proof of the strong connection between the Lower Yangzi tradition and the *YZFS*.

REGIONAL TRADITIONS AND THE HISTORY OF THE
SONG-YUAN TRANSITION

As stated above, Yuan architecture from each region of north China, Upper Yangzi, and Lower Yangzi has its own stylistic features regarding plan, columniation, bracket sets, and roof framing. Moreover, some shared features suggest connections between the regions. In order to provide a summary of how these three traditions are distinct yet still related to one another, this chapter concludes by comparing the three regional traditions.

First, squarish plans commonly were used in small-sized buildings in all three regions.[35] Squarish plans in the Lower Yangzi were slightly different from those in the Upper Yangzi in three aspects. In the Lower Yangzi, there were three bays on each side of the squarish plan; in the Upper Yangzi, on the other hand, there could be three or four bays. In addition, building facades in the Upper Yangzi are proportionally wider than those of the Lower Yangzi. In other words, squarish plans in the Lower Yangzi are a little "deeper" than those of the Upper Yangzi. Moreover, along the side of the buildings in the Lower Yangzi the front bay usually was expanded to the same width as the middle bay, which never happened in the Upper Yangzi.

Columniation is one major factor that differentiated the Lower Yangzi tradition from the Upper Yangzi and northern traditions. Four out of ten buildings in the Upper Yangzi were designed as either the eliminated-column structure or the displaced-column structure, or both. These two styles of columniations were often found in Yuan architecture in the north but never in the Lower Yangzi. It is worthy to note that the displaced-column structure and the eliminated-column structure are not mentioned in the YZFS, and yet both styles appeared in north China as early as the eleventh century during the Liao dynasty.[36] Therefore, the difference of columniation between north China and the Lower Yangzi likely began prior to the Yuan dynasty. The presence of the displaced-column and the eliminated-column structures in the Upper Yangzi, however, suggests an influence from north China. The lack of these two structures in the Lower Yangzi also explains why the front bay along the side of the building was expanded. This method seems to have been the only alternative that provided a more spacious room and kept all the columns in place.

As for the bracket sets, there are eight differences between the Upper Yangzi and the Lower Yangzi traditions:

1. Distribution of intercolumnar sets is irregular in the Upper Yangzi but regular in the Lower Yangzi.
2. In terms of the modular unit *cai,* the Lower Yangzi tradition has more similarity to the YZFS than the Upper Yangzi tradition does.

3. As for the proper use of single-unit and full-unit, the Lower Yangzi tradition follows the rule in the *YZFS* while the Upper Yangzi tradition does not.
4. In the Upper Yangzi, the crisscross-heart structure is dominant on the exterior steps and almost matches the number of the stolen-heart structures on the interior steps; whereas in the Lower Yangzi, the stolen-heart structure is more prevalent.
5. For the configuration of the buttress-bracket, six out of ten buildings in the Upper Yangzi do not follow the *YZFS*, while all the Lower Yangzi buildings do.
6. The *angting tiaowo* (where the cantilever is invisible) is more popular in the Upper Yangzi than the *angwei tiaowo* (where the cantilever is visible), whereas the *opposite* seems to be true in the Lower Yangzi.
7. The oblique arm, wing-shaped bracket and pseudo-cantilever exist in the Upper Yangzi but not in the Lower Yangzi; the outermost bracket, upward cantilever and rounded-off block, however, exist in the Lower Yangzi but not in the Upper Yangzi.

There were many differences in bracket sets between the Upper Yangzi and the Lower Yangzi traditions, and the Lower Yangzi tradition is clearly similar to the *YZFS* in many respects. The *YZFS* seems to have had little influence on the Upper Yangzi buildings; however, it has some connections with the Yuan architecture of the northern tradition.

It is not yet possible to generalize about the characteristics of bracket sets in north China because all the data have not been collected. Similarities or differences between north China and other regions, however, can still be found. Members such as the oblique arm, wing-shaped bracket, press-projection, and pseudo-cantilever that are found in the Upper Yangzi but not in the Lower Yangzi were also commonly used in north China. Things that are found only in the Lower Yangzi, such as the upward cantilever and rounded-off block, are not found in the north.

In terms of roof framing, there is more evidence indicating differences between the Upper Yangzi and the Lower Yangzi, as well as the connection between the northern tradition and the Upper Yangzi tradition. In a building of the conventional style, it is the transversal beams (the rafter beams that cross the short side of the building) that carry the main load and where the transversal beams are usually the thickest and strongest. The big-architrave style, on the other hand, is revolutionary because the load-bearing beams were shifted from the transversal beams to the longitudinal beams (architraves that cross the long side of the building, parallel to the facade). Therefore, the big architrave was designed to be the thickest and strongest beam. The conventional style and big-architrave style both exist in the north—the big-architrave style in the Upper Yangzi, and the conventional style in the Lower Yangzi. This major difference of roof framing is solid evidence that the Lower Yangzi tradition is very different from the Upper Yangzi tradition, and that the latter was influenced by the big-architrave style from the north.

In addition, a few architectural details also differentiate the Upper Yangzi and Lower Yangzi traditions but show connections between the Upper Yangzi and the northern ones. The crescent-moon beams are found in the Lower Yangzi but in neither the Upper Yangzi nor the north. Two beam-bearing members, the curtain-mounting joist and the press-projection, are found in both the Upper Yangzi and the north but not in the Lower Yangzi. The common beam-bearing element, the T-bracket, is unique to the Lower Yangzi. The shuttle-shaped column and column foot, both recorded in the *YZFS*, are also unique to the Lower Yangzi tradition.

Table 2.8 summarizes features that differentiate the three regional traditions with reference to the *YZFS*. The Upper Yangzi tradition is clearly different from that of the Lower Yangzi but shares many features with the northern tradition. The Lower Yangzi tradition follows many of the rules in the *YZFS*, but the *YZFS* did not seem to be influential in the Upper Yangzi tradition. The northern tradition also differs from the *YZFS* in many respects and is like a hybrid of local Song and Jin architecture.

A regional tradition of architecture is not created merely from local tradition. It can also be influenced by imported ideas and skills. The similarity between Yuan architecture in the Upper Yangzi and in north China can be explained through the migration history of peoples in the Upper Yangzi and north China during the Song, Jin, and Yuan periods.

In 1126, the Jurchen people of the Jin dynasty launched a full-scale invasion of the then Northern Song. Within the year, the Northern Song capital,

Table 2.8. Comparison of the features in the northern, the Upper Yangzi, and the Lower Yangzi traditions

	Upper Yangzi	Northern	Lower Yangzi	YZFS
Eliminated/displaced-column structure	X	X		
Conventional style		X	X	X
Big-architrave style	X	X		
Oblique arm	X	X		
Upward cantilever			X	X
Press-projection	X	X		
Wing-shaped bracket	X	X		
Curtain-mounting joist	X	X		
Crescent-moon-shaped beam			X	X
T-bracket			X	X
Shuttle-shaped column			X	X
Column foot			X	X

Bianliang, fell, and the Northern Song collapsed. The Jurchen captured the Northern Song emperors Huizong and Qinzong. Known as the Disorders of the Jingkang Period 靖康之亂, this gave rise to successive southward migrations into the Han-Chinese–held parts of central and south China. This third major migration wave in China's premodern history lasted for more than a hundred and fifty years until the fall of the Southern Song dynasty to the Mongols in 1279.[37] The Upper Yangzi area was one of the popular destinations for refugees from the north: the number of immigrants and refugees there ranked second only to the number in the Lower Yangzi area. Moreover, most immigrants in the Upper Yangzi were originally from the northwest, including the modern provinces of Shaanxi and Gansu.[38] The post-Jingkang migration wave may explain the similarity in architecture between the Upper Yangzi and north China, especially in the Shaanxi province.[39]

It is also interesting to note that the Lower Yangzi received even more immigrants from the north. Surprisingly, Yuan architecture there did not reflect much influence from the north. Instead, extant Yuan architecture in the Lower Yangzi shows a continuity of local tradition and adherence to the YZFS. The resistance to outside/northern influence likely was related to the reprinting of the YZFS in Suzhou in the fifteenth year of Shaoxing period (1145), the influence of which might not have traveled far enough to affect the architecture in the Upper Yangzi. Although it had been within the territory of the Southern Song court, instead of being influenced by the YZFS, Yuan dynasty architecture in the Upper Yangzi is rather similar to the Yuan architecture in the north. In terms of pre-Yuan regimes, there was more influence from the Jin dynasty in the north than from the Southern Song in the Lower Yangzi area. Refugees from the north who fled to the Upper Yangzi after the Jingkang period were actually from the territory of the Jin dynasty. It is reasonable to assume that they brought with them the architectural designs and techniques—such as the eliminated-column/displaced-column structures, the oblique arms, and so on—that were typical of Jin architecture in the north.

It is also possible that Yuan people in the Upper Yangzi might have had limited resources to use on architecture compared to those in the Lower Yangzi. The skills of the Upper Yangzi craftsmen is without question given the example of Feilai Hall of the Temple of Eastern Peak, which was so carefully designed and elegantly decorated. In some other cases, however, bracket sets were installed only on the facade, and the rest of the elevations were left simple and plain, as if unfinished. From the bracket sets on the facades of many buildings in the Upper Yangzi, the advanced carpentry technique is obvious; but from the simple and crude construction on the sides it is easy to assume possible financial difficulties.[40]

Buildings, especially religious structures such as temples and monasteries, require large amounts of manpower and materials. Historians have shown that the Upper Yangzi suffered a financial setback during the Yuan dynasty. In his article about Sichuan refugees of the Song to Yuan transition, Paul Smith described the Mongols' destruction of Sichuan and suggests that no devastation by premodern warfare was greater. The Mongol invasions from 1231 to 1280 reduced the self-contained Sichuan Basin, which had been the cultural and economic core of the empire for over a millennium, to "a backwater frontier." Before 1260, when Khubilai Khan had not yet been crowned, and Chinese or sinicized advisers were not present at court, the Mongols employed wholesale civilian massacre as a tactic of intimidation and control in Sichuan. This contrasted with the peaceful solution that Khubilai Khan later imposed on the Lower Yangzi. In the course of a half-century, roughly two million Sichuan families were slaughtered or forced to flee. Between 1223 and 1282, the region's population was reduced by over 95 percent.[41] Given the severe destruction in Sichuan caused by the Mongol invasion, it is understandable that many Yuan buildings in the Upper Yangzi were not as refined as contemporary buildings in the north and the Lower Yangzi.

Architecture in the Lower Yangzi did not seem to have a similar problem. The Yuan buildings there are stylistically independent from those in the north, but because of the Mongols' less destructive conquest of the Lower Yangzi, they still follow the orthodoxy of the *YZFS*. The Mongols occupied one town after another in southeast China without encountering any severe resistance. In many cases, the Song military and inhabitants simply surrendered, and the Song court had no other choice than to capitulate. In late January 1276, the empress dowager, who acted as regent of the emperor, handed over the dynasty's seal to the Mongols. They accepted the Song's surrender graciously, and the royal family was escorted to the north. Although the conquest of the Song was still not complete, as the Song loyalists who had fled farther south were constantly at odds with each other, by 1279 they were crushed by the Mongols. Not only was the conquest less destructive because of the easy concession of the Southern Song court, but Khubilai Khan also realized that in order to gain the allegiance of the Chinese he could not appear to be merely a "barbarian." Rather than exploiting the resources of southeast China as the Mongols had done in the north, he chose to retain the continuity in some policies and personnel that would ensure a smoother transition to Mongolian rule.[42]

Considering the history of the Mongols' conquest of the Southern Song, it is not surprising that many Song traditions are evident in Yuan buildings and the orthodoxy of the *YZFS* was followed by the Yuan craftsmen in the Lower Yangzi. Because of the peaceful resolution of the hostilities between the Chinese and the Mongol rulers, economic prosperity in the Lower Yangzi was not severely affected. With sufficient funding available, the Yuan buildings in the Lower Yangzi were still finely built and carefully decorated.

The preservation and continuation of the Song (Chinese) tradition in architecture in the Lower Yangzi, the heartland of the Southern Song, was also echoed in painting. As James Watt states, "in the prosperous south . . . arts and letters continued to flourish in areas of relative calm."[43] The "good and valid reasons why literati paintings survived and continued to develop in the Jiangnan (Lower Yangzi) area and came to be regarded as the mainstream" are due to the fact that "the Jiangnan (Lower Yangzi) area remained prosperous during and after the Yuan dynasty, while other parts of China became increasingly poor."[44] Although the design of the architectural remains in the Lower Yangzi was not mainstream during or after the Yuan, it illustrated the continuation of prosperity in the area; in contrast, extant Upper Yangzi buildings testify to the "increasingly poor" conditions in that area.

The diversity of Yuan architecture demonstrated by regional traditions was related closely to pre-Yuan local traditions. The regional traditions during the Yuan show the continuity of timber architecture rather than a "dynastic style." The dynastic style certainly is significant in discussing imperial authority and the top-down influence on architecture. Still, a clear-cut dynastic style may exist only in a court-enforced building code or in architectural projects that received direct supervision from the court.

In the Yuan dynasty, it seems that the Mongol rulers did not intend to regulate timber architecture nationwide, which seems to conflict with how craftsmen (jiang 匠) were strictly controlled by the court. Historical records demonstrate that the Mongol rulers did exert special protection and control over craftsmen. During the early years of the Mongols' conquest of the Jin dynasty in north China, they ruthlessly burned down cities and slaughtered people, but the craftsmen were spared.[45] As stated above, the course of the Mongols' takeover of the Southern Song was relatively peaceful. In addition to the political reason that made the Mongols seem less barbaric, this smooth transition of power allowed them to make use of the large and skilled population of craftsmen living in the south.

When the Mongols conquered Jin and later the Southern Song, they gathered all the craftsmen and registered them under the Yuan household system. Those officially registered craftsmen were exempt from taxes and civilian and military service, and sometimes were even provided with food and accommodations.[46] Mongol rulers' favorable treatment of craftsmen actually caused a tremendous increase in the number of craftsmen households. More than two hundred thousand households were recognized as craftsmen in the Yuan—2 percent of the entire population, and much more than that in the Song dynasty.[47]

In order to build and rule a new state, the Mongols relied on the skills of those Han-Chinese craftsmen. Under the household registration system of the Yuan, all craftsmen had to register in units of households. The craft-household registration (jiangji 匠籍) was on a hereditary basis, and no descendants of the family could convert to a different occupation.[48] Anyone who fled or changed profession, if caught, would be punished severely.

The craft-households (*jianghu* 匠户) were divided into different groups based on their skills and then administered by different offices in the government. As for craftsmen whose skills were related to architecture and urban construction, they had to report to the Regency Authorities (*Liushousi* 留守司) of Dadu or Shangdu, which suggests that they were strictly controlled by the central authority. This would not have been a problem if the central authority had tried to regulate and standardize timber-framed architecture, but neither extant buildings nor historic literature proves that this was the intention of the Mongol rulers.

The Yuan dynasty certainly was not the only time when regional traditions existed. In fact, they always played a part throughout the history of Chinese architecture. As we can see in these three regional traditions of the Yuan, there was considerable flexibility and creativity in the design of timber-framed structures. To further illustrate this diversity, the next three chapters provide detailed case studies of individual Yuan buildings in the Upper through the Lower Yangzi areas.

CHAPTER 3
TIMBER-FRAMED ARCHITECTURE OF THE UPPER YANGZI

This chapter explores ten case studies of Yuan timber-framed architecture located in the Upper Yangzi region—nine in Sichuan province and one in Chongqing municipality (plate 2).[1] The two westernmost buildings are the main hall of Qinglong Monastery 青龍寺 and Pingxiang Pavilion 平襄樓. Both are situated in a mountainous county called Lushan 蘆山.[2] The two southernmost buildings, one in Meishan City 眉山市 and one in Emei City 峨嵋市, are built along the Min River 岷江, a tributary of the Yangzi River in the Sichuan basin. The other six buildings are located in or near the area between the Jialing River 嘉陵江 (another tributary of the Yangzi River) and the Fu River 涪江 (a tributary of the Jialing River), the gateway from Sichuan to Shaanxi province. In terms of chronology, six buildings can be firmly dated to the Yuan dynasty on the basis of literary evidence. The other four are thought to be Yuan monuments because of their architectural features; a dearth of textual evidence, however, does not allow for precise dating. The rationale for the date of each building will be explained below.

Little scholarship on these buildings has been published. In his book on Yuan architecture, Pan Guxi briefly introduces Feilai Hall of the Temple of the Eastern Peak and the main hall of Qinglong Monastery.[3] Two articles about the Grand Temple at Mount Qiqu were published in 1984 and 1991 respectively,[4] and another two about the main hall of Yong'an Monastery in 1955 and 1991 respectively.[5] Some buildings, such as the main hall of Lifeng Temple and Yong'an Temple 永安廟, are just documented in the internal files of the local administrations, and their historical value has not been fully understood. Others, such as the Lord Wenchang Hall of Wulong Temple and the main hall of Bao'en Monastery 報恩寺, are mentioned only in journals published by the Sichuan Cultural Relics Administration (Sichuan wenwuju 四川文物局, hereafter SCRA) and are never the central subject matter.

In this chapter, the histories, designs, and details of critical components of the ten buildings will be enlarged upon. Through these case studies, the Upper Yangzi tradition, introduced in the previous chapter, will be further described. More detailed discussion will show the flexibility, the influence from the north, and the uniqueness of the Yuan timber architecture in the Upper Yangzi region.

THE MAIN HALL OF LIFENG (DAOIST) TEMPLE

The main hall of Lifeng (Sweet Spring Peak Daoist) Temple 醴峰觀 is the old-est of the Sichuan Yuan buildings that can be dated specifically. The temple was named after its location, the Sweet Spring Peak (Lifeng 醴峰), where sev-eral ancient wells with sweet springs were discovered. The peak, also known as Mount Empress (Huanghoushan 皇后山), is northwest of the county seat of Nanbu 南部.

The history of the temple is related to a ruler of Sichuan in the Western Jin dynasty (265–316). The prince of Chengdu, Li Xiong 李雄 (274–334), declared his independence from the Western Jin and claimed Sichuan to be the Dacheng Kingdom 大成國 (304–347).[6] Li Xiong became the emperor of Dacheng. During his reign, he traveled to Mount Empress and showed his fondness for the spring-water by honoring the wells with his personal favor. Though there is as yet no evidence for the exact date of the construction of the temple, it is likely that it was built soon after Li Xiong's visit. One indication is an alternative name of this temple, Lifengguan 李封觀, meaning a (Daoist) temple conferred by Li. The first character in this name, li 李, is the surname of Li Xiong, though it has the same pronunciation as the other li 醴, meaning sweet spring. Moreover, when Li Xiong's mother passed away, he built her a tomb right behind the temple, and in the early twentieth century local residents expanded the complex of the temple to create a symmetrical plan with three timber-framed buildings placed on the central axis. These buildings are, from south to north, the gatehouse (shanmen 山門), the main hall (Daxiongdian 大雄殿), and the Hall of Imperial Mother (Huangniandian 皇娘殿).[7]

The main hall is the earliest dated Yuan building that has been found in Sichuan. An inscription left by the Yuan builders on a major beam in the main hall states that it was built in the first month of 1307, the eleventh year of the Dade 大德 reign of Yuan.[8] It is a miracle that the main hall of the temple survives today. The building is on top of a mountain and could easily have been destroyed by wind, storm, or earthquake. It was restored several times during the Ming-Qing period, but its authenticity as a Yuan structure has been preserved.

The main hall is oriented north-south with its front entrance facing south. The three-by-three-bay plan is almost a square, with dimensions of 7.90 by 8.05 m. On each side of the building, the width of the central bay is approximately twice that of the side bay, which creates a spacious room in the center of the hall (fig. 3.1). Brick walls are built on the east and west sides, and the front entrance is built like a porch. A slim board, functioning as the background of the Daoist statues on the center altar, is placed in the rear side of the middle central bay. Though such a layout usually is supposed to have an arrangement of sixteen col-umns in the shape of two rectangular rings, this building has fourteen columns, which indicates that two front eave columns were purposely removed (figs. 3.1 and 3.2). This type of arrangement of columns, known as the eliminated-column structure (*jianzhuzao* 減柱造), as described in chapter 1, was popular among Yuan timber-framed buildings in north China.

The main hall of Lifeng Temple, built on a platform 20 cm high, is a one-story building with a hip-and-gable roof (fig. 3.2).[9] The eaves at the corners are highly propped up, like wings. The top ridge of the roof is decorated with ceramic dragons, cranes, horses, and other animals. Bracket sets are built at both corners, while three intercolumnar sets are installed evenly between the corner columns. Since two columns on the front elevation have been removed, the eave architrave (*yan'e* 檐額) is curved downward and thick enough to span the front elevation, which is about 8 m wide.[10] As argued above, the usage of the eave architrave is one unique feature of Yuan timber-framed architecture in the region of the Upper Yangzi.

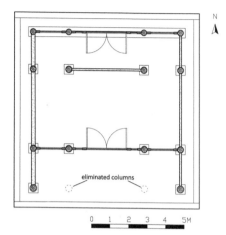

Fig. 3.1. Plan of the main hall of Lifeng Temple, Nanbu, Sichuan, 1307. (Drawing by author.)

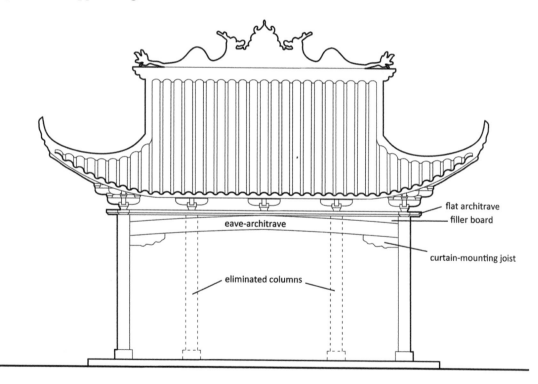

Fig. 3.2. Front elevation of the main hall of Lifeng Temple, Nanbu, Sichuan, 1307. (Drawing by author.)

Fig. 3.3. Bracket sets on the east side of the main hall of Lifeng Temple, Nanbu, Sichuan, 1307. (Photo by Jun Ye.)

Two types of bracket sets are found in this building. The first has two tiers of projecting brackets (*huagong* 華栱): a five-layer (*wupuzuo* 五鋪作) type according to the *YZFS*; the second type had only one tier: a four-layer (*sipuzuo* 四鋪作) type, a lower grade according to the *YZFS*. A pattern of distributing the two types can be observed: the style of bracket set degrades as its position moves from front to side to rear. On the front elevation, the bracket sets are all five-layer, as the front elevation is considered the most important and memorable part of a building. On the east side of the building, five-layer and four-layer types are mixed; and at the rear of the building, only four-layer bracket sets are used (figs. 3.3 and 3.4).

If viewed toward the front elevation, all three intercolumnar sets are identical to each other and all have two tiers of projecting brackets (fig. 3.5). The first tier of projecting bracket supports a short bracket (*guazigong* 瓜子栱); the second tier, with no projected inclined cantilever (*ang* 昂), immediately supports a square eave purlin (*liaoyanfang* 撩檐方). If viewed from the inside, however, the middle one is different from the two sides. Had the two front eave columns not been eliminated, the two side sets would have functioned as column-top sets. Thus, the side intercolumnar sets are built similarly to a column-top set, which often projects a bracket inward and is connected to the interior column by a horizontal beam that could be either a two-rafter eaves beam (*rufu* 乳栿) or a one-rafter beam (*zhaqian* 箚牽). In this building, such a horizontal beam is a one-rafter beam that passes

Fig. 3.4. Bracket sets on the rear side of the main hall of Lifeng Temple, Nanbu, Sichuan, 1307. (Photo by Jun Ye.)

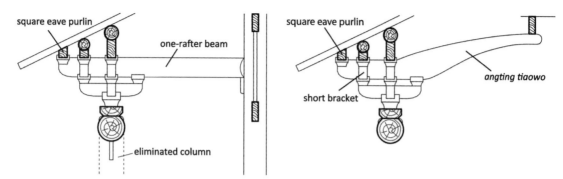

Fig. 3.5. Sectional views of the intercolumnar sets on the front elevation of the main hall of Lifeng Temple, Nanbu, Sichuan, 1307: (*left*) side intercolumnar set; (*right*) middle intercolumnar set. (Drawing by author.)

the load from the eaves to the interior columns (fig. 3.5, left). The middle bracket set, on the other hand, is structurally a real intercolumnar set. It has an inclined cantilever projected inward, but the cantilever does not project outward (fig. 3.5, right). This type of cantilever is called *angting tiaowo* 昂桯 挑斡, meaning a slating cantilever that does not project toward the outside of the building. Such a design is another local feature of Yuan architecture in the Upper Yangzi and occurs in other buildings discussed below.

The roof structure indicates that the main hall of Lifeng Temple is basically a mansion-style building (*tingtang* 廳堂), combined with some features in a palatial-style building (*diange* 殿閣). The interior columns (*wuneizhu* 屋內柱) are higher than the eave columns, which is a feature of the mansion style, but it still has a layer of bracket sets on top of the interior columns bearing the ceiling, which resembles the palatial style (fig. 3.6).

The north-south sectional view of the building is almost symmetrical. The front bay is crossed by a one-rafter beam projected from the bracket set to the interior columns. The structure of the rear bay is similar to that of the front bay except for their different types of bracket sets. The middle bay, of two-rafter width, has two beams. The lower one, a crescent-moon-shaped beam (*yueliang* 月梁) ties one interior column to the other; the top one is the upmost beam (*pingliang* 平梁) of a roof frame. A dwarf pillar (*shuzhu* 蜀柱) stands on the center of the crescent-moon-shaped beam and has a bracket set on top helping to support the upmost beam. It is noticeable that the bottom of this dwarf pillar is pointed. In addition, the upmost beam is sustained by two interior columns through two bracket sets and holds the upper purlins (*shangpingtuan* 上平槫) upon both ends. Another dwarf pillar is built on the center of the upmost beam to bear the ridge purlin (*jituan* 脊槫).

Last, the dimensions of the modular unit (*cai* 材) used in this building is 17.5 by 12 cm, suggesting it is a building between Grade Six and Grade Seven, according to the *YZFS*. The two-dimensional modular unit is close to a ratio of 3:2, the standard modular unit regulated by the *YZFS*.

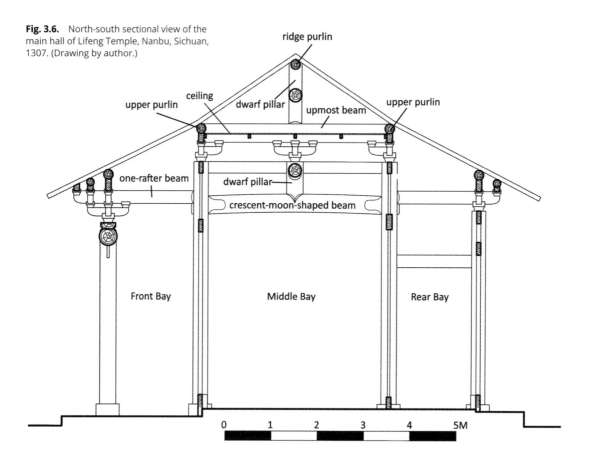

Fig. 3.6. North-south sectional view of the main hall of Lifeng Temple, Nanbu, Sichuan, 1307. (Drawing by author.)

The main hall of Lifeng Temple is exceptional in that the roof structure is a combination of the mansion and palatial styles. Its crescent-moon-shaped crossbeams in the middle bay are unique in the Upper Yangzi, where most crossbeams are straight. In some other details the main hall of Lifeng Temple is consistent with the local tradition: namely, in the squarish plan with eliminated columns, the crescent-moon-shaped eave architrave, the pointed bottom of the dwarf pillars, and the simplified bracket sets on the side and rear elevations of the building. This relatively small and humble building contrasts sharply with the next example, which is more lavish in design and construction.

FEILAI HALL OF THE TEMPLE OF THE EASTERN PEAK

Feilai (Flying-hither) Hall 飛來殿 is the main hall and oldest building of the Temple of the Eastern Peak (Dongyuemiao 東嶽廟) near the city of Emei 峨嵋, Sichuan province. The temple also is called "the Grand Temple" (Damiao 大廟), due to its popularity among the locals as a place for religious activities.[11] The temple complex, built along the hillside of Flying-hither Hill (Feilaigang

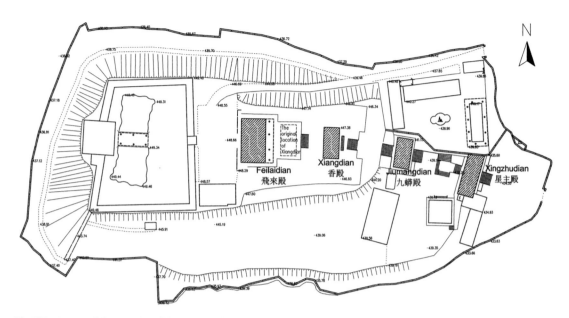

Fig. 3.7. Layout of the complex of the Temple of the Eastern Peak, Emei, Sichuan, Yuan to Qing. (Redrawn by author after a drawing provided by the administration office of the Temple of the Eastern Peak.)

飛來崗), is two kilometers to the north of the city of Emei. Nowadays, four buildings remain along the east-west central axis: the Astrid Lord Hall (Xingzhudian 星主殿, the gatehouse), the Nine Pythons Hall (Jiumangdian 九蟒殿), the Incense Hall (Xiangdian 香殿), and, at the west end, Feilai Hall (fig. 3.7).

Construction of the Temple of the Eastern Peak continued from the Yuan dynasty to the Qing dynasty: the oldest structure, Feilai Hall, is dated to 1327 of the Yuan; the newest buildings were constructed during the Qing dynasty. Religious affiliations of the temple changed throughout its history. Early in the Song and Yuan periods, the temple was built solely for worshipping the Eastern Peak (Taishan 泰山). Later, Daoist and Buddhist buildings were added to the temple complex.[12] Such transformation may be associated with the movement of the syncretism of the Three Teachings (*sanjiao heyi* 三教合一) that emerged in Yuan and was accepted widely in China after the Ming dynasty.[13] Neither of these religions, Buddhism or Daoism, were seen at odds and so could coexist.

Of all the buildings in the temple, Feilai Hall is the most legendary. According to *Emei xianzhi* 峨眉縣誌 (the gazetteer of Emei County), published in the Qing dynasty, Feilai Hall was originally established by the Lord of Eastern Peak himself. The story reads:

Feilai Hall is located five *li* to the northwest of the county seat. Its location is guarded by hills and surrounded by creeks. There are swamps and marshes everywhere except [for] a mound that has risen. The mound, being clear and reclusive, is natural scenery. [On the mound,] buildings impose and shrines cluster, the name of which is "flying hither" (*feilai*). The history of Feilai Hall is unknown. However, according to the inscriptions on a stele of the Taiding reign (1324–1328) and some stone tablets of the Chunhua (990–994) and Jingyou (1034–1038) reigns, the location of the temple was chosen by the Lord [of the Eastern Peak] himself.[14] One night, it was windy and thundering. When it cleared, a little lofty hall was standing there. After that, the people no longer suffered from disease and pestilence, and they had a bumper harvest every year. For this reason, the locals built double-layer eaves on to the hall. The story of *feilai* is more than conjecture. The temple is known as a historical site of the town. According to Qing gazetteers, the building was first built in Tang, renewed in Song and restored again in the Dade (1297–1307) period of Yuan. In the Hongwu reign of the Ming dynasty (1368–1398), the aged hall was about to fall. In the Dingwei and Wushen years of the Kangxi reign, the locals rescued the poor building and operated the temple again. It is lucky that the ancient timber is huge and good quality. People just needed to replace the rotten pieces. Though the fascinating color painting on the building is impossible to reproduce, at least there is no danger of leakage.[15]

In addition to the account in the gazetteer, the stele and the stone tablets mentioned were discovered and provide more information about the building. The title of the inscription on the Chunhua (Song) tablet, dated to 993, reads *Chongxiu beiji* 重修碑記 (The record of reconstruction). This tablet suggests that an earlier version of this building must have existed. Moreover, the inscription on the Taiding (Yuan) stele confirms that there was indeed an older Feilai Hall before 933, but it is not known what it was like. The text on this Yuan stele tells how Feilai Hall was completely rebuilt again during the early 1300s. This building, then, had at least three versions: one earlier than 933; one dated to 933; and one in 1327, which is the extant building.[16]

In 1984, when the building was being restored, an iron mortise bolt was found on a corner beam with an inscription, *Yuan Dade wuxunian* 元大德戊戌年, which means "the second year of Dade 大德, reign of Yuan" (1298).[17] Such a phrase inscribed on a construction element confirms that the extant building is an authentic Yuan structure. Given such an interesting history by various textual evidence, Feilai Hall is regarded as one of the most important examples of Yuan architecture in Sichuan. It is also important because of its well-preserved condition and fine timber-framed structure, which may even retain some structural features of the Song dynasty.[18]

Feilai Hall is oriented east-west, with its front entrance facing east. It has a five-by-four-bay plan (fig. 3.8). The front entrance is an open porch, and the rear central bay is designed to be an exit. The rectangular plan of Feilai Hall is about 18 m long and 13 m wide, close to a ratio of 3:2. The rectangular plan of Feilai Hall is exceptional when compared to other Yuan buildings surviving in Sichuan, most of which have either square or nearly square plans. The

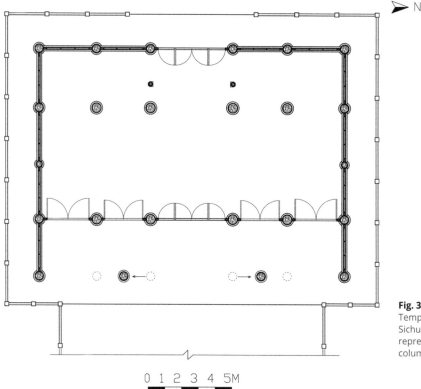

> N

0 1 2 3 4 5M

Fig. 3.8. Plan of Feilai Hall, Temple of the Eastern Peak, Emei, Sichuan, 1327. Dashed circles represent eliminated or relocated columns. (Drawing by author.)

dimension of each bay is identical and measures about 3 m wide, except that the central bay (*dangxinjian* 當心間) is about 5 m wide. The arrangement of the columns is somewhat creative. The technique, known as the displaced-column structure (*yizhuzao* 移柱造), was introduced in chapters 1 and 2, and is applied here. Two front eave columns were eliminated, and another two were relocated to the middle of the side bays. Therefore, the front porch has three bays instead of five, which widens the entrance.

Feilai Hall is a ten-meter hall and stands on a platform 1.5 m high with balustrades around it and a ten-step staircase in the front (fig. 3.9). It has a hip-and-gable roof covered by golden glazed tiles. Twelve bracket sets are distributed evenly under the front eave, and two vivid Chinese dragons coil along the middle front-eave columns.[19] A huge arched eave architrave crosses the central bay to tie the front columns that are inclined slightly toward the center. The height of the columns increases slightly and gradually from the central bay toward the corners. This way of handling the columns is called *shengqi* 生起 (rising-up), and is one of the characteristics of Song timber-framed architecture.[20]

As for the roof structure, Feilai Hall is a typical eight-rafter mansion-style building (fig. 3.10). According to the definition of the mansion style in the *YZFS*, its roof structure can be described as *qianhou rufu yong sizhu* 前後乳栿

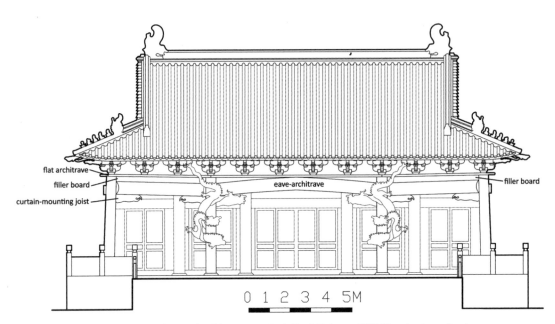

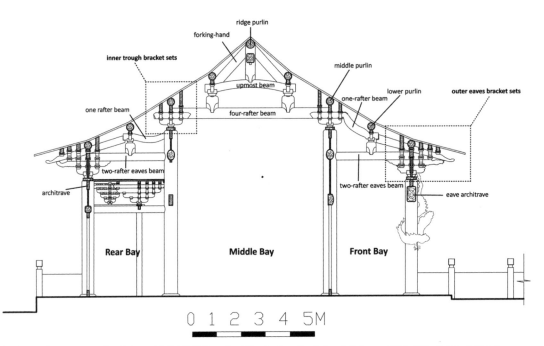

Fig. 3.9. Front elevation of Feilai Hall, Temple of the Eastern Peak, Emei, Sichuan, 1327. (Drawing by author.)

Fig. 3.10. East-west sectional view of Feilai Hall, Temple of the Eastern Peak, Emei, Sichuan, 1327. (Drawing by author.)

用四柱, meaning "a two-rafter eaves beam is used both in the front and back of the building, and there are four columns (two eave columns and two interior columns)." The front bay is crossed by a two-rafter eaves beam that was projected from the back of the bracket sets under the front eave. The other end of the beam is inserted into the shaft of an interior column. A dwarf pillar stands in the middle of the two-rafter eaves beam and supports a lower purlin (*xiapingtuan* 下平槫). A bracket set also tops the interior column to carry the load of the middle purlin (*zhongpingtuan* 中平槫). A diagonal one-rafter beam has been installed to reinforce the structure. The structure of the rear bay is quite similar to that of the front. The only two major differences are: first, the eave architrave of the rear bay is much thinner than that of the front bay; second, the one-rafter beam in the rear bay is curved downward instead of slanting as in the front bay. As for the middle bay, a four-rafter beam (*sichuanfu* 四椽栿) spans the distance between two interior columns. Two dwarf pillars are placed on the four-rafter beam to carry the load of the upmost beam, which is slightly curved, with another dwarf pillar atop supporting the ridge purlin. Two forking-hands (*chashou* 叉手), slanting struts used to support and stabilize the ridge purlin, compose a stable triangular composition.

With regard to the bracket sets, there are three major types in Feilai Hall. Each of them has a different modular unit in accordance with various functions. The outer-eaves bracket sets (*waiyan puzuo* 外簷鋪作) sit on the loop of eave columns. The outer-eaves bracket sets are six layered (*liupuzuo* 六鋪作), with two projecting brackets and one inclined cantilever (fig. 3.11). The upper tier projecting bracket is in the shape of an inserting cantilever (*cha'ang* 插昂), also known as pseudo-cantilever (*jia'ang* 假昂). The lower tier projecting bracket is carved in the shape of a cloud; the upper tier, the (inserting) pseudo-cantilever, is carved into a dragon's head; and the real inclined cantilever on the top looks like an elephant's trunk. Within the outer-eaves bracket sets, there are not many differences between the capital set (*zhutou puzuo* 柱頭鋪作) and the intercolumnar set (*bujian puzuo* 補間鋪作). The only distinction

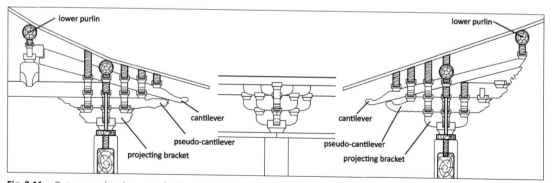

Fig. 3.11. Outer-eave-bracket sets of Feilai Hall, Temple of the Eastern Peak, Emei, Sichuan, 1327: (*left*) sectional view of the capital set; (*middle*) frontal view; (*right*) sectional view of the intercolumnar set. (Drawing by author.)

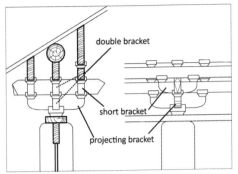

Fig. 3.12. Inner-trough bracket sets of Feilai Hall, Temple of the Eastern Peak, Emei, Sichuan, 1327: (*left*) sectional view; (*right*) frontal view. (Drawing by author.)

is that the capital set has a two-rafter beam projected toward the inside, and its inclined cantilever does not support the lower purlin directly. The intercolumnar set has no beam on its inner tiers, and the tail of the inclined cantilever props up high enough to support the lower purlin directly. The modular unit of the outer-eaves bracket sets is 21.5 by 14 cm. The ratio of the width to the thickness of the modular unit is 1.53, which is very close to the standard of 1.5 in the *YZFS*.

The second type, the inner-trough bracket sets (*shencaonei puzuo* 身槽內鋪作), are placed in lines along the two rows of interior columns (fig. 3.10). The inner-trough bracket sets help the interior columns and tie beams to support the load of the roof. The structure of the inner-trough bracket sets can be described as *chonggong jixinzao* 重栱計心造, meaning they have a double bracket sitting above the interior column and a short bracket crossing the end of the projecting bracket (fig. 3.12). The modular unit of this type of bracket sets is 18 by 11 cm, smaller than that of the outer-eaves ones.

The third type of bracket sets compose the small-scale carpentry (*xiaomuzuo* 小木作), the decorative and nonstructural carpentry of the building. Those brackets sets are found under the ceiling in the rear central bay of the building (fig. 3.13). The small-scale carpentry of this building is a highly complicated and exquisite object composed of five bracket sets—each has three tiers of projecting brackets with a short bracket on each tier. Its modular unit is the smallest of all, 13.5 by 8.5 cm. The function of this object is unknown. It may have been the canopy for a statue or part of a cabinet. The former explanation seems more reasonable, since it is known that Feilai Hall originally enshrined a copper statue of Dongyuedadi 東嶽大帝, the Lord of Eastern Peak, that was destroyed during the 1950s.[21]

The dragon columns, the various types of bracket sets, the small-scale carpentry, as well as the adjusted arrangement of columns indicate that Feilai Hall was designed elaborately, carefully decorated, and well preserved. So far, it is the most important example of Yuan architecture in the Upper Yangzi. It retains more features of Song architecture than any other building in the same area—such as the dearth of oblique arms, the joint of beams and columns decorated by bracket sets, and the usage of *angwei tiaowo* (with visible inclined cantilevers) instead of *angting tiaowo* (without visible inclined cantilevers). On the other hand, Feilai Hall also incorporates many local features—such as the curved eave architrave, the diagonal beams, and the absence of the uttermost bracket and the locust head. Moreover, influence from the northern tradition also is present.

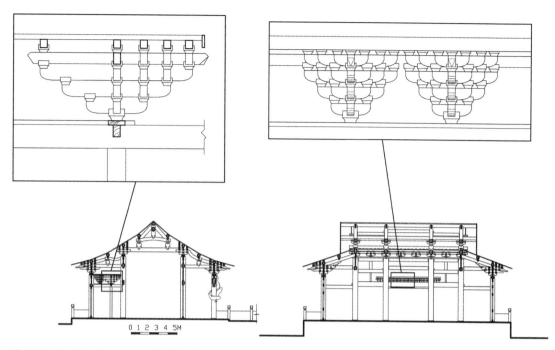

Fig. 3.13. Small-scale carpentry of Feilai Hall, Temple of the Eastern Peak, Emei, Sichuan, 1327: (*top left*) sectional view of the bracket sets; (*top right*) frontal view of the bracket sets; (*bottom left*) east-west sectional view of Feilai Hall; (*bottom right*) north-south sectional view of Feilai Hall. (Drawing by author.)

As discussed in chapter 2, the design of Feilai Hall is similar to those of some contemporary buildings in north China, such as the buildings in Yongle Palace 永樂宮 in Shanxi province.

THE MAIN HALL OF BAO'EN MONASTERY

In contrast to the exquisite Feilai Hall, the main hall of Bao'en (Requiting Kindness) Monastery 報恩寺 is a relatively humbler and simpler building. Bao'en Monastery is located in the village of Gaofeng 高豐, approximately 20 kilometers southeast of the city of Meishan. The main hall is the only building that survives today. According to an early twentieth-century version of *Meishan xianzhi* 眉山縣誌 (the gazetteer of Meishan County), the monastery was first built during the Tang dynasty. Later, a restoration took place in 1761, the twenty-sixth year of the Qianlong 乾隆 reign during the Qing dynasty.[22] The construction of Bao'en Monastery was sponsored by a lay Buddhist surnamed Wang; he named this monastery *bao'en* 報恩 as a memorial to his mother. Although the gazetteer does not document any construction activities in the Yuan dynasty, an inscription discovered on a beam in the main hall stating "the fourth year of Taiding (*taiding sinian* 泰定四年)" reveals that the current structure was built or completed in 1327. Structural features of the main hall further validate the possibility of it being a Yuan building.

The main hall of Bao'en Monastery is oriented north-south with its front on the south (fig. 3.14). The front-south side has three bays and is about 13 m wide. The east and west sides are 13.5 m wide, and each has four bays. The dimensions are close to a square. It is noteworthy that the east and west sides of the main hall are a little longer than the front side, which differentiates it from a more common situation wherein the front side is longer than its sides. The central bay on the south side is about one times wider than the side bays. In terms of the east and west sides, on the other hand, the first front bay is about one-and-a-half times the size of other bays. There are four interior columns in this building, and a brick wall is placed between the two interior columns of the rear row, creating a backdrop for the statues of some folk deities.

The main hall of Bao'en Monastery has a hip-and-gable roof and stands on a base of 0.9 m in height (fig. 3.15). The eave columns are about 3.7 m high and inclined slightly inward. The height of the columns

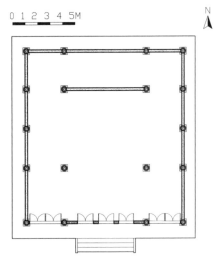

0 1 2 3 4 5M   N

Fig. 3.14. Plan of the main hall of Bao'en Monastery, Meishan, Sichuan, 1327. (Drawing by author.)

Fig. 3.15. Front elevation of the main hall of Bao'en Monastery, Meishan, Sichuan, 1327. (Photo courtesy of Zhao Yuanxiang.)

increases slightly and gradually from the central bay toward the corners. The frontal eave architrave is thick, and its section almost round, which is in contrast to the slim flat architrave (*pupaifang* 普拍方) atop (fig. 3.19). There are three intercolumnar bracket sets installed in the central bay and one in each side bay on the front elevation of the building.

The building basically has two types of bracket sets: the first type has two tiers of projecting brackets, and the second has no projecting bracket but a horizontal and flat cantilever instead. According to the *YZFS*, the former is a five-layer bracket set, while the latter is a simplified version of a five-layer set. The first type is used on the front elevation of the building as an intercolumnar set (fig. 3.16). Its style can be defined as the crisscross-heart structure (*jixinzao* 計心造) where a short bracket always intersects with the projecting bracket. The rear part of the bracket set has one tier of projecting bracket, atop which is installed a double bracket (*chonggong* 重栱) that is parallel to the elevation of a building and composed of a long bracket (*mangong* 慢栱) placed above a short bracket. A curvy slanting cantilever, *angting tiaowo*, is projected from the long bracket to support the load of the lower purlin. This type of bracketing in the main hall of Bao'en Monastery resembles those on the front elevation of the main hall of Lifeng Temple (fig. 3.5). The second type in the main hall of Bao'en Monastery, unusually, has no projecting bracket (fig. 3.17). It serves as the capital set all over the building and simply has the beams project outside.

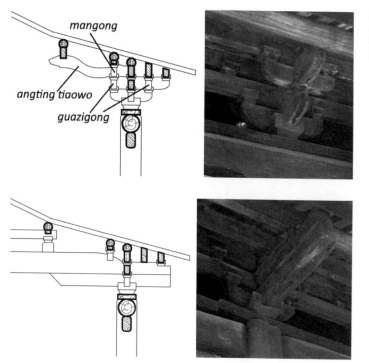

Fig. 3.16. Intercolumnar set of the main hall of Bao'en Monastery, Meishan, Sichuan, 1327. (Drawing by author. Photo by Jun Ye.)

Fig. 3.17. Capital set of the main hall of Bao'en Monastery, Meishan, Sichuan, 1327. (Drawing by author. Photo by Jun Ye.)

The second type seems to be too simple, as if it were unfinished. In fact, that may not have been the case.

The central intercolumnar set installed in the central bay of the main hall of Bao'en Monastery is special. It is similar to the other intercolumnar sets except that it has two additional oblique projecting brackets (*xiegong* 斜栱) at a 45° angle (fig. 3.18). Such oblique arms, at 30°, 45°, or 60°, are decorative members with little load-bearing function. As already discussed, similar examples also are found in other places in Sichuan, such as Wulong Temple and Yong'an Temple.

The roof frame of the main hall of Bao'en Monastery consists of ten rafters (fig. 3.19). In total, the roof frame has four columns and is crossed by three beams from south to north: a three-rafter beam (*sanchuanfu* 三椽栿) in the front bay, a five-rafter beam (*wuchuanfu* 五椽栿) in the middle bay, and a two-rafter eaves beam in the rear bay. The three-rafter beam in the front bay is supported by the capital bracket set at one end and is inserted into the shaft of the interior column at the other end. A small post stands on one-third of the beam to uphold the lower purlin. On top of this post, a slim two-rafter beam is built to tie in the interior column as well. Above this beam is a thick traversal tie beam, perhaps

xiegong

Fig. 3.18. Oblique arms in the main hall of Bao'en Monastery, Meishan, Sichuan, 1327. (Photo by Jun Ye.)

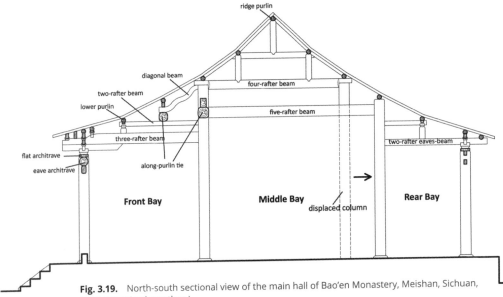

Fig. 3.19. North-south sectional view of the main hall of Bao'en Monastery, Meishan, Sichuan, 1327. (Drawing by author.)

an along-purlin tie (*shunshenchuan* 順身串). Another along-purlin tie is installed through the front interior columns to strengthen the structure. A curved diagonal beam (*xiefu* 斜栿) is built in the front bay to connect two purlins of different levels. Such a diagonal beam also is applied in many other positions of the building to strengthen the structure between purlins of different levels. The diagonal beam is considered unique to Sichuan.[23] The structure above the five-rafter beam is noteworthy for the design of the displaced-column structure. In the middle bay, an interior column was moved one rafter outward to provide more space in the center of the building, and the original four-rafter beam was extended to a span of five rafters. A short post to support the purlin replaced the original internal columns. The overall simplicity of the roof frame is remarkable—no bracket set is used to pass load between horizontal and vertical members.

The oblique arms, the diagonal beams, and the displaced-column structures are the three most important features of the main hall of Bao'en Monastery, suggesting that the builders abided by the Upper Yangzi tradition. Moreover, this building is somewhat extraordinary due to the simplicity in its roof frame. The sharp contrast between the simple roof frame and the elaborated intercolumnar bracket sets under the frontal eave may suggest that the roof frame was altered during the restoration during the Qing dynasty, and only the arrangement of the plan and the frontal bracket sets are credible remnants from the Yuan restorations. Alterations are often an obstacle in assigning a date. Such an issue also should be taken under consideration in the following example of Yong'an Monastery.

THE MAIN HALL OF YONG'AN MONASTERY

Yong'an (Eternal Peace) Monastery 永安寺 is located on a hill called Yellow Mud (黃泥崗 Huangnigang) 45 kilometers southeast of the city of Langzhong 閬中. The complex of Yong'an Monastery, built along the hillside, covers about 4,000 square meters. Along its south-north axis are the gatehouse (*shanmen* 山門), the Guanyin Hall (Guanyindian 觀音殿), and the main hall (fig. 3.20). Except for the main hall, which is dated to Yuan, all the other buildings were constructed in the Qing dynasty.

The history of Yong'an Monastery is presented in the *Langzhong xianzhi* 閬中縣誌 (The gazetteer of Langzhong) published during the Qing dynasty. In the gazetteer, a line reads: "Yong'an Monastery is 90 *li* to the east [of the county seat of Langzhong]. It was established in the Tang dynasty and restored during the Zhiping reign of the Song dynasty, the Zhizheng reign of the Yuan dynasty, and the Jiajing reign of the Ming dynasty respectively."[24] A similar record is found in the inscription on a "stele for deforestation warning" (*jinshanbei* 禁山碑) dated to the Qing dynasty and uncovered in the monastery.[25] Moreover, from earlier

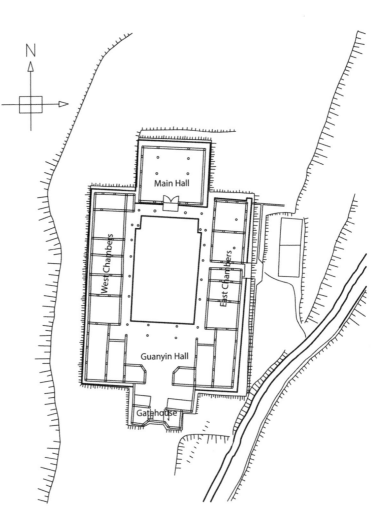

Fig. 3.20. Layout of Yong'an Monastery, Langzhong, Sichuan, Yuan to Qing. (Redrawn by author after the Langzhong Administration of Cultural Heritage.)

textual evidence, we learn that "Eternal Peace" is not the original name of this monastery. A stele dated to 1548, the twenty-seventh year of Jiajing 嘉靖 reign of Ming, has an inscription titled *Chongxiu chici benjueyuan ji* 重修敕賜本覺院記 (Record of the reconstruction of Benjue Monastery granted by the imperial order). The legible part is as follows:

Benjue Monastery is about sixty *li* east of Langzhong. It was established by a Song monk named Chu Linzhi. It was built under an imperial order in 1067, the fourth year of the Zhiping reign period of Song. In the second year of the Zhishun reign of Yuan, the main hall was expanded. . . . During the Hongwu period of Ming, an imperial monk, whose name is Li Yongyong and whose monastic title is Junxian, once restored the monastery. . . . In 1547, the Dingwei year during the Jiajing reign, [due to the poor condition of the monastery] a monk whose monastic title was Baofeng was anxious day and night. Because of this, he donated his property and recruited some craftsmen. Then the buildings and other monuments were erected one after another. The halls, the pavilions, the corridors, the platforms, and other structures were renovated as if they were new.[26]

This quotation indicates that the monastery originally was called Benjueyuan 本覺院 until the Qing dynasty, and a major restoration took place during the Ming. Besides the stelae and gazetteers that document the history of the monastery, an inscription written in ink is found on a four-rafter beam of the main hall confirming the architectural date of the Yuan period. Although some characters are missing from this inscription, it is clear that the existing characters bear the date *Dayuan Zhishun sinian* 大元至順四年, meaning "the fourth year of Zhishun reign of Yuan (1333)."[27]

Therefore, Yong'an Monastery, originally called Benjue Monastery, was first built in the early Tang. Supervised by some prestigious monks, it was restored several times during the Song, Yuan, Ming, and Qing periods. During the Yuan dynasty, the main hall, originally small, was expanded to its current size in 1333. Although several restorations took place during the Ming and Qing periods, the Yuan inscription that survives on its main beam indicates that the major structure of the main hall is a Yuan construction.

The main hall of Yong'an Monastery has a three-by-four-bay plan with the three-bay front porch facing the south (fig. 3.21). Each side measures about 15.5 m. The dimensions of the bays vary. On the front/south side, the width of the central bay is about twice that of the side bays. On the east and west sides, the dimensions of the four bays are quite irregular. The southernmost bay (the porch) and the northernmost bay are both 2.3 m wide. The bay next to the northernmost bay is about 3.6 m. The bay next to the southernmost bay is more than 7 m wide, very close to the central bay on the south side. The variety in the size of the bays indicates a flexibility in the design.

The main hall of Yong'an Monastery, with a hip-and-gable roof, is built on a two-storied platform (fig. 3.22). Four front eave columns stand on the lower level, which is 0.65 m above ground level; the majority of the building sits on the upper level, which is 1.8 m above ground. The upper and lower levels are connected by a six-step staircase. This unusual two-storied platform solves the problem of leveling the sloping ground. The front eave columns, built on the lower level, are about 5.47 m high, and their diameters are 50 cm. The architrave is slightly curved downward to span the central bay that

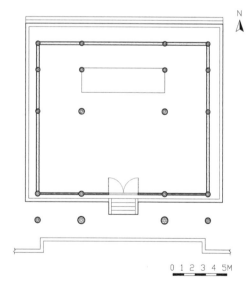

0 1 2 3 4 5M

Fig. 3.21. Plan of the main hall of Yong'an Monastery, Langzhong, Sichuan, 1333. (Drawing by author.)

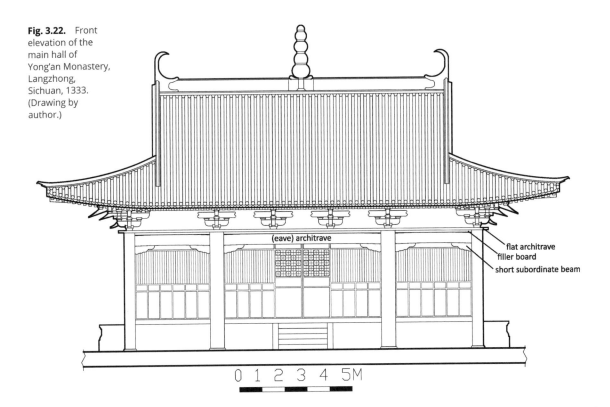

Fig. 3.22. Front elevation of the main hall of Yong'an Monastery, Langzhong, Sichuan, 1333. (Drawing by author.)

(eave) architrave

flat architrave
filler board
short subordinate beam

0 1 2 3 4 5M

was more than 7 m wide.[28] The architrave is made of a round log with a diameter of 40 cm. The flat architrave (*pupaifang* 普拍枋) on top is flat and slim, as usual. An uneven filler board (*dianban* 墊板) was installed between the architrave and the flat architrave to fill in the space between these two beams.

With regard to the bracket sets of this building, only those on the facade are well preserved. There are six bracket sets in total on the front elevation: two corner sets, two capital sets, and the two intercolumnar sets in the central bay. All the bracket sets under the frontal eave are six-layer sets. Each bracket set has one projecting bracket, which is in the guise of a pseudo-cantilever, and two tiers of real inclined cantilever (fig. 3.23).[29] On both the pseudo-cantilever and the first-tier inclined cantilever is a traversal bracket, appearing like a pair of bird's wings, known as wing-shaped bracket (*yixinggong* 翼形栱). The rear part of the projecting bracket on the capital directly supports the one-rafter beam, and a slanting cantilever of the type of *angwei tiaowo* 昂尾挑斡 (visible inclined cantilevers) is extended to the end of the four-rafter beam. The modular unit of the bracket sets is about 19 by 13 cm, approximately the Grade V in the *YZFS*.

The design of the bracket sets is neither complicated nor highly decorative. It is unique because it appears to have had three cantilevers, but one of them is a pseudo-cantilever. This type of bracket set is said to have been popular and influential in Sichuan during the Ming and Qing periods.[30] It is apparent that the bracket sets of the main hall in Yong'an Monastery are nothing like those of most other Yuan buildings in Sichuan with many common and local features, such as the main hall of Lifeng Temple, the Lord Wenchang Hall of Wulong Temple, and Yong'an Temple. Though these three buildings are not far from Yong'an Monastery, their bracket sets do not have any inclined cantilever. The bracket sets in the main hall of Yong'an Monastery possibly were altered during the Ming and Qing restorations.

The ten-rafter roof structure of the main hall is also extraordinary (fig. 3.24). Two bays at the ends are crossed by the above-mentioned one-rafter beam, supported by the eave columns, and inserted in the shaft of the interior columns.

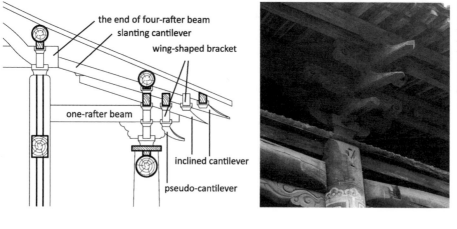

Fig. 3.23. A capital set on the front elevation of the main hall of Yong'an Monastery, Langzhong, Sichuan, 1333. (Photo by Jun Ye. Drawing by author.)

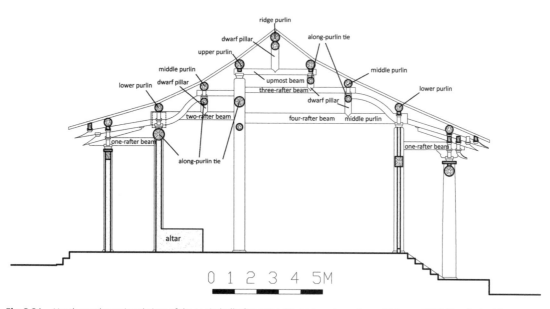

Fig. 3.24. North-south sectional view of the main hall of Yong'an Monastery, Langzhong, Sichuan, 1333. The dashed-frame shows the position of fig. 3.25 in the building. (Drawing by author.)

The structure of the two middle bays is not symmetrical. The tallest interior column divides the central space of the building into two areas. The left one, where an altar was installed to enshrine statues of the Buddha, is crossed by a two-rafter beam (*liangchuanfu* 兩椽栿). The right bay, which is wider and spanned by a four-rafter beam, seems to have been designed for worship because of its spaciousness. A dwarf pillar with bottoms carved to a point stands on the two-rafter beam and the four-rafter beam to uphold the middle purlins. The middle purlins are connected by curvy diagonal beams to the lower purlins. As discussed above, the diagonal beam connecting the purlins is a typical local feature in Sichuan, and was also found in the main hall of Bao'en Monastery and a few other examples.

It is noteworthy that several big interior tie beams, along-purlin ties (*shunshenchuan* 順身串), were added to this building to reinforce the structure. An along-purlin tie, literally meaning a tie beam parallel to the "body" of the building, usually connects two interior columns and is parallel to any purlins except for eave and ridge purlins. Since the dimension of the central bay on the front elevation is wider than 7 m, these along-purlin tie beams were built to stabilize the vertical members, such as interior columns and dwarf pillars. The along-purlin tie, as discussed in the previous chapter, is a typical feature of the Upper Yangzi tradition that has influence from the north. These along-purlin ties are made from roundish logs, the diameters of which are between 30 to 50 cm. Moreover, some four-layer bracket sets are built on one of these along-purlin ties to increase supporting points for the lower purlin (fig. 3.25). As discussed in chapter 2, the application of such thick interior tie beams is also a typical feature of Yuan timber-framed architecture in north China. It enabled a spacious area for worship without necessitating more interior columns.

The main hall once housed statues of Buddha Dīpaṃkara, Buddha Śākyamuni, and Buddha Maitreya on its central altar. In the middle, back to back with Buddha Śākyamuni, was a statue of Amitābha, facing in the opposite direction. Along the east and west walls were Bodhisattvas of the Ten Stages, five on each side and all standing on one base. Next to each window on the side bay stood a six-armed bodhisattva.[31] Unfortunately, none of the statues remain, and

Fig. 3.25. Bracket sets between the along-purlin tie and the lower purlin, the main hall of Yong'an Monastery, Langzhong, Sichuan, 1333. (Photo by Jun Ye.)

lower purlin ⎯

along-purlin tie ⎯

only the central altar is extant. By 1955, when the scholar Tao Mingkuan visited Yong'an Monastery, Yuan sculptures and wall paintings still remained in the main hall.[32] Perhaps the statues and wall paintings were damaged or lost during the Cultural Revolution (1966–1976).

According to Tao Mingkuan, images of *Tianlong babu* 天龍八部 (Eight divisions of gods and dragons) were painted in color on the east and west walls. An inscription dated to 1348 was once on the east wall and read:

> The abbot of this monastery decided to construct a place for the bhikṣu (Buddhist monks), with Masters Wuzhen and Wuli, and their apprentices Yongyong, Yongbao, Yongjian and Yonghe. . . . [We] use the good deeds and merits from building the temple and sculpting the statues to solicit a convenience to teach both the wise and the foolish. Since the autumn of the Guiyou year (1333), in order to provide a place for worship, we were about to reconstruct the main hall, and then we started. We sincerely intended to protect the building. Before our work was halfway done, the master passed away. Now that the restoration is finished, we should certainly celebrate. The timber and earth work has been accomplished and the sculptures and color paintings are all finished. . . . Wuzi year of the Zhizheng reign (1348).[33]

The inscription indicates that the statues and wall paintings were finished fifteen years after the completion of the building, and it further proves that the main hall was expanded or rebuilt in 1333. Although there are many texts that help to date the building to the Yuan, it seems that the Yuan building, especially its bracket sets, may have been altered significantly during the Ming and Qing restorations. This is especially evident when we compare it to the next structure that was built in the same year and located in the same county but looks very different.

LORD WENCHANG HALL OF WULONG TEMPLE

Lord Wenchang Hall (Wenchangdian 文昌殿) was the main hall and is the only extant building in Wulong (Five Dragons) Temple 五龍廟, located in the village of White Tiger (Baihucun 白虎村), thirty kilometers south of Langzhong. The temple was once a communal space for the villagers. The temple complex consisted of a gate, a stage, two side chambers, and the main hall that is called Wenchangdian and dedicated to Lord Wenchang, a Daoist deity.[34] Except for Lord Wenchang Hall, all the other buildings in Wulong Temple were pulled down in the 1960s.

A stele found in Lord Wenchang Hall has an inscription with a brief description of the hall's history. The inscription is titled *Chongxiu Wenchangge gongde-bei* 重修文昌閣功德碑 (Stele for the merits and virtues of the reconstruction of

Wenchang Pavilion).[35] One line reads: "Lord Wenchang Hall was first built in the Tang dynasty. It was reconstructed in the third year of the Zhizheng reign of the Yuan dynasty (1333)."[36] Since no evidence of later destruction or renovation was found, we can assume that the history of the temple can be traced back to the Tang dynasty and the current Lord Wenchang Hall was built during the Yuan dynasty. By studying its structural features, the Yuan date is validated further.

Lord Wenchang Hall is oriented north-south with its front entrance facing the south (fig. 3.26). It has a three-by-three-bay plan, the dimensions of which are 9.8 by 9.5 m. Although the front is a little wider than the sides, the layout was close to a square. The central bay on the front is one-and-a-half times each side bay; the dimension of the middle bay on the sides, however, is almost twice as wide as that of the side bays. The building has sixteen columns: twelve eave columns and four interior columns. Neither eliminated-column structure nor displaced-column structure was employed. The front three bays, which are semi-open, can be considered the porch of the building. The main entrance is installed between two front interior columns, with two windows on each side. Brick walls 30 cm thick are constructed on the rear, east, and west sides of the building.

Lord Wenchang Hall has a hip-and-gable roof and stands on a two-storied base, which also is found in the main hall of Yong'an Monastery, as mentioned above (fig. 3.27).[37] The four front eave columns stand on the lower level, which is 1.7 m above ground level and is a natural mound with rocks lying on the surface. The rest of the building is constructed on the second level, which is 0.65 m above the lower level and is made of irregular stone blocks. At the center, two staircases connect the ground and the two levels of the base. The eave architrave is made of a thick round log and curves downward. The flat architrave atop the eave architrave is 10 cm thick, and its edge is carved into lotus buds. A filler board is installed between the eave architrave and the flat architrave.

The bracket sets in Lord Wenchang Hall can be categorized into two groups—the first group, complicated and elaborate, is built on the front elevation; the second group, simple and modest, is built on the side and rear elevations. The first group has a total of five bracket sets: two corner sets, two capital sets, and one intercolumnar set (figs. 3.28 and 3.29). Each capital set has three projecting brackets with no cantilever. The first-tier projecting bracket intersects with a wing-shaped bracket. The second-tier projecting bracket intersects with a long bracket and projects two oblique arms of 45°. These oblique arms hold the square eave purlin together with the third-tier projecting bracket. The rear part

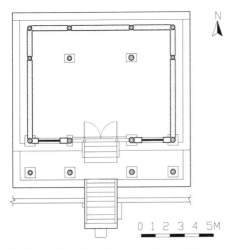

N

Fig. 3.26. Plan of Lord Wenchang Hall of Wulong Temple, Langzhong, Sichuan, 1333. (Drawing by author.)

0 1 2 3 4 5M

of the capital set is relatively simple, with no blocks and transversal arms. The only intercolumnar set is installed in the middle of the central bay, and its front view is covered partially by the wooden plaque. The intercolumnar set, more complicated than the capital set, also has three tiers of projecting brackets. The first tier intersects a double bracket and projects two layers of oblique arms at a 45° angle. The oblique arms help the middle-tier projecting bracket support the transversal arms on the second tier that also projects five brackets forward; three are orthogonal and two have a 45° angle. The rear part of the interco-lumnar set is similar to that of the capital set, except that, instead of bearing a one-rafter beam, the intercolumnar set has a slanting cantilever of the type of *angting tiaowo* to bear the lower purlin. A triangle wedge is inserted between the

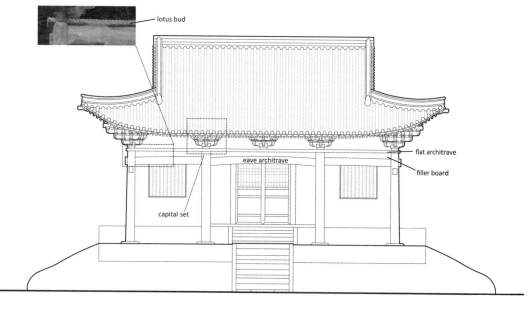

Fig. 3.27. Front elevation of Lord Wenchang Hall, Wulong Temple, Langzhong, Sichuan, 1333. (Drawing by author.)

0   1   2   3   4   5m

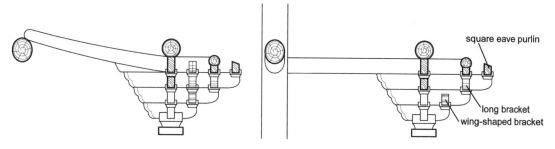

Fig. 3.28. Sectional views of the bracket sets in Lord Wenchang Hall, Wulong Temple, Langzhong, Sichuan, 1333: (*left*) intercolumnar set; (*right*) capital set. (Drawing by author.)

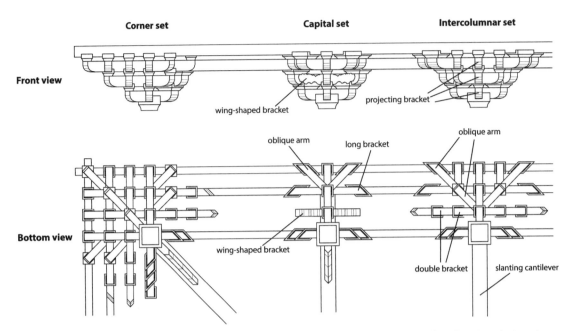

Fig. 3.29. Front (*top row*) and bottom (*bottom row*) views of the bracket sets in Lord Wenchang Hall, Wulong Temple, Langzhong, Sichuan, 1333: (*left*) corner set; (*middle*) capital set; (*right*) intercolumnar set. (Drawing by author.)

Fig. 3.30. Bracket sets on the east side of Lord Wenchang Hall, Wulong Temple, Langzhong, Sichuan, 1333. (Photo by Jun Ye.)

plank projected from the capital block and the slanting cantilever to stabilize the structure. The corner set on the front elevation also has a similar and complicated structure. Viewed from the bottom, the bracket arms from different directions are interwoven with oblique arms projecting at the sides.

In contrast to the first complex group, bracket sets on the east, west, and north/rear sides of the building are almost identical and quite simple. The second type of bracket set is crossed by a one-rafter beam from inside and only projects one tier of bracket to support the square eave purlin (fig. 3.30). This simplistic type is considered a four-layer bracket set and also is called "a jump from the mouth of the block" (*doukoutiao* 枓口跳), meaning that one tier bracket projects from the opening of the capital block. It is remarkable that no inclined cantilever can be seen from the outside in the bracket sets of this hall—this is a local feature shared by the main hall of Lifeng Temple, the main hall of Bao'en Monastery and the main hall of Qinglong Monastery, and Yong'an Temple, which has been discussed in Chapter 2.

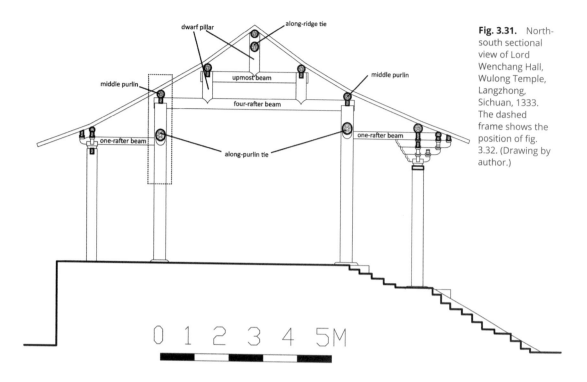

Fig. 3.31. North-south sectional view of Lord Wenchang Hall, Wulong Temple, Langzhong, Sichuan, 1333. The dashed frame shows the position of fig. 3.32. (Drawing by author.)

The roof structure of Lord Wenchang Hall is relatively simple. It has two interior columns dividing the hall into three bays (fig. 3.31). The front and rear bays are crossed by a one-rafter beam, and the middle bay is crossed by a four-rafter beam. Two dwarf pillars stand on the four-rafter beam to support the upmost beam, where another dwarf pillar holding up the ridge purlin is located. All dwarf pillars have a pointed bottom. Two

Fig. 3.32. The along-purlin tie of Lord Wenchang Hall, Wulong Temple, Langzhong, Sichuan, 1333. (Photo by Jun Ye.)

interior columns under the middle purlin are crossed by an along-purlin tie (fig. 3.32). The along-purlin tie is made of a thick round log and curves downward a little. A similar tie beam often is found in many other buildings in Sichuan but in a different position. The dwarf pillar on the upmost beam is crossed by an along-ridge tie (*shunjichuan* 順脊串), a tie beam parallel to the ridge purlin to stabilize the roof frame.

In sum, Lord Wenchang Hall is one of the best illustrative examples of the local tradition in the Upper Yangzi. It has the curved eave architrave that is unique to the area. Its bracket sets include oblique arms and the structure of *angting tiaowo* (no cantilever seen from the outside); they lack the uttermost bracket and the locus head, and the distribution of single and double brackets. The bracket sets on the side and rear elevations are also simplified. Those along-purlin ties found in Lord Wenchang Hall are an important feature of the Upper Yangzi tradition that suggests some connection to north China.

The five Yuan buildings described here have a specific date in the Yuan dynasty. The buildings in the following sections, however, are from the Yuan dynasty but cannot be dated to an exact year.

THE MAIN HALL OF QINGLONG MONASTERY

Qinglong (Azure Dragon) Monastery 青龍寺 is located in Qinglong Village 青龍村, twenty kilometers northeast of the Lushan county seat. It was originally built in 1344, the fourth year of the Zhizheng 至正 period of the Yuan dynasty.[38] The monastery used to enshrine statues of Śākyamuni, Maitreya, and the Eighteen Arhats (*Shiba luohan* 十八羅漢). Unfortunately, except for the architecture of the main hall, all other buildings and art in the monastery were demolished in the early 1950s.[39] At that time, the main hall was used as a classroom for the local school and so was not destroyed; it did not suffer any damage until an earthquake in 2013.[40]

There are a few sources proving that the main hall of Qinglong Monastery was originally a Yuan building. First, an inscription found on one of the stone pivot bearers of the main hall reads: "the ninth year of the Zhizheng reign of Yuan (*Dayuan Zhizheng jiunian* 大元至正九年, 1349)."[41] Second, four roof tiles that show inscriptions dated to the Yuan period were uncovered.[42] Although we do not know exactly what year in Yuan the building was completed, from these textual sources and the architecture itself, it is certain that the main hall originally dated to the Yuan, and the construction probably took place from the late 1330s to the early 1350s.[43] Although major restorations or reconstructions took place during the Ming and Qing periods, it is believed that part of the original Yuan construction has remained, especially that from the bracket sets and below.[44]

The main hall of Qinglong Monastery is oriented north-south with its front side facing south (fig. 3.33). The dimensions of the plan are 15.1 by 14.95 m, which is very close to a square. Its south and north sides have three bays and are a little wider than the east and west sides. The central bay on the south side is almost twice as wide as the side bays.

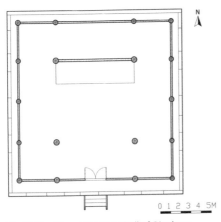

N

0 1 2 3 4 5M

Fig. 3.33. Plan of the main hall of Qinglong Monastery, Lushan, Sichuan, Yuan. (Drawing by author.)

The dimensions of the four bays on the east and west sides, however, are almost identical. A total of eighteen columns were used in this building—fourteen eave columns and four interior columns. The arrangement of columns is fairly normal; no column was eliminated or displaced. An altar, 7 m long and 2 m wide, is installed in front of the wooden board between the rear interior columns.

The building has a hip-and-gable roof. It is about 8.6 m tall and constructed on a 0.8-meter-high base (fig. 3.34). Since the central bay is much wider than the side bays, there are three intercolumnar bracket sets in the central bay and only one in each side bay. In order to stabilize the structure of the central bay that is wider than 7 m, a roundish and thick eave architrave, slightly curved downward, is built to span the width of the central bay. The eave architraves in the side bays are of the same thickness as that in the central bay. Because the heights of the eave columns are slightly and gradually increased from the center toward the corners, there is more space between the eave architrave and the flat architrave on the side than in the center. Therefore, a dwarf pillar is installed in the side bays between the eave architrave and flat architrave to stabilize the structure.

The bracket sets in the main hall of Qinglong Monastery are very diverse. There are five types of bracket sets on the front side of the building: the capital set, the corner set, and three types of intercolumnar sets. The capital set has two tiers of projecting brackets (fig. 3.35). The first-tier projecting bracket supports a wing-shaped bracket, while the second-tier projecting bracket sustains the eave lintel directly, with no traversal bracket. With regard to the interior

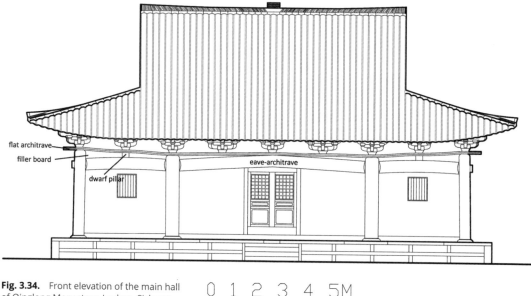

Fig. 3.34. Front elevation of the main hall of Qinglong Monastery, Lushan, Sichuan, Yuan. (Drawing by author.)

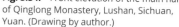

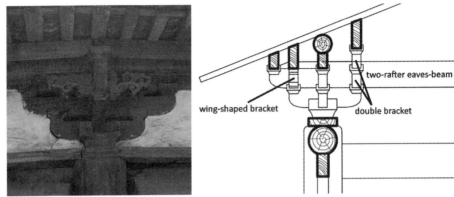

Fig. 3.35. The capital set on the front elevation of the main hall of Qinglong Monastery, Lushan, Sichuan, Yuan. (Photo by Jun Ye. Drawing by author.)

two-rafter eaves-beam

wing-shaped bracket

double bracket

Fig. 3.36. Intercolumnar sets in the central bay of the main hall of Qinglong Monastery, Lushan, Sichuan, Yuan. (Photo by Jun Ye.)

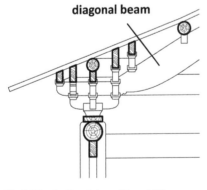

diagonal beam

Fig. 3.37. Sectional view of the middle intercolumnar set in the central bay of the main hall of Qinglong Monastery, Lushan, Sichuan, Yuan. (Drawing by author.)

part of the capital set, the first projecting bracket supports a double bracket, and a two-rafter eaves beam is connected with the second tier. It should be again noted that no inclined cantilever is used.

The three intercolumnar sets in the central bay belong to two types (fig. 3.36). From the outside, the one in the middle looks the same as the capital set. From the inside, however, the only difference from the capital set is that the two-rafter eaves beam in the capital set is now replaced by a diagonal beam (fig. 3.37). The other two intercolumnar sets on the side are quite different from the middle one: they have two tiers of projecting brackets that are orthogonal to the plane of wall, and two tiers of oblique arms at a 45° angle flanking the projecting bracket. The intercolumnar set in the side bay belongs to a third type. It looks almost the same as the middle

Fig. 3.38.
Intercolumnar set
in the side bay on
the front elevation
of the main hall
of Qinglong
Monastery, Lushan,
Sichuan, Yuan.
(Photo by Jun Ye.)

intercolumnar set in the central bay except that the wing-shaped arm in the former was replaced by a regular short bracket in the latter to provide support to the square eave purlin above (fig. 3.38). Last, in addition to the front side of the building, the bracket sets on the rear of the building are very simple. A two-rafter eaves beam crosses the eave column to support the square eave purlin and is supported by a projecting bracket both inside and outside (fig. 3.39).

It is extraordinary that the roof structure of the main hall is built with a series of thick diagonal beams that are constructed to connect one purlin with another, creating a strong inverted V-shaped frame (fig. 3.40). It seems that these diagonal beams were made of un-hewn timber, which is known as one of

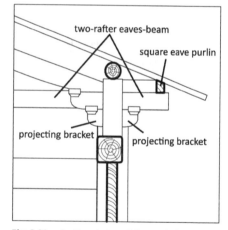

Fig. 3.39. Sectional view of the capital set on the rear side of the main hall of Qinglong Monastery, Lushan, Sichuan, Yuan. (Drawing by author.)

the characteristics of Yuan timber-framed architecture in north China. In addition to these diagonal beams, the front and rear bays of the building are spanned by a two-rafter eaves beam, and the middle bay is crossed by a four-rafter beam. Above the four-rafter beam are two dwarf pillars sustaining the upmost beam.

Another remarkable feature in this building is the application of tie beams that were installed under and parallel to the purlins to connect posts and/or

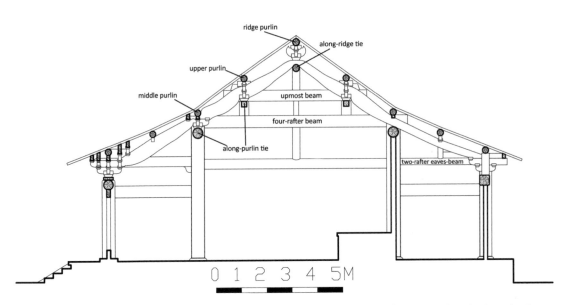

Fig. 3.40. North-south sectional view of the main hall of Qinglong Monastery, Lushan, Sichuan, Yuan. (Drawing by author.)

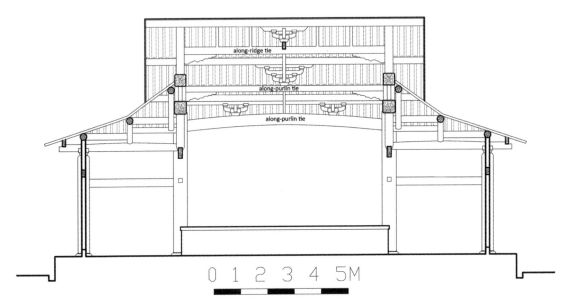

Fig. 3.41. East-west sectional view of the main hall of Qinglong Monastery, Lushan, Sichuan, Yuan. (Drawing by author.)

interior columns; this also has been used in other examples. One along-ridge tie crosses the dwarf pillar on the upmost beam (fig. 3.41). Several along-purlin ties, under either the upper purlin or the middle purlin, cross the dwarf pillars and the interior columns. Along the east-west direction, these tie beams have increased the stability of the building, especially the large span of the central bay.

The two most striking features in the main hall of Qinglong Monastery are the huge and curved eave architrave and the inverted V-shaped frame composed of huge diagonal beams. Both are used to support the wide-span central bay. The eave architrave and the diagonal beams are also found in other Yuan buildings in the same area, but the large size of these elements in the main hall of Qinglong Monastery is exceptional. Moreover, the bracket sets at different positions are differentiated by using oblique arms, perpendicular arms, or wing-shaped arms. These differences between the capital set and the intercolumnar set is also found in other Yuan buildings in the Upper Yangzi, such as Lord Wenchang Hall and Yong'an Temple. The main hall of Qinglong Monastery, however, has the most varieties. The main hall of Qinglong Monastery has a number of features that are exceptional but understandable within the context of the local tradition.

PINGXIANG PAVILION

All the buildings discussed so far are one-storied. Pingxiang Pavilion 平襄樓 is the only multistoried building in our discussion. Located in the city of Lushan in southeast Sichuan, this two-storied timber-framed building is the centerpiece of Marquis Jiang Shrine (Jianghouci 姜侯祠). The shrine is in memory of Jiang Wei 姜維, a famous general of the state of Shu Han 蜀漢 during the Three Kingdoms era (220–280), and today it serves as a public park for the local community.[45] The pavilion is named after Jiang Wei's honorific title, Pingxiang 平襄.

The date of the Pingxiang Pavilion is problematic. The earliest record of the building is in a Ming book titled *Shuzhong mingshengji* 蜀中名勝記 (Records of places of interest in Sichuan), by Cao Xuequan 曹學佺. In the entry of Lushan 蘆山, it records: "In the twenty-third year of the Shaoxing reign (1153), Xu Hongzhong wrote: 'The native people commemorated Boyue (the style name of Jiang Wei) with a temple.[46] The horizontal inscribed board on the temple reads *pingxiang* (the honorific title of Jiang Wei).'"[47] Accordingly, some people argue that the building mentioned above is the same building that survives. There is no additional evidence to identify the building as Song architecture. Considering that it served not only as the shrine of Jiang Wei but also as the center of the community since the Song dynasty, it could have been restored or rebuilt frequently.[48]

In the early 1940s, architectural historian Liu Dunzhen 劉敦楨 (1897–1968) investigated Pingxiang Pavilion. He discovered an identical inscription on several pieces of roof tiles, which read "*Zhengtong shinian* 正統十年, the tenth year of Zhengtong reign of the Ming dynasty" (1445). Liu could not date the building to an exact year either, but he confirmed that the building had been repaired in 1445. Later on, another Ming inscription and a Qing stele documenting restoration events were uncovered; these verify that restoration was carried out during the Ming-Qing period. Although it is generally agreed that the building was first built in the Song, its structure has been altered since then.

It is quite difficult to date Pingxiang Pavilion to a specific dynasty. The reason it is discussed here as a "Yuan" building is that China's State Administration of Cultural Heritage (SACH) designated it a state heritage building in 2006 and dated it to the Yuan period. Nevertheless, further studies are needed to confirm that it is indeed an authentic Yuan building.

Pingxiang Pavilion is a two-storied building with a hip-and-gable roof and three layers of eaves (fig. 3.42). The middle eaves are not part of the main structure and are attached only to protect the balcony and balustrade on the second floor, it does not suggest a real floor. The building was set on a low-rise base of 17.5 cm, and the building itself is about 11 m high. In the central bay of the ground level, the thick and round architrave is slightly curved downward, as the central bay is much wider than the side bays. Instead of placing a filler board into the space between the architrave and the flat architrave as in previous cases, the builders of Pingxiang Pavilion installed two dwarf pillars, each under the intercolumnar set, to increase stability. This may be a local feature of Lushan County, as a similar structure is also found in the Main Hall of Qinglong Monastery in the same county.

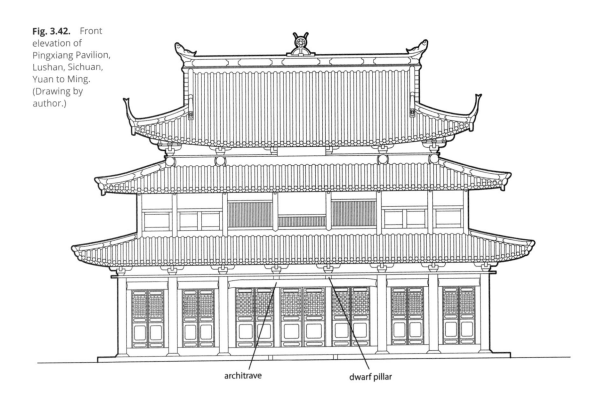

Fig. 3.42. Front elevation of Pingxiang Pavilion, Lushan, Sichuan, Yuan to Ming. (Drawing by author.)

architrave   dwarf pillar

Pingxiang Pavilion is oriented north-south with entrances on both the north and south sides (fig. 3.43). A small staircase on its south side suggests that it is the front. The front side is about 14 m wide and has five bays. The east and west sides are about 10 m wide and have four bays. It is interesting that the plan of Pingxiang Pavilion is symmetrical on both the east-west and north-south axes. On its long side, the central bay is 6 m wide, three times wider than the side bays of the front and back, all of which are about 2 m. Each bay on the long side has a two-panel door. Along the short side, the two middle bays are 3 m wide, and the dimensions of the end bays are both 2 m. There are no interior columns in line with the center columns on the east and west sides, which provides a large space in the center of the building.

The bracket sets of Pingxiang Pavilion appear more standardized than those of other Yuan buildings in Sichuan. Among the thirty-eight bracket sets in this building, twenty-two are on the ground floor, including four intercolumnar sets. Each central bay of the south and north sides has two intercolumnar sets. The other sixteen sets are built on the second floor under the top eave, four of which are intercolumnar sets, two on each central bay of the south and north sides.

The structures of the capital and intercolumnar sets are nearly identical when viewed from the outside. They both have two projecting brackets, one short bracket on the first tier, and the upper projecting bracket supporting a square eave purlin through a block (fig. 3.44). Along the wall

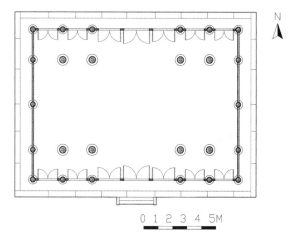

Fig. 3.43. Plan of the ground floor of Pingxiang Pavilion, Lushan, Sichuan, Yuan to Ming. (Drawing by author.)

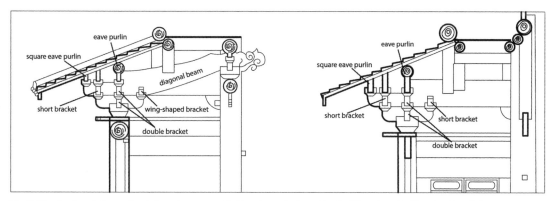

Fig. 3.44. Sectional views of an intercolumnar set (*left*) and a capital set (*right*) of Pingxiang Pavilion, Lushan, Sichuan, Yuan to Ming. (Drawing by author.)

plane, both the capital and intercolumnar sets support a double bracket to sustain the eave purlin (*yantuan* 檐槫) through a lintel. An inclined cantilever is not used here, as in other Yuan buildings previously discussed. Viewed from the inside, however, there are still some differences between a capital set and intercolumnar set. A short bracket is placed on the first-tier projecting bracket of the capital set, but the intercolumnar set has a wing-shaped bracket at the same position. Moreover, the capital set is connected by a horizontal beam to the interior column, but the intercolumnar set is connected to a tie beam by a diagonal beam.[49]

Regarding the structure of Pingxiang Pavilion, the ground floor is divided into three parts. The side bays on the ground floor are spanned by a two-rafter eaves beam, and the central part is crossed by a four-rafter beam and covered by a ceiling (fig. 3.45). Instead of being supported by interior columns, the four-rafter beam spans two transversal tie beams that are supported by interior columns. The second floor has only one bay. A four-rafter beam joins one column to another with an along-beam tie (*shunfuchuan* 順栿串) built beneath it. On the four-rafter beam stand three dwarf pillars, all of which are connected by another tie beam. The short post in the middle is sort of irregular. It is feasible

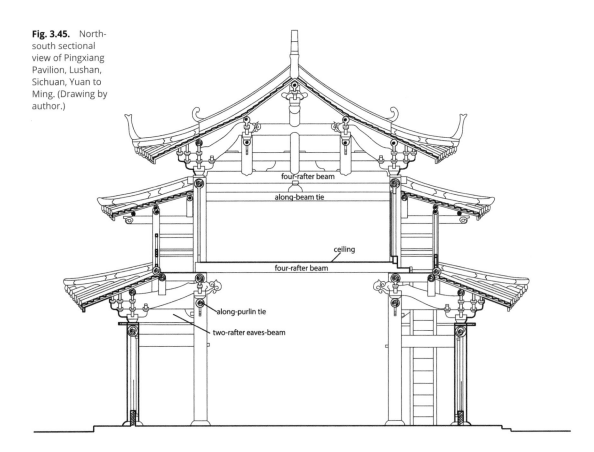

Fig. 3.45. North-south sectional view of Pingxiang Pavilion, Lushan, Sichuan, Yuan to Ming. (Drawing by author.)

four-rafter beam

along-beam tie

ceiling

four-rafter beam

along-purlin tie

two-rafter eaves-beam

that the middle one was not part of the original design but was added later to strengthen the upmost beam.

The multistoried structure of Pingxiang Pavilion is built by the technique called the "through-column method" (*tongzhufa* 通柱法). In order to build the upper floor(s), interior columns are extended from the ground floor to the second or even the third floor. This method is different from the techniques used in other multistoried buildings that are earlier than the Yuan period. Pre-Yuan buildings usually have separate columns on each floor. In Pingxiang Pavilion, two interior columns are tall enough to reach the bracket sets under the top eave. Generally, the through-column method is regarded as a common technique often used in Ming-Qing multistoried buildings, which weakens the theory that the main part of Pingxiang Pavilion is earlier than Ming.[50]

As stated above, it is difficult to identify the exact age of Pingxiang Pavilion due to its frequent renovations. Moreover, its standardization of bracket sets and the style of *tongzhuzao* are atypical of Yuan architecture in Sichuan. Its similarities with the main hall of Qinglong Monastery are probably local rather than dynastic features. Nonetheless, Pingxiang Pavilion provides some information about the transformation of timber structure from Yuan through Ming in Sichuan.

PANTUOSHI HALL OF THE GRAND TEMPLE AT MOUNT QIQU

Pantuoshi (Uneven Stone) Hall 磐陀石殿 is located in the complex of the Grand Temple at Mount Qiqu (Qiqushan damiao 七曲山大廟), which is nine kilometers north of the City of Zitong 梓潼. Similar to Lord Wenchang Hall, Pantuoshi Hall also is related to the cult of Wenchang. The Grand Temple at Mount Qiqu is known as the pilgrimage site of the cult of Wenchang and is one of the most popular historical and scenic sites in north Sichuan. The Grand Temple houses a shrine of the Divine Lord Wenchang (Wenchang Dijun 文昌帝君), also called the Divine Lord of Zitong (Zitong Dijun 梓潼帝君). Wenchang is the patron Daoist deity of literary arts. His short biography can be found in the *Mingshi* 明史 (History of Ming), and it reads:

> The deity, surnamed Zhang and named Yazi, lived at Mount Qiqu in Sichuan. As he served the Western Jin rulers and died on the battlefield, people built a temple in memory of him. During the Tang and Song dynasties, he was granted honorific titles several times and then was entitled the King of Heroic Manifestation. According to the Daoist canon, the Jade Emperor appointed the Divine Lord of Zitong (the posthumous Zhang Yazi) to take charge of affairs in the House of Literary Arts, and at the same time to manage official ranks and scholarly honors in the mortal world. Therefore, he was granted the title "the Divine Lord" in the Yuan dynasty, and schools all over the country also worship him.[51]

According to the aforementioned reference, the cult of Wenchang has been very popular since the Yuan dynasty. This esteem certainly resulted in active construction in his home shrine at Zitong. The complex of the Grand Temple was first built during the Western Jin (266–316) and was significantly expanded during the Yuan dynasty. Due to occasional damage caused by fire and war, construction work on the temple was continual from the Ming to the Qing dynasties. Today, buildings dated to Yuan, Ming, and Qing coexist in the temple complex of 10,000 square meters.[52] Dated to the Yuan dynasty, Pantuoshi Hall is the oldest one and was located across the road west of the main compound. The name *pantuoshi* means "uneven stone" and refers to a huge monolith discovered at the place where the building is constructed. It is said that Lord Wenchang once meditated on the monolith himself and attained his Dao there. The dimensions of this oblong monolith are about 4 by 2.8 by 0.85 m. It is kept in the hall today as the altar to enshrine the statue of Lord Wenchang. Unfortunately, the original statue was destroyed.

There is no clear evidence that determines the exact age of Pantuoshi Hall. Although two Qing dynasty stelae are embedded in the side wall of the building, they merely record irrelevant information regarding the construction. According to the history of the Wenchang cult, Emperor Renzong 仁宗 of the Yuan dynasty conferred the title *dijun* 帝君 (the Divine Lord) on the deity in 1316, and the Grand Temple was expanded at that time. Originally the temple was called "shrine" (*ci* 祠) and later, after 1316, upgraded/renamed as a "palace" (*gong* 宮), which also may suggest a promotion of Wenchang in the Daoist pantheon.[53] It is very possible that Pantuoshi Hall was built during this expansion together with the main complex of the temple. Moreover, in a gazetteer of Zitong published in 1858, a fire was documented as follows: "In the winter of the fourth year of Yongzheng reign (1726), the main hall, the Prayer Hall, the Bell Tower, the gatehouse and the Zhongxiao Pavilion (of the Grande Temple) were all destroyed by the fire, the cause of which was unknown."[54] According to the gazetteer, Pantuoshi Hall was not destroyed in this disaster. It certainly predates the buildings of the main complex of the temple.

Pantuoshi Hall is a small timber-framed hall facing southeast with an approximately square plan, measuring 8.4 by 8.3 m (fig. 3.46).[55] The plan is basically three by three bays. On the front side, the central bay is nearly twice as wide as the side bays. The building does not have a rear entrance, and the oval monolithic altar is placed against the rear wall. The eliminated-column structure is applied here: two front eave columns and two rear interior columns have been removed. Such a design of columns is found elsewhere in Sichuan.

The building sits on a base and has a hip-and-gable roof with single-layer eaves, which are covered by yellow glazed tiles (fig. 3.47). Two round and decorative windows are installed on the front wall. The front corner columns are about 35 cm thick and 3.25 m high. The ratio of its diameter to its height is about

1:9, which makes the column appear a little thick. A batter (*cejiao* 側腳) is applied on these two corner columns by making the top of the column lean 8 cm inward, nearly 2.4 percent of the height of the column itself. The eave architrave is curved slightly downward and is round in section, the diameter of which is 35 cm. Since there are no columns between the corners, the eave architrave would have been strong enough to cross the whole width of the front. It is also remarkable that there is no flat architrave on top of the eave architrave. *Ludou* 櫨枓, the capital block of the intercolumnar bracket sets, sits directly on the eave architrave. Because the flat architrave is not mentioned in the *YZFS*, an absence of a flat architrave usually is associated with architecture before the twelfth century.

Five bracket sets are built on the front elevation: two corner sets and three intercolumnar sets.[56] The intercolumnar set is a five-layer bracket set (fig. 3.48). Its two tiers of projecting brackets are replaced by two tiers of inclined cantilever, which is worth special

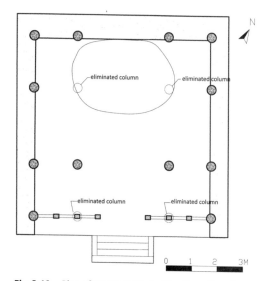

Fig. 3.46. Plan of Pantuoshi Hall of the Grant Temple at Mount Qiqu, Sichuan, Yuan. (Drawing by author.)

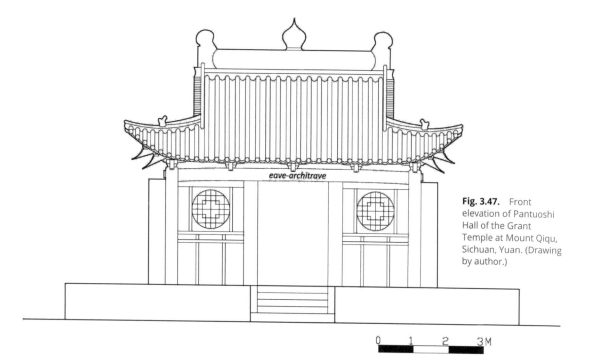

Fig. 3.47. Front elevation of Pantuoshi Hall of the Grant Temple at Mount Qiqu, Sichuan, Yuan. (Drawing by author.)

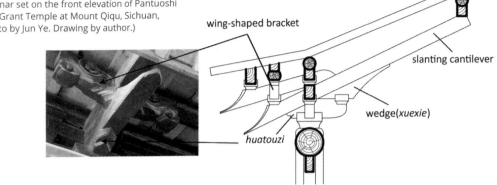

Fig. 3.48.
Intercolumnar set on the front elevation of Pantuoshi Hall of the Grant Temple at Mount Qiqu, Sichuan, Yuan. (Photo by Jun Ye. Drawing by author.)

wing-shaped bracket

slanting cantilever

wedge(*xuexie*)

huatouzi

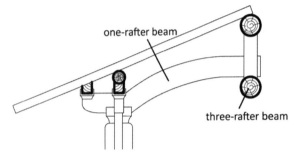

one-rafter beam

three-rafter beam

Fig. 3.49. Sectional view of the capital set on the flank side of Pantuoshi Hall, the Grant Temple at Mount Qiqu, Sichuan, Yuan. (Drawing by author.)

attention because the inclined cantilever is absent in many other Yuan buildings in the Upper Yangzi. The lower-tier inclined cantilever carries a wing-shaped bracket, and a member called *huatouzi* 華頭子 projects from the capital block bearing the lower inclined cantilever. According to the *YZFS*, *huatouzi* usually has a two-scroll profile; the one here is quite similar to that in the *YZFS*. The upper tier of inclined cantilever does not have any traversal bracket on top and sustains the square eave purlin through a block.

The rear part of the intercolumnar set projects one tier of bracket from the capital block. Between the projecting bracket and the cantilever, a triangular member that functions as a boot-shaped wedge (*xuexie* 鞾楔) is inserted to adjust the angle.[57] The inner end of the inclined cantilever is extended long enough to bear the lower purlin. The upper tier of inclined cantilever is much shorter than the lower one.

The capital set on the flank side of the building is much simpler than the bracket sets on the front. There is only one projecting bracket toward the outside, and a one-rafter beam curves downward, connecting the capital to a three-rafter beam. Such a concise bracket set can be identified as a four-layer type (fig. 3.49).

The modular unit, *cai,* of the bracket sets in Pantuoshi Hall is 17 by 12 cm, close to Grade VII in the *YZFS.*

The roof structure of Pantuoshi Hall is four rafters deep (fig. 3.50). The only interior column divided the space into two rooms. The composition of the front (smaller) room is unique. In most other Yuan buildings in Sichuan, the front room usually is spanned by a horizontal beam of either one or two rafters. In Pantuoshi Hall, however, the lower inclined cantilever of the bracket set is

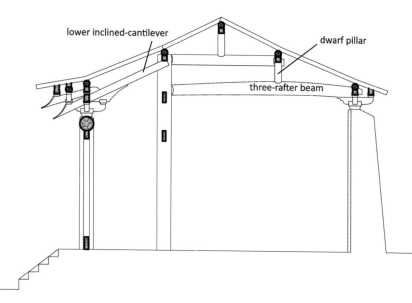

Fig. 3.50. North-south sectional view of Pantuoshi Hall of the Grant Temple at Mount Qiqu, Sichuan, Yuan. (Drawing by author.)

Labels on figure: lower inclined-cantilever; dwarf pillar; three-rafter beam

extended all the way to the lower purlin, and there is no horizontal beam connecting the bracket set to the interior column. The rear bigger room is spanned by a three-rafter beam from the interior column to the rear eave column. A dwarf pillar is built on the three-rafter beam to bear the upmost beam together with the interior column. Since two rear interior columns are eliminated, there is enough space to accommodate the huge monolithic altar.

Pantuoshi Hall retains a few features from Song architecture, such as the lack of flat architrave, the usage of *huatouzi,* and the design of the inclined cantilevers. More importantly, Pantuoshi Hall had a special function—to enshrine the monolith that was an embodiment of Lord Wenchang. Therefore, four columns were removed to make room for the huge monolith, and a long and one-piece eave architrave became necessary to support the front entrance.

THE MAIN HALL OF DUBAI MONASTERY

Dubai (Sole Cypress) Monastery 獨柏寺 is located in a village in Tongnan County 潼南县 more than a hundred kilometers northwest of downtown Chongqing. The monastery is now part of an elementary school. *Tongnan xianzhi* 潼南縣 誌 (Gazetteer of Tongnan County) written by Xia Huang 夏璜 in 1915 records: "Dubai Monastery is fifty *li* north of the county seat. It was first built in Tang and was once known as Huiriyuan. [The monastery] enshrines a statue of Buddha, the height of which is more than one *zhang* (1 *zhang* = 3.33 meters). The Buddha is carved from a cypress and is decorated with gold. Accordingly, the monastery is given its current name."[58]

Fig. 3.51. The front elevation of the main hall of Dubai Monastery, Tongnan, Chongqing, Yuan to Ming. (Photo by Jun Ye.)

The main hall of Dubai Monastery is the only structure surviving from the Yuan dynasty. When surveyed in 2007, the main hall was being used as a warehouse and was in poor condition (fig. 3.51). In 2013, the building was included in the seventh list of national cultural heritage sites announced by SACH and was dated to the Yuan dynasty, even though no literary source about the building has as yet been discovered.

The building has a three-by-three-bay square plan and is oriented north-south (fig. 3.52). On each side of the building, the central bay is twice as wide as the side bay. Sixteen columns are arranged in two rings, none of which was displaced or eliminated. The roof frame has a total transverse span of eight rafters. A two-rafter eaves beam is installed between the eave column and the interior column, with a short pillar standing atop it to support the lower purlin (fig. 3.53, top left). The space between the two interior columns is spanned by a four-rafter beam with two short pillars standing atop it to bear the two-rafter upmost beam (fig. 3.53, top right). Moreover, two along-purlin ties, parallel to the front wall, are slightly curved upward and built to connect the interior columns with the short pillars from one bay to another (fig. 3.53, bottom).

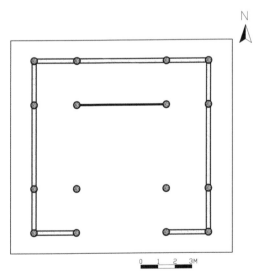

Fig. 3.52. Plan of the main hall of Dubai Monastery, Tongnan, Chongqing, Yuan to Ming. (Drawing by author.)

front eave column

front interior column

rear interior column

along-purlin tie

Fig. 3.53. Details in the roof frame of the main hall of Dubai Monastery, Tongnan, Chongqing, Yuan to Ming. (Photo by Jun Ye.)

With regard to the bracket sets on the front elevation, the capital set and intercolumnar set look identical from the outside (fig. 3.54). They both have two tiers of inclined cantilever with no projected arm, such as a projecting bracket or an oblique arm. A short bracket intersects the first-tier inclined cantilever, and a small block is put on the second-tier inclined cantilever to support the eave lintel immediately above. The rear part of the capital set differs from that of the intercolumnar set (fig. 3.55). The capital set has one tier of an orthogonal arm projecting inward to support the two-rafter eaves-beam. The intercolumnar set, however, projects one tier of bracket inward as well, and atop the projecting bracket is a slanting cantilever of the type *angwei tiaowo*. The upper end of the slanting cantilever upholds the lower purlin. This cantilever is the tail of the upper-tier inclined cantilever projecting toward the outside. Therefore, from the sectional views, it is evident that both inclined cantilevers in the capital set and the lower inclined cantilever in the intercolumnar set are in fact projecting brackets in disguise as pseudo-cantilevers, and only the upper-tier inclined cantilever at the intercolumnar set is a functioning inclined cantilever.

Although the main hall of Dubai Monastery is dated to the Yuan dynasty by SACH, its structural details might suggest otherwise. The bracket sets and roof framing do not resemble the other Yuan buildings in the same area. The

Fig. 3.54. Bracket sets on the front elevation of the main hall of Dubai Monastery, Tongnan, Chongqing, Yuan to Ming. (Photo by Jun Ye.)

Fig. 3.55. Sectional views of the capital (*left*) and intercolumnar (*right*) sets in the main hall of Dubai Monastery, Tongnan, Chongqing, Yuan to Ming. (Drawing by author.)

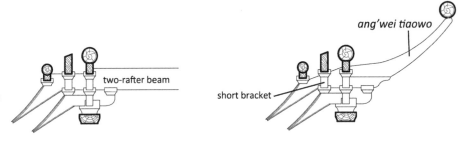

four intercolumnar sets installed in the central bay on the facade outnumber all examples of Yuan architecture that have been discovered so far in the Upper Yangzi area. This building very likely was built toward the end of the Yuan dynasty.

YONG'AN TEMPLE

The last example in this chapter is a small timber-framed building that lacks textual evidence and is not yet officially recognized as a Yuan building. Through comparison with the Yuan buildings discussed up to now, the author tends to classify it as a Yuan building because of its architectural features.

Yong'an (Eternal Peace) Temple 永安廟 was built on a hillside in a remote and backward village a hundred kilometers northwest of the city of Nanbu in Sichuan. There is no reliable source yet to indicate the date of the temple. A Qing dynasty stele dated to 1804 was discovered that bears the dates and circumstances of the temple's earliest construction in the Tang dynasty and a later restoration in the Qing dynasty. The inscription on the stele is titled *Peixiu Yong'anmiao beiji* 培修永安廟碑記 (Record of the restoration of Yong'an Temple), and it reads:

> Yong'an Temple is located in the ancient town of Yong'an. In the second year of the Yonghui period (651) during Emperor Tang Gaozong's reign, a local official appealed to the royal court to build a temple in order to keep the people away from flood, drought, and pestilence. The emperor consented and the official constructed the temple in response to the imperial decree. Although it has been more than a thousand years [since it was first built] and the graceful decree has also been lost for a long time, the temple still retains the main beam, which is inevitable due to the increasing miraculous brightness of this place.[59]

According to the inscription, the temple was first built in the Tang dynasty. A major beam, which possibly could be dated to the Tang, still remained when the Qing stele was inscribed. Furthermore, two inscriptions written in ink on the beams are still legible. They record, respectively, two inconsequential alterations in the Qing dynasty—one in 1724 and the other in 1759. Since no evidence can date the temple precisely, some scholars, on the basis of their own understanding, tend to identify it as an early Ming building.[60] Now, by comparing Yong'an Temple to other Yuan buildings, such as the main hall of Lifeng Daoist Temple and Lord Wenchang Hall, I shall argue that there are a number of similarities between them and Yong'an Temple, possibly identifying Yong'an Temple as a Yuan building.

The temple is oriented to the southeast and has a square and three-by-three-bay plan measuring 8.2 by 8.2 m (fig. 3.56). On each side of the building, the central bay is twice as wide as the side bays, which resembles the layout of the main hall of Lifeng Temple and Lord Wenchang Hall. In the front is a three-bay porch 2.1 m wide. There are fourteen columns in total—two interior columns and twelve eave columns that compose the outer ring. Another two interior columns were eliminated, and the characteristic technique of Yuan, the eliminated-column structure, is employed.

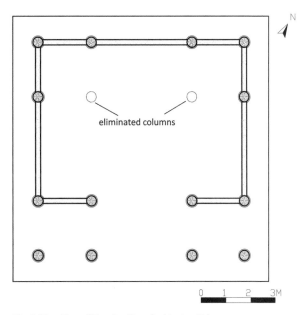

Fig. 3.56. Plan of Yong'an Temple, Nanbu, Sichuan, Yuan. (Drawing by author.)

Yong'an Temple has a hip-and-gable roof, and its front eave columns are connected to each other by a flat architrave (fig. 3.57). The eave architrave, however, merely spans the central bay, while the side bays are crossed by an associate architrave (*you'e* 由額) that is placed lower than the eave architrave. In addition, both the eave architrave and the associate architrave are curved downward

The arrangement of bracket sets on the front elevation of Yong'an Temple resembles those on Lord Wenchang Hall. There are two corner sets, two capital sets and one intercolumnar set, all of which have 45 oblique arms without any inclined cantilever. The capital set has two tiers of brackets projecting outward (fig. 3.58). A double bracket sits on the octagonal capital block, and two oblique arms of 45° project from the capital block as well. The length of the oblique arms is much shorter than the orthogonal brackets. Atop the first tier of projecting bracket is a hexagonal block, which supports one traversal bracket, two symmetrical oblique arms, and the top orthogonal bracket. The transversal bracket, interestingly, has a zigzag profile that differs from either a regular bracket or a wing-shaped bracket. The top tier of the oblique and orthogonal brackets immediately supports the eave purlin. The rear part of the capital set is simple—only one tier of projecting brackets is installed to bear a one-rafter beam that is inserted into the shaft of the interior column (fig. 3.59).

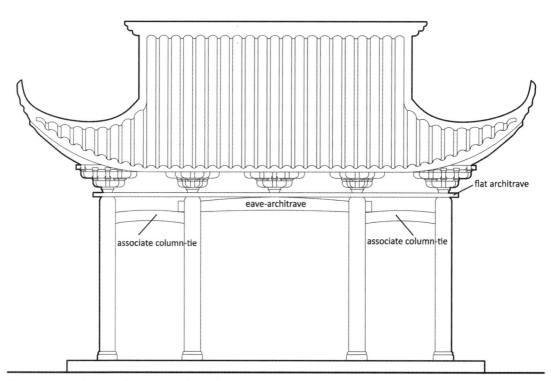

Fig. 3.57. Front elevation of Yong'an Temple, Nanbu, Sichuan, Yuan. (Drawing by author.)

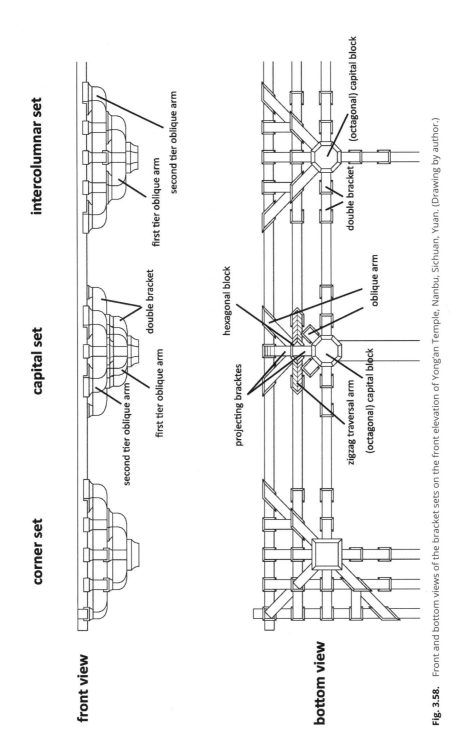

corner set

capital set

double bracket

second tier oblique arm

first tier oblique arm

intercolumnar set

second tier oblique arm

first tier oblique arm

front view

hexagonal block

oblique arm

projecting bracktes

zigzag traversal arm

(octagonal) capital block

double bracket

(octagonal) capital block

bottom view

Fig. 3.58. Front and bottom views of the bracket sets on the front elevation of Yong'an Temple, Nanbu, Sichuan, Yuan. (Drawing by author.)

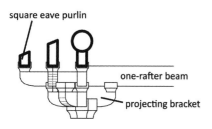

Fig. 3.59. Sectional view of the capital set on the front side of Yong'an Temple, Nanbu, Sichuan, Yuan. (Drawing by author.)

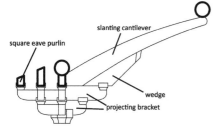

Fig. 3.60. Sectional view of the intercolumnar set on the front side of Yong'an Temple, Nanbu, Sichuan, Yuan. (Drawing by author.)

The intercolumnar set is five-layer as well, but more complicated than the capital one (fig. 3.58). Its octagonal capital block radiates one orthogonal bracket and two oblique arms of 45°. Both the projecting bracket and oblique arm jointly support a transversal bracket. Each of these arms on the first-tier projects more arms on the second tier toward the front, side, and obliquely. On the top tier are five bracket arms—three orthogonal brackets and two oblique—upholding the square eave purlin. The rear part of the intercolumnar set has two tiers of projecting brackets instead of one as in the capital set (fig. 3.60). A slanting cantilever of the type of *angting tiaowo* is built to bear the lower purlin. A wedge is inserted between the upper tier projecting bracket and the slanting cantilever to stabilize the structure. The configuration of the rear part of the intercolumnar set recalls the same formation of bracketing in Lord Wenchang Hall. With regard to the corner set, it resembles the intercolumnar set in many respects, but its capital block is four-sided as opposed to octagonal as in the capital and intercolumnar sets (fig. 3.58).

The roof structure of Yong'an Temple has two noteworthy features (fig. 3.61). An interior column that was supposed to be installed in the building was eliminated and replaced by a dwarf pillar. A three-rafter long tie beam is employed to link the rear eave column to the interior column to compensate for the eliminated column. This is a typical eliminated-column structure, and the interior space is therefore enlarged. Moreover, recalling the main hall of Lifeng Temple, a layer of bracket sets is built above the interior column covering the central space of the building.

Although in the official documents Yong'an Temple has hitherto been dated to early Ming, many of its architectural features suggest a similarity with other Yuan buildings in Sichuan. Its bracket sets on the front elevation are analogous to those of Lord Wenchang Hall. A typical Yuan timber-framing technique in north China, the eliminated-column structure, is applied to the roof structure.

The ten Yuan buildings in the Upper Yangzi discussed in this chapter are quite different from one another. From reviewing the history of each building, it is evident that the structural design and decorative details largely depended on their function, audience, and available resources. The Yuan builders in the Upper Yangzi seemed flexible in their choices of designs, plans, bracket sets, and roof frames. Nevertheless, overall these ten buildings testify to several regional features that were unique to this area during the Yuan: the eave architrave,

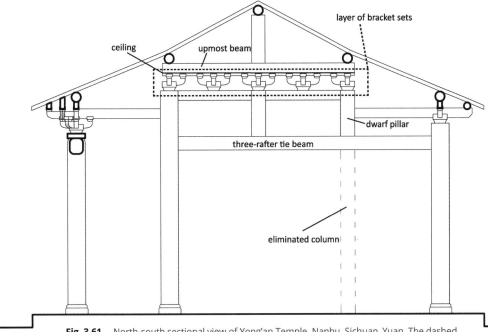

Fig. 3.61. North-south sectional view of Yong'an Temple, Nanbu, Sichuan, Yuan. The dashed frame indicates the layer of bracket sets. (Drawing by author.)

diagonal beams, bracket sets devoid of the uttermost bracket, and the locust head. The preference for *angting tiaowo* (invisible inclined cantilevers) over *angwei tiaowo* (visible inclined cantilevers) also differentiates the Upper Yangzi tradition from the rest. Moreover, as discussed in chapter 2, influence from the north is present in the Yuan buildings of the Upper Yangzi. This influence is distinguished by, but not limited to, the oblique arm, the wing-shaped bracket, the along-purlin ties, and eliminated/displaced-column structure. In general, Yuan buildings in the Upper Yangzi retained some legacy from the local and northern Song-Jin architecture but less from the idealistic Song style represented by the *YZFS*, in contrast to the five examples introduced in the next chapter, which demonstrate a strong inheritance from the *YZFS*.

CHAPTER 4

TIMBER-FRAMED ARCHITECTURE OF THE LOWER YANGZI

The Lower Yangzi region is usually called "Jiangnan," the area of modern Zhe-jiang province, south Jiangsu, and Anhui provinces, and Shanghai Municipality. During the Southern Song (1127–1279) "Jiangnan" was composed of three *lu*—West Liangzhe *lu* 兩浙西路, East Liangzhe *lu* 兩浙東路, and East Jiangnan *lu* 江南東路.[1] Lin'an 臨安 (modern Hangzhou), the capital city of the Southern Song, was located in the center of this area. In the beginning of the Yuan dynasty, these three *lu* were incorporated into one "branch secretariat" (*xingsheng* 行省), called Jianghuai Branch Secretariat 江淮行省. The Lower Yangzi was considered the heartland of the Han-Chinese culture and played a significant role in both economy and culture throughout the history of China. This chapter explores the five Yuan timber buildings that have survived in this area; their locations are shown in plate 3.

Modern research and fieldwork on these five timber-framed buildings started as early as the 1930s when *Zhongguo Yingzao Xueshe* 中國營造學社 (the Society for Research in Chinese Architecture) was active. Early monographs based on primary sources and fieldwork mostly were published before the Cultural Revolution (1966–1976) when academic activities had to cease. Since academic research resumed in the 1980s, these timber-framed buildings have been studied in a broad context. In *Zhongguo gujianzhu jishushi* 中國古建築技術史 (History and development of ancient Chinese architectural technology), a major 1986 publication on Chinese architectural history, the author included the main hall of Zhenru Monastery and the main hall of Yanfu Monastery to exemplify features of a small Yuan Buddhist hall.[2] In another book, *Zhongguo gudai jianzhushi* 中國古代建築史 (History of Chinese ancient architecture), the main halls of Yanfu, Tianning and Zhenru Monasteries were used to represent Yuan timber-framed Buddhist halls in the Lower Yangzi delta.[3] Two pioneering scholars studying this subject were Liu Dunzhen (1897–1968) and Chen Cong-zhou (1918–2000). The most recent research has been done by a contemporary scholar, Zhang Shiqing. In his book *Zhongguo Jiangnan Chanzong siyuan jianzhu* 中國江南禪宗寺院建築 (Architecture of Chan Buddhist monasteries in Jiang-nan, China), Zhang Shiqing compares Yuan buildings to both Song buildings in the Lower Yangzi and *karayo* 唐樣 architecture in Japan.[4] His research focuses on the scale, the worship space, the bracket sets, the roof structure, decorative carpentry, etc. Case studies on the timber-framed buildings in this chapter partially follow Zhang's method and presents the local tradition of the Lower Yangzi distinguished by its connection to the *YZFS*.

THE MAIN HALL OF YANFU MONASTERY

Yanfu (Extended Blessing) Monastery 延福寺 is located in the village of Taoxi (Peach Brook) 桃溪 in Wuyi county 武義縣 of Jinhua 金華 city in central Zhejiang province.[5] The main hall of Yanfu Monastery was first mentioned in Chen Congzhou's article on Tianning Monastery that was published in 1954.[6] Chen briefly stated that the main hall of Yanfu Monastery was one of the Yuan buildings remaining in the Lower Yangzi and was dated to 1326. In 1963 Chen surveyed and measured the monastery, and in 1966 published an article about its main hall.[7] This article is the earliest available source providing information on the history of Yanfu Monastery and details of its architecture.[8] During 1999 and 2002, the main hall was repaired and maintained by Zhejiang Provincial Institute of Cultural Relics and Archaeology (*Zhejiang wenwu kaogu yanjiusuo* 浙江文物考古研究所).[9] My observation and documentation of this building is based on the condition after the reparation.

In 1966, Chen changed his dating of the main hall from 1326 to 1317 because he found an inscription on a stele in the monastery. The inscription, written in 1324, is titled *Chongxiu Yanfuyuan beiji* 重修延福院碑記 (Record of the reconstruction of Yanfuyuan). Part of the inscription is transcribed as follows:

In the early Jiazi year of the Taiding reign (1324), Master Dehuan visited me and said, "My grandmaster said, 'You build the new based on the old. There is nothing left around. Only the main hall looks lofty. Then I think it could endure and there is no need to change it.' As time passed by, the main hall suddenly decayed. My master then instructed his grandson Yongguang, with deep emotion: 'The main hall is a big project. If you do not take it as your priority, I will not take the leadership.' Then they led a group of people with one purpose, expanded the old foundation, and renewed the relic site. A fellow villager Zheng was touched by them and was willing to sponsor the project. In the Dingsi year of the Yanyou reign (1317), the sky circled and the earth gushed. The main hall was brightly renewed. They inherited the rules and gathered at the hall by hours. The sound of chanting is clear and melodious, with cymbals and chime stones intermittently played. Without [jarring] highs and lows [in the melody/voices], it gradually ferments into a pure style. These sounds were brewed as wind of wine, without difference in tones. Monks came from different places. People with no accommodations were all admitted."[10]

In addition to the inscription, the history of Yanfu Monastery also was documented in the local gazetteers. In a Qing dynasty version of *Xuanping xianzhi* 宣平縣誌 (Gazetteer of Xuanping County) written in 1878, the entry about Yanfu Monastery is included in *juan* nine and reads:

> Yanfu Monastery is 25 *li* to the north of the county seat and was [first] built in the second year of Tianfu reign of [the Later] Jin (937) by Monk Zongyi. During the Tianshun reign of the Ming dynasty, Monk Jianqing restored the monastery. The rear hall, Guanyin Pavilion, and two corridors were rebuilt by Monk Zhaoying in the ninth year of the Kangxi reign (1670). During the eighth year of the Yongzheng reign (1730) and the thirteenth year of the Qianglong reign (1748), Monk Tongmao and his apprentice Dingming repaired the main hall several times and established the Hall of Heavenly Kings and twenty-one chambers of bays on the two corridors. They also decorated and sculpted four golden statues of the Heavenly Kings. Because of this, the power of the Buddha was caused to prosper. There once were six scenic spots: the Emerald Screen Mountain, the Five Willows Creek, the Hanging Musical Stone, the Wooden Fish Mountain, and the Stony Brook Well. In the eighteenth year of the Daoguang reign (1838), abbot Hanshu rebuilt the main gate. Abbot Miaoxian supervised another restoration in the fourth year of Tongzhi reign (1865).[11]

A passage written by a Ming fellow villager, Tao Mengduan 陶孟端, also was attached to the main entry, and it reads:

> [Yanfu Monastery] is about twenty *li* from the county seat. It is surrounded by mountains and brooks. It was called Futian in the second year of the Tiancheng reign of the Tang dynasty (927). During the Shaoxi reign of the Song dynasty, it was given its current name. At that time, Master Shouyi from Zixuan Sect was authorized to construct [the monastery] and the construction was roughly done. The [main] hall was not built until the Yuan, when Rishi and Dehuan purchased land and reestablished the stele. Monk Zongpu and Weiqian maintained the buildings one by one, and their apprentices, Wenbi and Jianqing, were busy cultivating the land. Their stockpile began to accumulate. An uprising broke out during the Zhengtong reign (1435–1443) of the Ming. Bandits destroyed the buildings and used the wood as fuel. The monastery was not renovated until the Jiajing reign (1521–1535). Wenbi and his fellow monks devoted themselves to cultivating the land. All kinds of work were quickly done and the demolished buildings were rebuilt. They also bought more fertile land. During the spring of the Guiwei year of the Tianshun reign (1463), Monk Jianqing asked me to write a memoir on stone. Therefore, I have recorded their reviving work.[12]

To summarize the history of Yanfu Monastery based on these primary sources, it was first built in 937, called Futian 福田, and renamed Yanfu 延

Fig. 4.1. Front elevation of the main hall of Yanfu Monastery, Wuyi, Zhejiang, 1317. (Photo by author.)

福 during the Song. It was not until 1317 that the main hall was built, and at the same time the abbot expanded the monastic territory. The main hall was restored once during the Ming dynasty and several times during the Qing dynasty, but it was never recorded that it had been "torn down" or "reconstructed" after the Yuan. Except for the textual evidence recorded in the gazetteers and the stele inscription, the main hall generally is dated to 1317 because a family name, Zheng, that was mentioned as the sponsor of the main hall in the 1324 inscription is also found in an inscription on a two-rafter beam in the building.[13] This suggests that at least the structure on the same level as or below the two-rafter beam was not significantly changed after 1317; otherwise, the two-rafter beam that bears the inscription would not fit where it is.

Due to the many restorations during the Ming and Qing periods, the extant main hall of Yanfu Monastery is a one-story hall. It has a five-by-five-bay plan with double eaves, which was not its original appearance in the Yuan dynasty (fig. 4.1). The lower eaves and outermost ring of columns were added during later restorations (fig. 4.2). To differentiate the original building from its later addition, Chen Congzhou explained that the structure of the

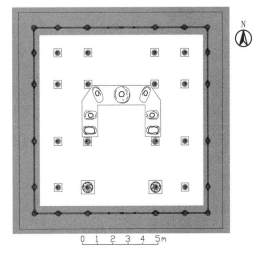

Fig. 4.2. Plan of the main hall of Yanfu Monastery, Wuyi, Zhejiang, 1317. The gray area shows the later addition. (Redrawn by author after Chen Congzhou, "Zhejiang Wuyixian Yanfusi Yuangou dadian," 33.)

lower eaves and the upper eaves were made in different ways, and the proportions of the bracket sets also vary.[14] As the purpose here is to discuss the Yuan period of the building, only its original part built during the Yuan dynasty will be discussed.[15]

The main hall of Yanfu Monastery is oriented north-south, and its front entrance faces south. The Yuan part of the building consists of two rings of columns that formed a four-sided hall with three bays on each side. The central bay (*dangxinjian* 當心間) on the front/south side is 4.60 m wide, and the side bay (*cijian* 次間, the bay next to the central bay) is 1.95 m wide. The middle bays on the east and west sides are 3.70 m wide, with a front bay of 2.90 m and a rear bay of 2 m. Three intercolumnar bracket sets are installed in the central bay on each side of the building, and one intercolumnar set is installed on each side bay. According to the measurement of the bracket sets, the dimensions of the modular unit (*cai* 材) are 15.5 by 10 cm, which is very close to the ratio of 3:2 as regulated in the YZFS.

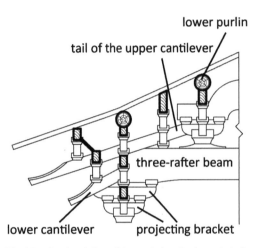

Fig. 4.3. Sectional view of the capital set in the main hall of Yanfu Monastery, Wuyi, Zhejiang, 1317. (Redrawn by author after Chen Congzhou, "Zhejiang Wuyixian Yanfusi Yuangou dadian," 36.)

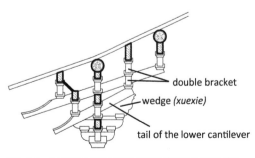

Fig. 4.4. Sectional view of the intercolumnar set in the main hall of Yanfu Monastery, Wuyi, Zhejiang, 1317. (Redrawn by author after Chen Congzhou, "Zhejiang Wuyixian Yanfusi Yuangou dadian," 36.)

The dimensions of the squarish plan are 8.5 by 8.6 m. A C-shaped altar for Buddhist sculptures is installed in the center of the hall.

The bracket sets of the building appear identical from the outside: the capital set looks the same as the intercolumnar set (figs. 4.3, 4.4). They both have one projecting bracket (*huagong* 華栱) and two inclined cantilevers (*ang* 昂) installed in order to support the load of the eave. The rear part of the bracket sets, however, varies due to different functions. The capital set has two projecting brackets facing inward to support a three-rafter beam (*sanchuanfu* 三椽栿) (fig. 4.3). The lower cantilever of the capital set is truncated at the position above the column, and the tail of the upper cantilever extends to sustain the lower purlin. The intercolumnar set, on the other hand, has two projecting brackets facing inward to support the tail of the lower cantilever that upholds a set of double brackets (*chonggong* 重栱). The upper cantilever of the intercolumnar set is composed in the same way as that of the capital set. Between the upper tier projecting bracket and the tail of the lower cantilever, a boot-shaped wedge (*xuexie* 鞾楔) is placed to adjust the bevel between the cantilever and the projecting bracket (fig. 4.4).

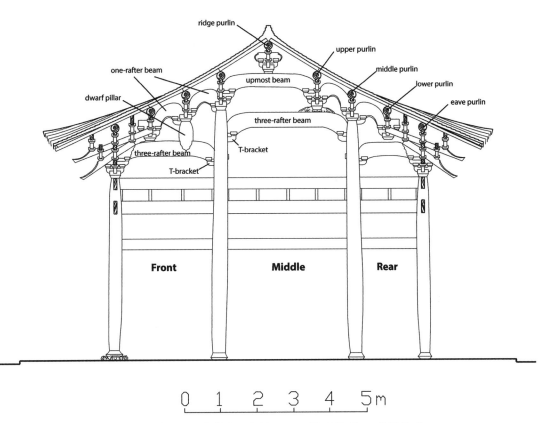

ridge purlin
upper purlin
middle purlin
lower purlin
eave purlin
one-rafter beam
upmost beam
dwarf pillar
three-rafter beam
three-rafter beam
T-bracket
T-bracket

Front   **Middle**   **Rear**

0 1 2 3 4 5 m

Fig. 4.5. North-south sectional view of the main hall of Yanfu Monastery, Wuyi, Zhejiang, 1317. (Redrawn by author after Chen Congzhou, "Zhejiang Wuyixian Yanfusi Yuangou dadian," 36.)

The roof structure of the building has eight rafters and nine purlins (fig. 4.5). The interior columns are higher than the eave columns, which defines the hall as a mansion-style (*tingtang* 廳堂) building. The front bay is crossed by a crescentic three-rafter beam that connects to the eave column with one end and fastens to the shaft of the interior column with the other end. A T-bracket (*dingtougong* 丁頭栱) is a half-projecting bracket with its tenon at the rear mortised into a column. Here in the main hall of Yanfu Monastery, a T-bracket projects from the shaft of the interior column to bear the three-rafter beam. Above the three-rafter beam, the tail of the upper inclined cantilever is bearing a block to uphold the lower purlin (*xiapingtuan* 下平槫). Moreover, a dwarf pillar stands on the three-rafter beam and holds up the middle purlin (*zhongpingtuan* 中平槫) as well. Two highly curved slanting beams, which cross a one-rafter span, are built to connect the capital of the interior column, the capital of the dwarf pillar, and the tail of the inclined cantilever. The middle bay of the main hall has two crescent-moon-shaped beams: the lower one, a three-rafter beam, crosses the full span from one interior column to the other; and the top one, the upmost beam (*pingliang* 平梁), crosses a two-rafter span. One end of the upmost beam is placed on the capital of the interior column to prop up the upper purlin (*shang-pingtuan* 上平槫), and the other end is supported by a bracket set built on the lower three-rafter beam to bear another upper purlin. Between this bracket set and the rear interior column is another highly curved and slanting one-rafter beam (*zhaqian* 劄牽). On the upmost beam, instead of a dwarf pillar, a bracket set is built on the center to uphold ridge purlin (*jituan* 脊槫).[16] It is remarkable that all beams in the direction along the rafters, such as the one-rafter beams, the (two-rafter) upmost beam, and the three-rafter beams, made in the shape of a crescent moon, are named the crescent-moon-shaped beams (*yueliang* 月梁).

One structural feature that distinguishes the main hall of Yanfu Monastery as a sample of local tradition is the lack of a flat architrave (*pupaifang* 普拍方). Here, the eave columns are tied by two architraves: a railing architrave (*lan'e* 闌額) at the top and an associate architrave (*you'e* 由額) at the bottom (fig. 4.6). The flat architrave, however, is not installed above the railing architrave, which also is found on some other Song-Yuan buildings in the area, such as the main hall of Tianning Monastery, the second gatehouse of Yunyan Monastery, and the main hall of Baoguo Monastery.[17]

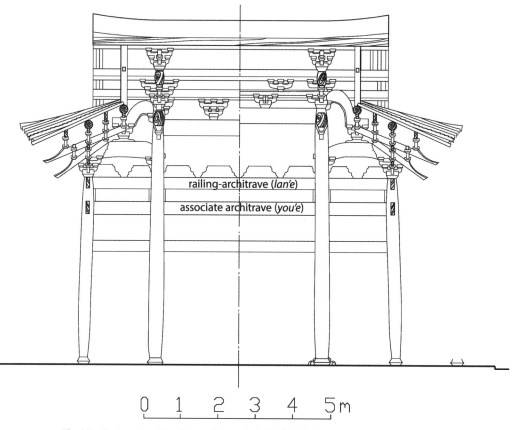

railing-architrave (*lan'e*)

associate architrave (*you'e*)

0 1 2 3 4 5 m

Fig. 4.6. East-west sectional view of the main hall of Yanfu Monastery, Wuyi, Zhejiang, 1317. (Redrawn by author after Chen Congzhou, "Zhejiang Wuyixian Yanfusi Yuangou dadian," 36.)

The last notable items in this building are the shuttle-shaped columns that taper on both ends in order to present the appearance of entasis. This type of column is called "shuttle-shaped column" (suozhu 梭柱), and it is one of the characteristics of timber-framed buildings in the Lower Yangzi, especially after the Song dynasty. As already discussed, the shuttle-shaped column is not found in north China among any post-Song timber buildings but lasted in the south even until the Ming dynasty. The shuttle-shaped columns discovered in the Lower Yangzi also differ little from the record in the YZFS. In the YZFS, however, a column has only one tapered end instead of two.

The plinth also is noteworthy. The plinth of this front eave column is composed of an overturned bowl (fupen 覆盆) at the bottom, which is carved with a lotus in high relief, and another block of stone above. Only the two plinths under the front eave columns in this building are made this way. The others do not have the decorative bottom part. Such a special treatment given to the plinths of the front eave columns stresses the importance of the front entrance. The same design is also found in the main hall of Tianning Monastery 天寧寺 in Nantong 南通, Jiangsu province. The column plinths in this monastery are believed to be remains from the Song dynasty.[18]

Overall, the main hall of Yanfu Monastery showcases several local characteristics of timber-framed buildings that can be traced to the YZFS, such as the crescent-moon-shaped beams, the cantilevers, the shuttle-shaped columns, and the joints that are delicately made of bracket sets. Features of its plan and bracket sets as well as the roof structure also are shared by the main hall of Tianning Monastery that is about sixty kilometers away.

THE MAIN HALL OF TIANNING MONASTERY

Tianning (Heavenly Peace) Monastery 天寧寺 is located in the center of Jinhua city. A brief monastic history was recorded in the 1894 version of Jinhua xianzhi 金華縣誌 (Gazetteer of Jinhua County) and it reads:

Tianning (Heavenly Peace) Wanshou (Longevity) Chan Monastery is located at the northwest of the city and used to be called Dazangyuan (Tripiṭaka Monastery). It was named Chengtian [by the imperial court] during the Dazhong Xiangfu reign (1008–1016) of the Song dynasty when it was first built. It was given its present name during the Zhenghe reign (1111–1118). In the eighth year of the Shaoxing reign (1138), it was granted the name Bao'enguang (Repaying Broad Kindness) Monastery 報恩廣寺 in respect of Emperor Huizong, and it was later renamed as Bao'enguang (Repaying Bright Kindness) Monastery 報恩光寺. The monastery was rebuilt during the Yanyou reign of the Yuan dynasty and was restored during the Zhengtong reign of the Ming dynasty. It was renamed Tianning Wanshou Monastery at that time. It once had a stone pagoda. Dabei (Great Compassion) Pavilion stands behind the main hall.[19]

Unfortunately, except for the main hall, no other architecture of the monastery remains. Buildings like the gatehouse (*shanmen* 山門), Tianwang (Heavenly King) Hall 天王殿, and Dabei Pavilion 大悲閣, which were built during the Qing dynasty, were demolished during the Cultural Revolution.[20]

Since the 1950s, modern scholars have studied the main hall, the only surviving building of the complex. Chen Congzhou wrote the first article about Tianning Monastery, published in *Wenwu* in 1954. In 1981, another important article about the main hall of Tianning Monastery was published in a collection of archaeological reports by the Institute of Cultural Relics and Archaeology of Zhejiang Province (Zhejiangsheng wenwu kaogu suo 浙江省文物考古所). Compared to Chen's 1954 article, this 1981 study includes a more detailed description of the timber-framed structure and provides more diagrams and charts showing the dimensions of the structural members. It also documents the alterations that were made during the 1980 restoration.

Chen was invited to visit and survey Tianning Monastery in 1954 because the local administrators suspected that the main hall might be a Yuan building. After Chen's visit, the speculation was confirmed by his discovery of a Yuan inscription written on the east three-rafter beam of the central bay. It reads: "Congratulations on the reestablishment [of the main hall] on the propitious Gengshen day of the sixth month of the Wuwu year, the fifth year of the Yanyou reign of Yuan (1318)."[21]

This inscription, as well as additional contemporary inscriptions on other architectural members, demonstrates that the current building is generally that remaining from 1318 in spite of later restorations. Moreover, the result of radiocarbon dating on some architectural members indicates that some timber pieces date to the Northern Song and Southern Song. During the reconstruction of 1318, they were carefully removed from the Song version of the building and reinstalled into the Yuan building.[22] Reusing a timber member from an older/destroyed building was quite common in ancient China.

The main hall of Tianning Monastery has a square plan with the front entrance facing southwest (fig. 4.7). Its plan is similar to that of the main hall of Yanfu Monastery. The dimensions of the plan are 12.72 by 12.72 m. Sixteen columns are arranged in two rings to form three bays on each

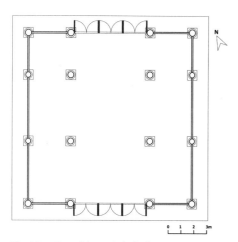

Fig. 4.7. Plan of the main hall of Tianning Monastery, Jinhua, Zhejiang, 1318. (Redrawn by author after Chen Congzhou, "Jinhua Tianningsi Yuandai zhengdian," 103.)

side. The central bay on the front/south side is 6.16 m wide with two side bays of 3.28 m wide. The middle bay on the flank side is 4.93 m wide with a front bay of 4.65 m and a rear bay of 3.14 m. It is likely that an altar was once placed in the center. Unfortunately, there is no longer any trace of the original altar.

The bracket sets in this building are also similar to those of the main hall of Yanfu Monastery. The capital set and the intercolumnar set appear identical from the outside: they are both six-layer bracket sets (*liupuzuo* 六鋪作), with one projecting bracket reaching outward and two inclined cantilevers installed to support the load of the eave (fig. 4.8). A set of double bracket crosses on the lower cantilever, and one tier of outermost bracket (*linggong* 令栱) crosses on the upper cantilever. Between the projecting bracket and the lower inclined cantilever is a transitional member called *huatouzi* 華頭子, a bracket arm with a two-scroll profile that also is considered a variety of projecting bracket (fig. 4.9).

The rear parts of the capital and intercolumnar sets inside the building are different. The capital set has one bracket projecting inward to support the three-rafter beam, and the tail of its upper inclined cantilever extends to the capital of the dwarf pillar (*shuzhu* 蜀柱) to uphold the lower purlin. The intercolumnar set, on the other hand, has one bracket projecting inward, and an upward-cantilever (*shangang* 上昂) is installed to adjust the inclination of the regular cantilever (fig. 4.10). The lower purlin here is supported by the tail of the

Fig. 4.8. Capital and intercolumnar sets on the front elevation of main hall of Tianning Monastery, Jinhua, Zhejiang, 1318. (Photo by author.)

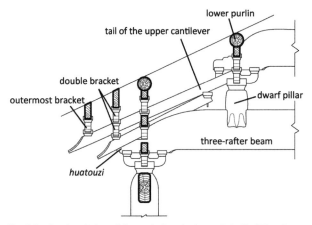

Fig. 4.9. Sectional view of the capital set in the main hall of Tianning Monastery, Jinhua, Zhejiang, 1318. (Redrawn by author after Zhejiang sheng wenwu kaogusuo wenbaoshi, "Jinhua Tianningsi dadian de gouzao ji weixiu," 179.)

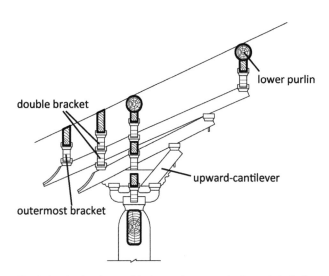

Fig. 4.10. Sectional view of the intercolumnar set in the main hall of Tianning Monastery, Jinhua, Zhejiang, 1318. (Redrawn by author after Zhejiangsheng wenwu kaogusuo wenbaoshi, "Jinhua Tianningsi dadian de gouzao ji weixiu," 178.)

upper cantilever. As already noted, the upward cantilever, although mentioned in the *YZFS,* is not often seen in Song-Yuan buildings in north China.

With regard to the distribution of intercolumnar sets, the central bay of the front side has three intercolumnar sets, and the side bays have only one. On the flank side, two intercolumnar sets are installed in the front and middle bay, and only one is built in the rear bay.

Similar again to the main hall of Yanfu Monastery, the roof structure of the main hall of Tianning Monastery has eight rafters and nine purlins (fig. 4.11). The interior columns are higher than the eave columns, which defines the building as mansion style. The front bay that spans three rafters is crossed by a three-rafter beam that is slightly curved on its ends. The three-rafter beam connects the eave column at one end and fastens the shaft of the interior column to the other end. Two T-brackets project from the shaft of the interior column to bear crescent-moon-shaped beams above. The same structure is also found in the main hall of Yanfu Monastery. Above the three-rafter beam is a two-rafter eaves beam (*rufu* 乳栿) across from the capital of a dwarf pillar that stands on the three-rafter beam to hold the lower purlin to the shaft of the interior column. A small bracket set, instead of a dwarf pillar, is built on top of the two-rafter eaves beam in order to bear the middle purlin. Between the interior column and this small bracket set, a horizontal one-rafter beam is installed.

The structure in the rear bay is simpler than that of the front bay. It is spanned by a two-rafter eaves beam that supports a dwarf pillar to hold the lower purlin. The dwarf pillar and the interior column are connected by a

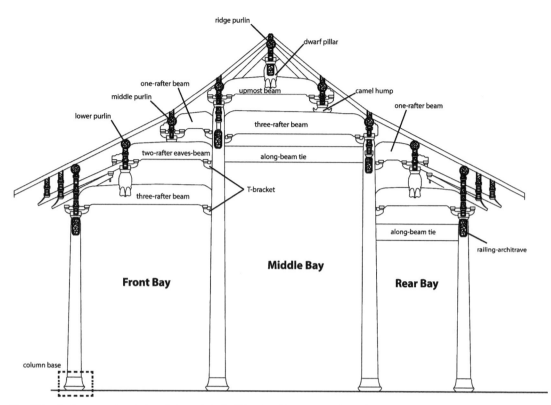

Labels in figure: ridge purlin, dwarf pillar, one-rafter beam, middle purlin, upmost beam, camel hump, one-rafter beam, lower purlin, three-rafter beam, two-rafter eaves-beam, along-beam tie, three-rafter beam, T-bracket, along-beam tie, railing-architrave, Front Bay, Middle Bay, Rear Bay, column base

Fig. 4.11. East-west sectional view of the main hall of Tianning Monastery, Jinhua, Zhejiang, 1318. (Redrawn by author after Zhejiangsheng wenwu kaogusuo wenbaoshi, "Jinhua Tianningsi dadian de gouzao ji weixiu," 177.)

horizontal one-rafter beam. Different from the front bay, an along-beam tie (*shunfuchuan* 順栿串), which is two-rafter long, is added beneath the two-rafter eaves beam to tie the eave column and the interior column. The middle bay, crossed by three rafters, has two beams: the lower one, the three-rafter beam, crosses the full span from one interior column to the other; and the top one, the upmost beam, crosses two-thirds of the span. One end of the upmost beam is put on the capital of the interior column to prop up the upper purlin, and the other end, bearing another upper purlin, is supported by a bracket set that was built on a "camel hump" (*tuofeng* 駝峰), a solid block or plank curved at the top in the shape of a camel hump. On the middle of the upmost beam stands a dwarf pillar to uphold the ridge purlin. Under the three-rafter beam, there is an along-beam tie between the interior columns in order to provide additional stability as it does to the rear bay.

There are many similarities between the main halls of Tianning Monastery and Yanfu Monastery. First, both the front and middle bays of these two buildings span a distance of three rafters, which results in the enlargement of the entrance and central worship space. Second, neither has a flat architrave atop the eave columns, and only a railing architrave is used to tie the eave columns. Third, all the major beams, including the three-rafter beam, two-rafter eaves beam, one-rafter beam, and upmost beam, are shaped like a crescent moon. The beams in the main hall of Yanfu Monastery are even more curved than those in the main hall of Tianning Monastery. Moreover, the style of the column plinth in the main hall of Tianning Monastery also resembles one type in the main hall of Yanfu Monastery (fig. 4.11, dashed frame lower left). Regarding the modular units of both buildings, the width of both is 10 cm; but the length of that of Tianning Monastery is 17 cm, 1.5 cm longer than that of Yanfu Monastery. It is clear that both buildings of Yanfu and Tianning Monasteries were influenced by the same local tradition that may have differed from the Yuan building in Shanghai to be discussed next.

THE MAIN HALL OF ZHENRU MONASTERY

Zhenru (Thusness) Monastery 真如寺 is located in Zhenru Town 真如鎮, a small town in northwest Shanghai.[23] The *Zhenru lizhi* 真如里志 (Gazetteer of Zhenru), written in the Qing dynasty, provides a brief history of the monastery:

> Zhenru Monastery, also known as Wanshou Monastery, or the "Grand Temple," was originally located at Guanchang. During the Jiading reign of the Southern Song (1208–1224), Monk Yong'an rebuilt the monastery and named it Zhenruyuan. During the Yanyou reign of the Yuan dynasty (1314–1320), Monk Miaoxin relocated the monastery to a place called Taoshupu and appealed for a new plaque to change the name from *yuan* to *si*. Through the Hongwu reign (1368–1398) and the Hongzhi reign (1488–1505) of the Ming dynasty, Monk Daoxin and Monk Falei restored the monastery twice.[24]

The architectural complex of the extant Zhenru Monastery is based on an earlier layout. Except for the main hall, most buildings were built in recent decades. Although the Main Hall has been restored several times, since the Yuan dynasty it has never been demolished completely. Liu Dunzhen first studied the main hall in the 1950s. In 1951, Liu stated that a local administrator discovered a Yuan inscription on an architectural member of the main hall in August 1950. It was then that Liu was invited to investigate the building.[25] This inscription, found on an interior tie beam, indicated that the building was built in 1320, the seventh year of the Yanyou reign. The inscription reads: "[The hall] is built on the third day of the seventh month, the seventh year of Yanyou reign of Yuan (1320)."[26]

In addition to this inscription, during a restoration between 1963 and 1964 other inscriptions in ink left by Yuan craftsman on other architectural members were found.[27] These inscriptions, mostly concerning technical terms, not only increased our understanding of the timber-framed structure of the building and the architectural terminology of the day but further proved the main hall's authenticity as a Yuan building.

The main hall of Zhenru Monastery is oriented north-south with its main entrance facing the south (fig. 4.12). The plan is similar to those of the main halls of Yanfu Monastery and Tianning Monastery—it is composed of two rings of columns that formed a square and three-by-three-bay plan, the total dimensions of which is 13.4 by 13 m. The central bay on the south/front side is 6.1 m wide, and the side bay is 3.65 m wide. The dimensions of the bays on the flank side, from south to north, are 5.3, 5.1, and 2.6 m respectively. A rectangular altar for Buddhist statues occupies three-quarters of the space of the very center bay.

Although the plan of the main hall of Zhenru Monastery is almost the same as the main halls of Yanfu Monastery and Tianning Monastery, its roof structure is extraordinary and more complicated (fig. 4.13). In

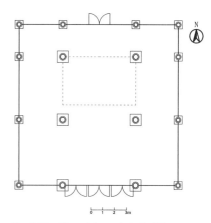

Fig. 4.12. Plan of the main hall of Zhenru Monastery, Shanghai, 1320. (Redrawn by author after Shanghaishi wenwu baoguan weiyuanhui, "Shanghai shijiao Yuandai jianzhu Zhenrusi zhengdian zhong faxian de gongjiang mobizi," 24.)

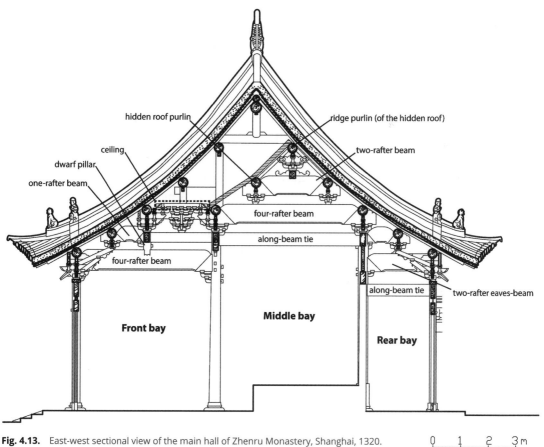

Fig. 4.13. East-west sectional view of the main hall of Zhenru Monastery, Shanghai, 1320. (Redrawn by author after Shanghaishi wenwu baoguan weiyuanhui, "Shanghai shijiao Yuandai jianzhu Zhenrusi zhengdian zhong faxian de gongjiang mobizi," 23.)

contrast to the other two Yuan buildings of a similar size, each of which has an eight-rafter roof, the main hall of Zhenru Monastery is a ten-rafter hall. The front bay is crossed by four rafters and thus is very spacious. A crescent-moon-shaped four-rafter beam (*sichuanfu* 四椽栿) spans the front bay and connects the eave column and the interior column. Above this four-rafter beam is a small bracket set and a dwarf pillar; each supports a purlin and they are connected by a crescent-moon-shaped one-rafter beam. Between the dwarf pillar and the interior column, a ceiling lintel (*pingqifang* 平棊枋) is installed, which supports the ceiling above. The ceiling, decorated by bracket sets on all sides, spans only the rear half of the front bay and hides the upper roof from the audience in the building.

The middle bay of the main hall of Zhenru Monastery is crossed by four rafters, and its front half is canopied by a hidden roof (fig. 4.13, shaded area). This type of hidden roof is quite rare in China but often seen in Japan; it is called *noyane* 野屋根 in Japanese. A four-rafter beam connects two interior columns of the middle bay and is accompanied by a slim along-beam tie beneath. Two small bracket sets are built on the four-rafter beam to hold a regular purlin and a hidden-roof purlin, called *nogeta* 野桁 in Japanese. These two bracket sets also are connected by a two-rafter beam, above which is another bracket set upholding the ridge purlin of the hidden roof. The structure above the hidden roof is called a "rough frame" (*caojia* 草架) that is not as refined as the part below the hidden roof. The roof structure under the hidden roof is called an "exposed roof frame" (*cheshang mingzao* 徹上明造). In his article, Liu Dunzhen pointed out that in China the hidden roof had become outdated even before the Yuan period and had already disappeared completely in north China. The hidden roof found in Zhenru Monastery was unique in the Lower Yangzi, or even all of China.[28] Since the twelfth century in Japan, on the other hand, a hidden roof built over an entire building was popular. This may suggest some connection between the main hall of Zhenru Monastery and architecture in Japan.[29]

The rear bay of the main hall is crossed by two rafters. The rear bay is similar to the front half of the front bay. A two-rafter eaves beam spans from the eave column to the interior column and is accompanied by a two-rafter along-beam tie beneath. A small bracket set on the two-rafter eaves beam holds up the lower purlin and also is tied to the interior column by a crescent-moon-shaped one-rafter beam. Liu Dunzhen believed that the roof structure of the building—except for the columns, the ceiling, and the hidden roof, and a number of members—could have been replaced during the later restorations.[30]

The arrangement of the bracket sets along the ring of eave columns is as follows: on the front side, four intercolumnar sets are installed in the central bay, and two installed in each side bay (fig. 4.14). On the flank side, each of the front and middle bays has three intercolumnar sets, and only one intercolumnar set is installed in the rear bay.

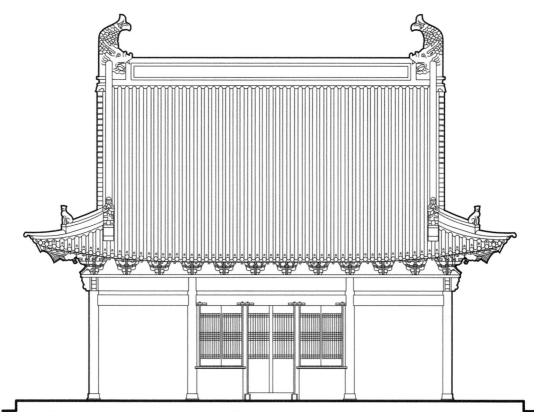

Fig. 4.14. Front elevation of the main hall of Zhenru Monastery, Shanghai, 1320. (Redrawn by author after Zhongguo kexueyuan ziran kexueshi yanjiusuo, *Zhongguo gujianzhu jishushi*, 195.)

Similar to the main halls of Yanfu Monastery and Tianning Monastery, the capital set and the intercolumnar set in the main hall of Zhenru Monastery look identical from the outside. Both the capital set and the intercolumnar set project, but one tier of projecting bracket is disguised as a pseudo-cantilever (*jia'ang* 假昂). The projecting bracket is overhung by a locust head (*shuatou* 耍頭), an overhanging bracket-end and the topmost member parallel to, and above, the projecting bracket and inclined cantilever. With regard to the rear part, the capital bracket set has one tier of the projecting bracket reaching inward to support the thick four-rafter beam

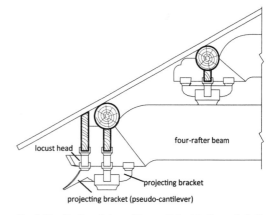

Fig. 4.15. Sectional view of the capital set in the main hall of Zhenru Monastery, Shanghai, 1320. (Redrawn by author after Zhongguo kexueyuan ziran kexueshi yanjiusuo, *Zhongguo gujianzhu jishushi*, 195.)

(fig. 4.15). The intercolumnar set, on the other hand, projects one tier of projecting bracket, and an upward cantilever is installed on the projecting bracket

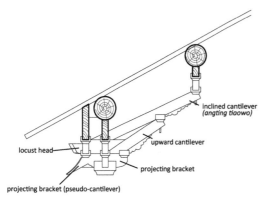

inclined cantilever
(angting tiaowo)

upward cantilever

locust head

projecting bracket

projecting bracket (pseudo-cantilever)

Fig. 4.16. Sectional view of the intercolumnar set in the main hall of Zhenru Monastery, Shanghai, 1320. (Redrawn by author after Shanghaishi wenwu baoguan weiyuanhui, "Shanghai shijiao Yuandai jianzhu Zhenrusi zhengdian zhong faxian de gongjiang mobizi," 25.)

to adjust the bevel of the upper inclined cantilever of the type of *angting tiaowo* 昂桯挑斡 (fig. 4.16).

After his personal investigation of the building, Liu Dunzhen believed that the bracket sets along the ring of the eave columns had little chance of being Yuan remains. He suggested that the bracket sets at the south side, and some at the east and west sides, were rebuilt during the restoration of the Guangxu reign, and others could not be earlier than the Ming dynasty.[31] Liu's evidence was the inconsistency of the style of inclined cantilever in the different bracket sets. Unfortunately, after the recent restoration, the bracket sets that Liu observed in the 1950s were altered again. Today, each bracket set looks exactly the same from the outside. Nevertheless, evidence remains to prove the younger age of the bracket sets. Considering the dimensions of the modular unit measured from the bracket sets, those of the main hall of Zhenru Monastery are 13.5 by 9 cm, much smaller than Yanfu Monastery and Tianning Monastery. Given a smaller modular unit on a building of a similar scale, it is obvious that the bracket sets of Zhenru Monastery, although they may retain some earlier features, do not date from 1320.

Although the bracket sets of the main hall of Zhenru Monastery were not originally from the Yuan, its roof frame provides several features that are shared in the local area. More important, the roof frame of the main hall of Zhenru Monastery is extraordinary. It is a combination of the mansion style and the palatial style, and its hidden roof, which is not found elsewhere in China during the Yuan dynasty, suggests some connection to Japan.

THE SECOND GATEHOUSE OF YUNYAN MONASTERY

Yunyan (Cloudy Cliff) Monastery 雲巖寺 was built along the south hillside of the Tiger Hill 虎丘 in the city of Suzhou, Jiangsu province. The Pagoda of Yunyan Monastery, also called Tiger Hill Pagoda, is one of the most famous landmarks of Suzhou. Yunyan Monastery has a long tradition that can be traced back to early in the Eastern Jin dynasty (317–420). In a Qing dynasty *Suzhou fuzhi* 蘇州府志 (Gazetteer of Suzhou Prefecture), the history of the monastery was recorded as follows:

The Chan Monastery of Yunyan is built on the Tiger Hill outside the outer city [of Suzhou]. It was a villa belonging to Wang Xun, Minister of the Masses of the Jin dynasty, and his younger brother Wang Min. It was donated to serve as a Buddhist temple in the second year of Xianhe reign (327). During the Renshou reign (601–604) of the Sui dynasty, a seven-story pagoda was established behind the [main] hall. The monastery was at first divided by the Sword Pool into an east section and a west section that were later united. Reconstruction work took place during the Zhidao reign (995–997) of the Song dynasty. The chief of the prefecture, Wei Xiang, presented a memorial to the emperor, and then the monastery was granted its current name. The Pavilion of Imperial Books was built during the middle Jingyou reign (1034–1037) and the Sutra Library was built in the middle Shaoxing reign (1131–1162). They were both demolished by the [Song-Yuan] war after a short while. As recorded by Huang Jin, [the monastery] was rebuilt in the fourth year of Zhiyuan reign (1338) of the Yuan dynasty. A fire occurred in the middle Hongwu reign (1368–1398) and the abbot Fabao presided over a reconstruction in the early Yongle reign (1403–1424). The pagoda was damaged by the fire in the middle Xuande reign (1426–1435) and was reconstructed by the provincial governor Zhou Chen in the Zhengtong reign (1436–1449). According to Zhang Yiyou's record, on the day when the dew plate was just installed on the pagoda finial, dozens of white cranes were hovering above the pagoda for a long time.[32] Zhou Chen noted by himself that a five-bay sutra library was also built at the same time to preserve the classic sutra of Tripiṭaka conferred by the emperor. The monastery was again burned in winter in the second year of Chongzhen reign (1629). The provincial governor Zhang Guowei rebuilt the main hall. A garrison commander Yang Chengzu reestablished the Hall of Heavenly Kings in the early years of Shunzhi reign (1644–1661). During the Kangxi reign (1662–1722), the emperor visited the monastery during his inspection tour to the south and granted a plaque. The main hall was again on fire in the fifty-third year of Kangxi reign (1714) and was renewed by Li Xu, an official censoring the salt industry. Emperor Gaozong (Emperor Qianlong) visited the monastery several times during his tour to the south and bestowed [upon it] his poem, prose, couplet, inscribed board, Tibetan incense, and sacrifice vessels. In the thirtieth year of the Qianlong reign (1765), the Empress Dowager visited the place and donated silver and gold to the monastery twice. In the fiftieth year [of the Qianlong period] (1785), Monk Zutong raised a fund for restoration. The monastery was destroyed again in the tenth year of the Xianfeng reign (1860). In the third year of the Tongzhi reign (1864), a military officer, Liu Qifa, donated some money to build a stone hall for Bodhisattva Avalokiteśvara and noted by himself. In the tenth year (1871), a native of Suzhou, Chen Deji, raised a fund to build the Hall of Heavenly Kings.[33]

According to this text, Yunyan Monastery has served as an important Buddhist institution in Suzhou ever since the Song dynasty and, at different times, received attention from imperial courts. It was ranked ninth among the ten Buddhist monasteries (*shicha* 十剎) in the Lower Yangzi during the Southern Song and Yuan, indicating its premier position in the area.[34] Although it suffered its share of chaos and turbulence between dynasties, restoration and reconstruction of this monastery was continuous. Most of these restorations were supervised by a provincial governor or officials of similar rank.

Given such a rich and complicated history, the second gatehouse (*ershanmen* 二山門) is considered the oldest timber-framed building and the only surviving building from the Yuan dynasty. A historical record concerning the construction of the monastery during the Yuan dynasty is found in an account written in the sixth year of Zhizheng reign (1344) by Huang Jin 黃溍. Dedicated to the reestablishment of Yunyan Monastery in 1338, Huang's account reads:

> In the fourth year of the [second] Zhiyuan reign (1338), the Institute of Buddhist and Tibetan Affairs ordered Puming, the Chan Master of Huideng Yuanzhao, to supervise the monastic affairs [of Yunyan Monastery]. Then divine sculptures of Buddha, Bodhisattva, Arhat, and Vajra were decorated. Statues of the Three Great Bodhisattvas, Mañjuśrī, Samantabhadra, and Avalokiteśvara, were made. The pagoda of the Buddha's relics and the sutra library of Tripiṭaka were repaired. Copper of nice quality was casted to produce huge bells. The architecture was renewed or restored depending on the severity of damages. Masonry and other labor were carried out at the same time. The Buddha Hall, the Pavilion of Thousand Buddhas, the Hall of Three Great Bodhisattvas, the Court of Sutra Library, the Meditation Hall, the accounting house, three gatehouses, two corridors, ancient trees, the Cold Spring, the Sword Pool, and other pavilions all retain their old conditions. The ancestors' pagodas, the dormitories, the storehouse, the kitchen, the bathroom, as well as the dining hall, were repaired. The building that can be seen from Pingyuan Hall and stands in front of the Little Wuxuan Hall is the second gatehouse. Then people reconstructed it like a new building.[35]

In this paragraph, the author recorded details of the reconstruction of 1338. He particularly pointed out that the second gatehouse, which he referred to as the "double gate" (*chongmen* 重門), was rebuilt as a brand-new building during the 1338 reconstruction. Among all premodern gazetteers of Suzhou or of Yunyan Monastery, this is the only information about the construction history of the second gatehouse. Moreover, even though later restorations during the Ming-Qing era also were recorded in as much detail as possible, the second gatehouse was never mentioned as having been rebuilt or restored.[36] In addition to the textual evidence, when Liu Dunzhen first investigated the building in the 1930s, he believed that, based on features and dimensions of its timber structure, the majority of the building remained from 1338. The following overview of the building will further substantiate Liu's opinion.

The second gatehouse is oriented north-south; its front entrance receives visitors from the south, and a rear exit leads people to the main compound of Yunyan Monastery at the north (fig. 4.17). Instead of having a squarish, three-by-three-bay plan like other Yuan buildings just discussed, the plan of the second gatehouse is arranged as three bays on the long side and two bays on the short side. The width of the central bay on the south/front is nearly 1.5 times that of the side bay. The width of the side bays on the front side also is equal to those of the two bays on the flank sides. The whole ratio of the plan is approximately 7 to 4, which is a typical proportion for the plan of a gatehouse. The interior space of the second gatehouse further differentiates itself from all other Yuan buildings, which mostly are main/worship halls. The central bays on the front and rear sides all are installed with arches

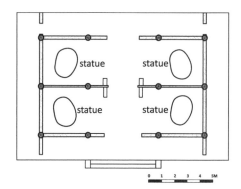

Fig. 4.17. Plan of the second gatehouse of Yunyan Monastery, Suzhou, Jiangsu, 1338. (Drawing by author.)

(fig. 4.18), while the side bays are divided by slim walls into four separated rooms that once housed statues of the four Heavenly Kings.[37] Today, the two rooms at the back preserve several steles dated from the Yuan and Ming; these bear relevant information about the monastery.

The arrangement of the bracket sets is as follows. Two intercolumnar sets are installed in each central bay on the long sides, and one intercolumnar set is installed in any other bay. The intercolumnar set and the capital set look the same from the outside. They both have only one tier of the projecting bracket and can be defined as four-layer bracket sets (*sipuzuo* 四鋪作) (figs. 4.19 and 4.20). Atop the projecting bracket is an outermost bracket that supports the square eave purlin (*liaoyanfang* 撩簷枋) through three blocks. No inclined cantilever can be seen from the outside of the building, which differs from other

Fig. 4.18. Front elevation of the second gatehouse of Yunyan Monastery, Suzhou, Jiangsu, 1338. (Photo by author.)

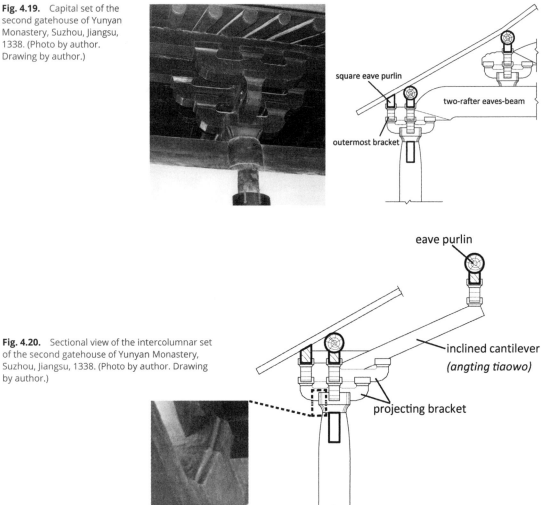

Fig. 4.19. Capital set of the second gatehouse of Yunyan Monastery, Suzhou, Jiangsu, 1338. (Photo by author. Drawing by author.)

square eave purlin

two-rafter eaves-beam

outermost bracket

eave purlin

Fig. 4.20. Sectional view of the intercolumnar set of the second gatehouse of Yunyan Monastery, Suzhou, Jiangsu, 1338. (Photo by author. Drawing by author.)

inclined cantilever
(angting tiaowo)

projecting bracket

Yuan buildings in the Lower Yangzi, all of which have inclined cantilevers projecting toward the outside.

In terms of the rear part of the bracket sets, each capital set has one tier of the projecting bracket reaching inward, supporting the crescent-moon-shaped two-rafter eaves beam (fig. 4.19). The intercolumnar set, on the other hand, projects two tiers of the projecting bracket in the style called "stolen-heart structure" (*touxinzao* 偷心造), meaning a successive projection of brackets without traversal arms (fig. 4.20). A diagonal cantilever of the type *angting tiaowo* is built above the projecting bracket to pass the load from the purlin to the eave column. A decorative detail on the capital block of each bracket set should be noted. Each angle of the square capital block is carved into two curved segments. Such decoration also is found on the capital block of the main hall of Xuanyuan Palace 軒轅宮, which is also located in Suzhou.

In contrast to a main hall of a monastery where bays along the south-north direction are composed differently to meet a particular spatial arrangement, figure 4.21 displays a perfect symmetry in its timber frame. This gatehouse is a four-rafter mansion-style building using three columns. The front bay, as well as the rear bay, is crossed by a crescent-moon-shaped two-rafter eaves beam that is supported by the bracket set on the eave column at one end and inserted into the shaft of the interior column at the other. A T-bracket is projected from the shaft of the interior column to buttress the two-rafter eaves beam. An along-beam tie, which ties the eave column and the interior column, is built beneath and parallel to the two-rafter eaves beam. Between the two-rafter eaves beam and along-beam tie is a structure called *yidou sansheng* 一鬥三升, a simplified bracket set using one capital block, one short bracket (*guazigong* 瓜子栱), and three small blocks to support a beam. Above the two-rafter eaves beam stands another bracket set that is crossed by the one-rafter beam and supports the purlin. The other end of the one-rafter beam also is inserted into the shaft of the interior column and is supported by another T-bracket. The upmost beam that usually bears a short post to hold the ridge of the building is not used here. The ridge purlin is supported by six sets of two-layer bracket sets from end to end (fig. 4.22).

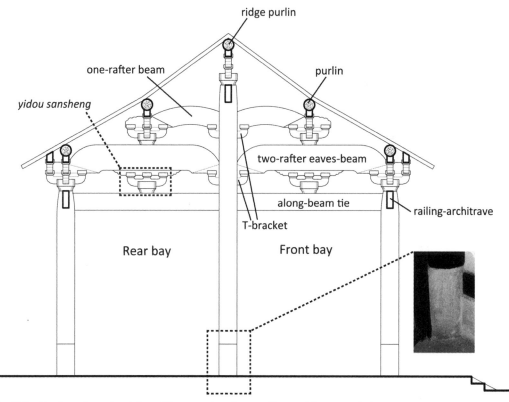

Fig. 4.21. North-south sectional view of the second gatehouse of Yunyan Monastery, Suzhou, Jiangsu, 1338. (Photo by author. Drawing by author.)

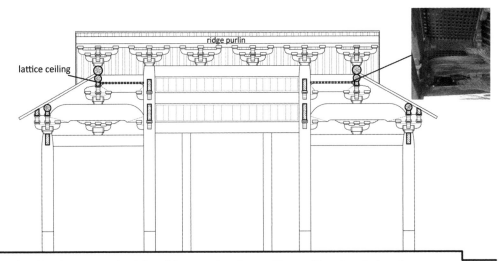

Fig. 4.22. East-west sectional view of the second gatehouse of Yunyan Monastery, Suzhou, Jiangsu, 1338. (Photo by author. Drawing by author.)

Three issues of the roof structure of the second gatehouse are worth extra attention. First, there is no flat architrave built on the eave column top, only a railing architrave is installed, which resembles the main halls of Yanfu Monastery and Tianning Monastery. Second, the plinth of the column is simply a plain stone cylinder 70 cm high, not similar to any other Yuan building in the Lower Yangzi (fig. 4.21). Moreover, a lattice ceiling (*ping'an* 平闇) is built in the side bays above the one-rafter beam (fig. 4.22). This is the only lattice ceiling of the Yuan period found in the Lower Yangzi. Due to the special function of this building as a gatehouse, a couple of structural designs seem unique compared to other Yuan buildings in the same area. It is an exceptional case to see how the timber frame was adjusted to meet the different spatial requirement.

THE MAIN HALL OF XUANYUAN PALACE

Xuanyuan ("the Yellow Emperor") Palace 軒轅宮, also known as Yangwan Temple 楊灣廟, is located in Yangwan 楊灣, a village on a peninsula called Dongshan 東山 (East Mountain) that is southeast of Lake Taihu.[38] The temple first was built in memory of Wu Zixu 伍子胥, an apotheosized official who lived in the Spring and Autumn era (722–481 BCE) and was prime minister of the State of Wu 吳國, approximately modern Jiangsu province. Wu Zixu was worshipped by natives of Suzhou for his virtues and contributions to the city and also as a river god with the title "the God of Waves" (Taoshen 濤神). Therefore, the temple used to be called Xuwang (King Xu) Temple 胥王廟, or Lingshun (Efficacy and Smoothness) Palace 靈順宮. The history of the temple is available in *Taihu beikao* 太湖備考 (References to Lake Taihu), a gazetteer of Lake Taihu written in the Qianlong reign of the Qing dynasty. It reads:

> Xuwang Temple, also known as Lingshun Palace, is located at Yangwan of Dong-shan. When the temple was first built is unknown. During the Yuan dynasty, a person named Wang Lanchao rebuilt the temple, and a front hall was established in the late Ming. As the temple enshrines Wu Zixu, the prime minister of Wu, it is called the Temple of King Xu. The above is recorded by Chen Hu.[39]

In addition, the author of *Taihu beikao* also annotated this entry with a record from another earlier source. Although it is not yet clear what the source is, the quotation is surely informative, and it reads:

> Lingshun Palace at Dongshan enshrines the prime minister Wu Zixu. It was first built in the second year of the Zhenguan reign of the Tang dynasty (628). During the time when Emperor Gaozong of Song fled to the south, the military officers and soldiers who were escorting the emperor parted and crossed the lake. The waves were too stormy to sail. Then the God of Waves (in this case, the apotheosized Wu Zixu) immediately responded to the prayers. Thus, the emperor later sent some officials to restore the temple and upgraded Wu Zixu from "minister" (*yuan*) to "king" (*wang*).[40]

According to this textual evidence, the temple was first built during the Tang dynasty to worship Wu Zixu, and then it was called Lingshun Palace. After Emperor Gaozong of the Song dynasty fled to the south, he bestowed a major restoration upon the temple, and it was renamed Xuwang Temple. In the Yuan dynasty, Wang Lanchao, a native of Suzhou, rebuilt the temple complex. Last, the front hall of the temple was constructed during the late Ming. Although the temple had been used to enshrine Wu Zixu ever since the seventh century, it was converted to worship the Yellow Emperor in order to escape demolition during the early twentieth century.[41] This is why it is now called Xuanyuan (the Yellow Emperor) Palace.

The main hall of Xuanyuan Palace is the oldest building that survived. Assigning it an exact date is complicated. The legible inscriptions written in ink on the major beams of the building indicate that two restorations took place in the sixth (1649) and twelfth (1655) years of the Shunzhi reign of Qing, respectively. This means that the beams bearing those inscriptions and the structure above the beams would be dated no earlier than 1649.[42] Chen Congzhou pointed out that some of the columns and all of the column bases look like remains from the Yuan dynasty. Therefore, regardless of later restorations, the main hall of Xuanyuan Palace still bears information about Yuan architecture.

The main hall of Xuanyuan Palace is oriented east-west, and its front entrance faces west toward Lake Taihu (fig. 4.23). This three-by-three-bay building stands

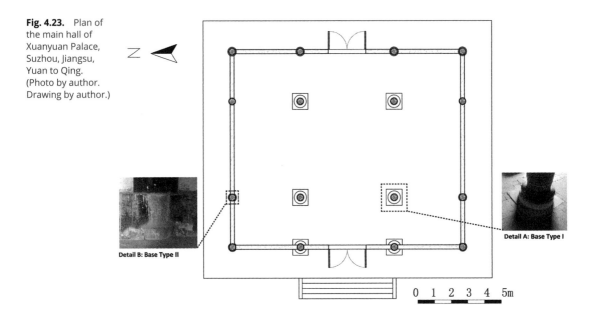

Fig. 4.23. Plan of the main hall of Xuanyuan Palace, Suzhou, Jiangsu, Yuan to Qing. (Photo by author. Drawing by author.)

Detail B: Base Type II

Detail A: Base Type I

0 1 2 3 4 5m

on a platform 64 cm high. The facade is 13.8 m wide with a central bay of 5.6 m and two side bays of 4.1 m. The side elevation of the building is 11.4 m wide, the central bay is 5.6 m wide, and two side bays are nearly half as wide as the middle one. The ratio of the facade to the side elevation is therefore about 5:4.

Two types of column base are used in this building. Type I, used under the four interior columns and two eave columns alongside of the front central bay, has a thick timber *zhuzhi* 柱櫍, a transitional block between the timber column and the stone column base. The square plinth underneath the column base is of 94 cm wide. The diameter of the ovolo molding part of the column base is 74 cm. Column bases of Type II are used under the rest of the columns. A *zhuzhi* made of stone with a bowl-shaped bottom is aligned with the column and directly put on the plinth on the ground. The Type II *zhuzhi* is seen more often in other Yuan buildings in the Lower Yangzi.

The arrangement of the bracket sets is as follows. On the facade, four intercolumnar sets are installed in the central bay, and two are installed in each side bay. On the side, however, only three intercolumnar sets are installed in the middle bay, and one is installed in the side bay. The number of intercolumnar sets in this building, similar to that of the main hall of Zhenru Monastery, surpasses most other Yuan buildings of a similar scale in the Lower Yangzi. This is evidence that the bracket sets of the main hall of Xuanyuan Palace could have been built during the Ming dynasty.

The capital set and the intercolumnar set share an identical appearance from the outside (fig. 4.24). They both project two tiers of inclined cantilever and one tier of the locust head on the top. In terms of the sectional views, the capital set and the intercolumnar set are different. Due to their different functions, the

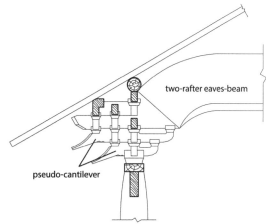

two-rafter eaves-beam

pseudo-cantilever

Fig. 4.24. Capital (*left*) and intercolumnar (*right*) sets of the main hall of Xuanyuan Palace, Suzhou, Jiangsu, Yuan to Qing. (Photo by author.)

Fig. 4.25. Sectional view of the capital set in the main hall of Xuanyuan Palace, Suzhou, Jiangsu, Yuan to Qing. (Drawing by author. Photo by author.)

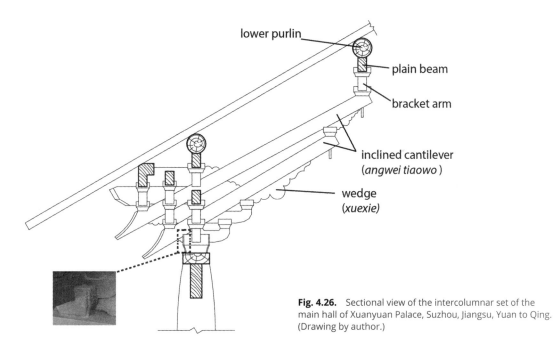

lower purlin

plain beam

bracket arm

inclined cantilever (*angwei tiaowo*)

wedge (*xuexie*)

Fig. 4.26. Sectional view of the intercolumnar set of the main hall of Xuanyuan Palace, Suzhou, Jiangsu, Yuan to Qing. (Drawing by author.)

inclined cantilever in the capital set is a pseudo-cantilever—it is actually a projecting bracket disguised as a cantilever (fig. 4.25). The inclined cantilever in the intercolumnar set, on the other hand, is a real inclined cantilever and functioned as such (fig. 4.26). Moreover, two tiers of projecting bracket of the capital set projected inward to buttress the crescent-moon-shaped two-rafter eaves beam, while those of the intercolumnar set also projected inward, but to support the tails of cantilevers. In regard to the two tiers of the inclined cantilever in the intercolumnar set, the upper inclined cantilever extends until the position right beneath the lower purlin and carries the load of the purlin through a plain beam (*sufang* 素方) and one layer of bracket arm; the lower cantilever, not parallel to the upper one, reinforces the angle of the upper inclined cantilever and is fit with a boot-shaped wedge at the bottom.

Another noteworthy thing about the intercolumnar set is that only the capital block (*ludou* 櫨枓) of the intercolumnar set on the center of the facade has its angles carved into two curved segments. No other bracket sets of this building have the same decoration. This special decoration on the capital block indicates two things. First, since such a decoration is also found in all bracket sets of the second gatehouse of Yunyan Monastery, this is no doubt a regional feature of Suzhou. Second, due to the inconsistency in the capital blocks in the main hall of Xuanyuan Palace, it is highly possible that the bracket sets here were not built during the same time or by the same people.

The roof framing of the building, which may be the product of a later restoration, seems quite symmetrical. The front bay has the same composition as the rear bay: they both are crossed by a moon-shaped two-rafter eaves beam that is supported by two tiers of T-brackets and the capital bracket set (fig. 4.27). Above the two-rafter eaves beam is a small bracket set supporting a lower purlin. A one-rafter beam, which also is shaped like a crescent moon, spans the distance

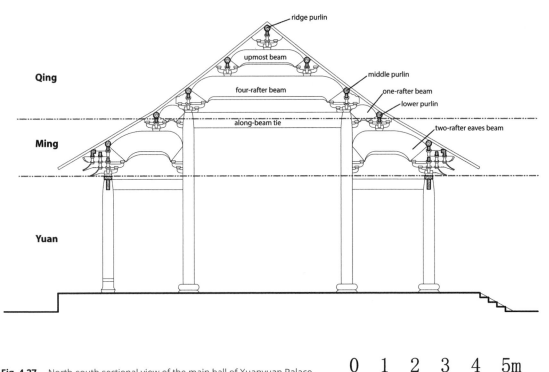

Fig. 4.27. North-south sectional view of the main hall of Xuanyuan Palace, Suzhou, Jiangsu, Yuan to Qing. (Drawing by author.)

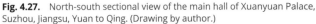

between the lower purlin and the interior column. The middle bay of the building is spanned by a crescent-moon-shaped four-rafter beam, above which is the upmost beam. The two interior columns also are connected by an along-beam tie. Each interior column upholds the middle purlin through a bracket set. Similarly to the second gatehouse of Yunyan Monastery, there is no dwarf pillar installed in this building to uphold the ridge purlin. Instead, the ridge purlin is sustained by a bracket set with a set of double brackets.

With regard to the exact date of the building, the main hall of Xuanyuan Palace exemplifies a hybrid of Yuan, Ming, and Qing architecture. Because the inscriptions discovered on the four-rafter beam are dated to the Qing dynasty, the roof frame above the four-rafter beam is no earlier than that. In comparison to the other Yuan buildings in Jiangnan, the bracket sets on the eave columns are more likely to be Ming. The layout of the columns, the tapered columns, and the column bases can be the only things surviving from the Yuan dynasty.

Although the majority of the timber structure in the main hall of Xuanyuan Palace was not originally from the Yuan, this building is still significant to our discussion. The main hall of Xuanyuan Palace shares a lot of features that belong to other Yuan buildings in the area, such as the crescent-moon-shaped beams, the column base, and the bracket sets that connect beams and columns. Especially in the bracket sets, features such as the rounded-off block, the boot-shaped wedge, and the style of the cantilevers show a strong connection to the local tradition.

The five timber-framed buildings described in this chapter share many local features of the Lower Yangzi. Especially, the main halls of Yanfu Monastery, Tianning Monastery, Zhenru Monastery, and Xuanyuan Palace all have a similar size and function. They also exhibit a consistency in terms of their spatial arrangement, bracket sets configuration, and some details in the roof frame. Most of these local features indicate a profound influence from the YZFS that mostly concerns timber-framed architecture. In the next chapter, five non-timber-framed Yuan buildings, one made of metal and four of stone, will present a rather diverse tradition in non-timber-framed architecture.

CHAPTER 5
NON-TIMBER-FRAMED ARCHITECTURE

Pre-modern Chinese architecture, especially buildings of political and/or religious significance, such as palaces and temples, are dominated by the timber-frame system. Non-timber-framed structures, mostly made purely of stone and/or brick, either aboveground or underground, usually are connected with ideas of an afterlife—taking form as underground palaces for deceased emperors, house-shaped sarcophagi preserving corpses, and shrines venerating ancestors. Pagodas, many of which were built of stone and brick, were related to the death of the Buddha or to deceased monks. Non-timber-framed architecture built for living people, such as temples or palaces, has rarely been discovered dating earlier than the Ming dynasty.

Since the late 1970s, several non-timber-framed buildings dated to the Yuan dynasty have been rediscovered and archaeologically surveyed by Chinese scholars. It is surprising to find that these buildings, one made of copper and the others of stone, were not related to any tomb or funerary ritual. They are actual-size buildings instead of miniature architecture such as the house-shaped containers or sarcophagi discovered in tombs. These non-timber-framed Yuan buildings, being part of a temple or a monastery and built within the context of Han-Chinese tradition, probably are the earliest extant examples of this kind, which further suggests the diversity of Yuan architecture.

To illustrate such diversity in regard to building materials, this chapter will explore five examples of non-timber-framed buildings in the Mid-and-Lower Yangzi area. I shall use these buildings to analyze their construction history and structural features, especially when compared to contemporary timber-framed buildings, and to determine how to contextualize them in historical and religious practice. The locations of the five buildings are shown in plate 4: one stone and one metal building are located in Hubei province of the mid-Yangzi area, one stone building is located in Jiangsu province of the Lower Yangzi, and two stone buildings are found in Fujian province on the southeast coast. I will begin with the earliest metal building discovered so far.

Both the metal and the stone buildings from Hubei province are located at Mount Wudang 武當山, a small mountain range along the middle Yangzi. Mount Wudang is well known for its many Daoist monasteries and is regarded as a center for the research, teaching, and practice of Daoism. Mount Wudang attracted attention from the imperial court as early as the Eastern Han (25–220). The first site constructed for the worship of Daoism was built in the Tang dynasty (618–907).[1] Later on during the Northern Song, Mount Wudang became the pilgrimage site of a particular Daoist deity, Xuanwu 玄武.[2] Xuanwu was first portrayed in the Daoist scripture titled *Yuanshi tianzun shuo beifang zhenwu miaojing* 元始天尊說北方真武妙經 (Sublime scripture of the Primeval Lord of Heaven explaining the Northern True Warrior) that was composed and disseminated during the Northern Song. Accordingly, Mount Wudang, called Taihe Mountain 太和山 in the scripture, was the place where Xuanwu practiced his arts and attained immortality. Mount Wudang gradually developed into the ongoing pilgrimage site for honoring Xuanwu. Due to the popularity of Xuanwu, architectural construction at Mount Wudang was quite active during the Song and Yuan dynasties, and most buildings there are related to Xuanwu.

Although monasteries and palaces in Mount Wudang were damaged and abandoned during the chaos of the Mongol invasion in the late thirteenth century, the cult of Xuanwu was revived by the Yuan imperial court. In the seventh year of the Dade 大德 reign (1303), Yuan emperor Chengzong 成宗 granted Xuanwu another honorific title, "the Dark Heavenly Emperor of Primal Sagehood and Might" (Yuansheng renwei xuantian shangdi 元聖仁威玄天上帝).[3] Construction of monasteries and temples became active on Mount Wudang again. Many worship sites built during the Yuan period were dedicated explicitly to Xuanwu. Regrettably, only a few buildings dating from this Yuan revival survive today; one is built of copper and two of stone. These structures are also the only credible Yuan buildings discovered hitherto in Hubei province. Interestingly, none of them was built of timber, which explains why they are extant, given that stone and copper buildings are much more durable. This is probably one reason for people to have chosen stone or metal, although they are much more time-consuming materials to work with. Because it was supposed to symbolize the residence of Xuanwu in heaven, the building had to be as long-lasting as the immortal himself.

THE LITTLE COPPER HALL

The copper building, the earliest extant metal building that has survived from the Yuan dynasty is now known as Xiaotongdian 小銅殿, the Little Copper Hall. According to the inscription found on the building, it is dated to 1307 of the Yuan dynasty. The hall originally was located on the Peak of Heaven Pillar (Tianzhufeng 天柱峰), the highest peak in Mount Wudang. It was an ideal location for a building dedicated to the worship of Xuanwu, because, as legend has it, Xuanwu ascended to heaven from this very peak. During the Yongle reign of the Ming dynasty (1403–1424), the Little Copper Hall was replaced by another larger copper hall and then relocated to its current place, the Little Lotus Peak (Xiaolianfeng 小蓮峰). Since then, it has been called "the Little Copper Hall" to differentiate it from the new one.[4]

The Little Copper Hall is oriented east-west with an entrance facing east. It has the same orientation as its larger Ming replacement on the Peak of Heaven Pillar. Its squarish plan is about 2.61 m long and 2.56 m wide. The front side is one bay wide, and the flank side is divided by one column into two bays. A *sumeru* altar of bluestone including a statue of Xuanwu is at the rear center of the hall (fig. 5.1). The Little Copper Hall we see today is not a freestanding structure. It is enclosed by another timber-framed building, Zhuanyun (Rotating Luck) Hall 轉運殿, also called Zhuanchen (Rotating Time) Hall 轉辰殿. The outer building, is merely a little bigger than the copper hall, which creates a narrow corridor between the copper hall and the outer building. The corridor is so narrow that it allows only one person to pass through at a time. The relocated Little Copper Hall not only functions as a structure to enshrine an idol but becomes an idol itself. When people enter Zhuanyun Hall with the Little Copper Hall standing in the center, they can circle around the copper hall in order to *zhuanyun*, meaning "change luck."

The Little Copper Hall is built on a *sumeru* terrace that is about one meter high (fig. 5.2). Four door panels are installed on the front. The corner columns are built on drum-type plinths with lotus pedal patterns all over it. The building is covered by a two-sloped roof (*xuanshan* 懸山) that projects beyond the gable walls at both ends. More intriguingly, the ridge of the building is decorated with images of constellations in positive scribing. From left to right, as labeled in figure 5.2, there are the Southern Dipper (Nandou 南斗, also known as Sagittarius), a three-star image representing the Three Daoist Purities (Sanqing 三清), and the Northern Dipper (Beidou 北斗).

The roof framework is composed of alloy members and imitates timber members in many ways. It is two bays deep and has one tie beam spanning each

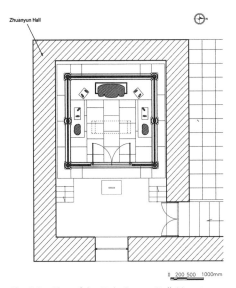

Fig. 5.1. Plan of the Little Copper Hall, Mount Wudang, Hubei, 1307. (Drawing by Zhang Jianwei in Zhang Jianwei, *Zhongguo gudai jinshu jianzhu yanjiu*, 141. Courtesy of Zhang Jianwei.)

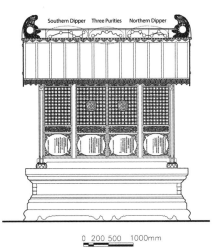

Fig. 5.2. Front elevation of the Little Copper Hall, Mount Wudang, Hubei, 1307. (Drawing by Zhang Jianwei in Zhang Jianwei, *Zhongguo gudai jinshu jianzhu yanjiu*, 142. Courtesy of Zhang Jianwei.)

bay (see right image of fig. 5.3). Two eave purlins and one ridge purlin rest directly on the columns without any transitions of bracket sets. A crescent-moon-shaped interior column-top tie beam (*yueliangzao wunei'e* 月梁造屋內額) is visible in the left image of figure 5.3. Such a simple roof structure can be defined as the "post-and-tie construction style" (*chuandou* 穿鬥), a type of structure with purlins resting directly on columns and with tie beams connecting the columns together in the transverse direction. Its lack of rafters is the only thing that differentiates the copper building from a timber-framed building. Flat roof tiles, also made in alloy, directly rest on the purlins instead of on rafters.

The Little Copper Hall is an excellent example of Yuan metal architecture. Since no later alteration has been done to this building, it preserves exceptionally authentic information about what a small-scale Yuan building might have looked like in the mid-Yangzi area. There are two possibilities for explaining why no bracket sets were used in this building. First, as the structure of the bracket sets is extremely complicated, the technique of metal casting at that time might not have been advanced enough to make bracket sets. People probably simplified the building by removing bracket sets for economic reasons. Second, it is also possible that the post-and-tie construction style involving no bracket sets was common for small-scale buildings even among timber-framed architecture in the area.

Metal architecture, usually built with an alloy of copper, tin, and lead, is rather unique in ancient China. The Little Copper Hall in Mount Wudang is the oldest

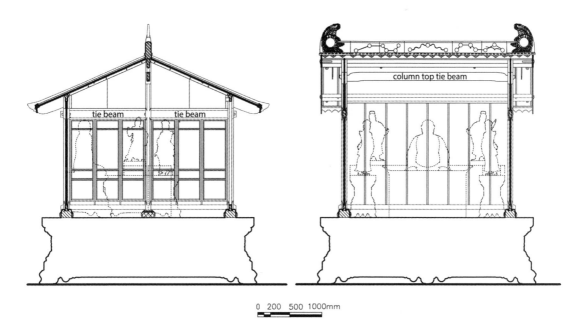

Fig. 5.3. East-west (*left*) and north-south (*right*) sectional views of the Little Copper Hall, Mount Wudang, Hubei, 1307. (Drawing by Zhang Jianwei in Zhang Jianwei, *Zhongguo gudai jinshu jianzhu yanjiu*, 142. Courtesy of Zhang Jianwei.)

extant metal building in China. Since there is no evidence of copper buildings prior to the Yuan dynasty, it is probably the earliest copper building that has ever been in China.[5] The Little Copper Hall's mimicking of timber-framed architecture also can be seen in many ways in a stone building also located in Mount Wudang.

TIANYI ZHENQING PALACE

Tianyi Zhenqing Palace 天乙真慶宮 (hereafter Zhenqing Palace), located at Mount Wudang, is the largest extant stone building known in China that imitates a timber-framed structure. Zhenqing Palace was named after the palace where Xuanwu was supposed to have lived in heaven. Construction of this building went on for thirty years—from the twenty-first year of the Zhiyuan reign (1284) to the first year of the Yanyou reign (1314)—much longer than the time involved to construct any timber-framed building.[6] The enormous time and effort dedicated to the construction of Zhenqing Palace are understandable due to Xuanwu's popularity and the endorsement of his cult in Mount Wudang by the Yuan court.

Although Zhenqing Palace is built completely of stone, it imitates timber-framed architecture in several aspects. Eight identical five-layered bracket sets (*wupuzuo* 五鋪作) without an inclined cantilever (*ang* 昂) are built on the front elevation (fig. 5.4).[7] Remarkably, six oblique arms (*xiegong* 斜栱) at a 45° angle are installed on each bracket set and are arranged in two tiers: four on top and two at the bottom (fig. 5.5). On the first/lower tier, a perpendicular projecting bracket (*huagong* 華栱) in the middle is flanked by two oblique arms projected from the capital block. All together, they support the traversal bracket on the second/upper tier that also projects five brackets forward. As to the five brackets, one is orthogonal toward the front; the other four, two on each side, are oblique toward a 45° angle to the facade. All five bracket arms, if built in a timber-framed building, would have

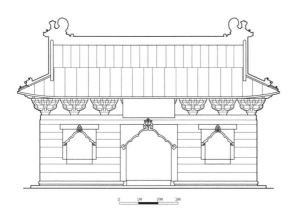

Fig. 5.4. Front elevation of Tianyi Zhenqing Palace, Mount Wudang, Hubei, 1314. (Drawing by author.)

Fig. 5.5. Bracket set of Tianyi Zhenqing Palace, Mount Wudang, Hubei, 1314. (Photo courtesy of Zhang Jianwei.)

Plate 1. Map of China displaying the three regions of north China, the Upper Yangzi, and the Lower Yangzi. (Drawing by author.)

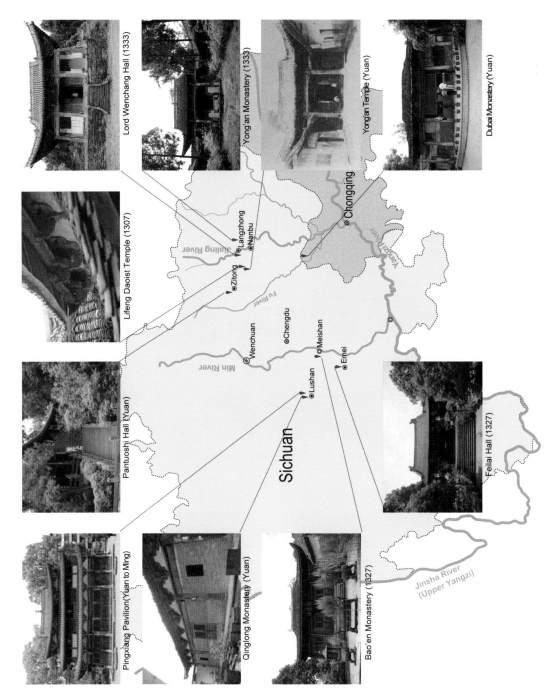

Plate 2. Locations of Yuan buildings in the Upper Yangzi, including Sichuan and Chongqing. (Photos and drawing by author.)

Lord Wenchang Hall (1333)

Yong'an Monastery (1333)

Yong'an Temple (Yuan)

Dubai Monastery (Yuan)

Lifeng Daoist Temple (1307)

Pantuoshi Hall (Yuan)

Feilai Hall (1327)

Pingxiang Pavilion (Yuan to Ming)

Qinglong Monastery (Yuan)

Bao'en Monastery (1327)

Jialing River

Zitong

Langzhong

Nanbu

Chongqing

Yangzi River

Fu River

Wenchuan

Chengdu

Meishan

Emei

Min River

Lushan

Sichuan

Jinsha River
(Upper Yangzi)

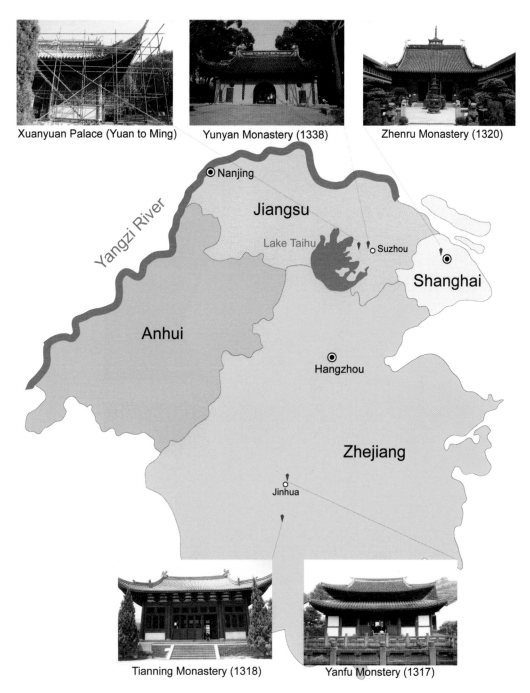

Xuanyuan Palace (Yuan to Ming)   Yunyan Monastery (1338)   Zhenru Monastery (1320)

Tianning Monastery (1318)   Yanfu Monstery (1317)

Plate 3. Locations of Yuan buildings in the Lower Yangzi, including Jiangsu, Zhejiang, and Shanghai. (Photos by author.)

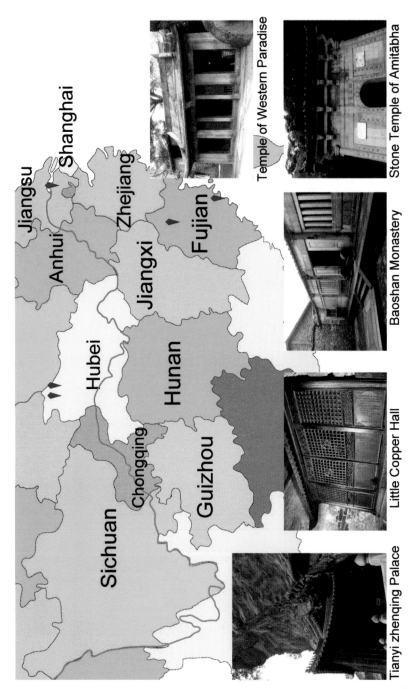

Tianyi zhenqing Palace   Little Copper Hall   Baoshan Monastery   Stone Temple of Amitābha

Temple of Western Paradise

Plate 4. Locations of non-timber-framed Yuan architecture in the Mid-and-Lower Yangzi. (Drawing by author. Photos by author, Zhang Jianwei, and Li Xinjian. Courtesy of Zhang Jianwei and Li Xinjian.)

carried the load of the eave purlin. In Zhenqing Palace, however, it is the stone-and-brick walls that bear the load. The bracket sets, on the other hand, do not seem to help the mechanics and structure of this stone building, but illustrate the simulation of an elaborated timber-framed structure.

The bracket sets of Zhenqing Palace truly reflect contemporary timber-framed buildings in the Upper Yangzi (see chapter 3). For example, the bracket sets of the main hall of Qinglong Monastery (see fig. 3.36) and Yong'an Temple (see fig. 3.58) are similar to those in Zhenqing Palace: they both have 45° oblique arms, and no inclined cantilever is installed. This type of five-layered bracket set with 45° oblique bracket arms is complicated to make even in timber.

The interior structure of Zhenqing Palace also includes typical members common in a timber-framed building: a crescent moon-shaped one-rafter beam (*zhaqian* 劄牽) with an along-beam tie (*shunfuchuan* 順栿串, a horizontal timber that connects a pair of columns, located below and parallel to the main beam to provide additional resistance to the movement of columns) underneath, and a cicada's abdomen joist (*chanduchuomu* 蟬肚綽幕, a joist with an underside shaped with a succession of rings like a cicada's abdomen) under an interior column-top tie beam (fig. 5.6). Again, a similar crescent moon-shaped

Fig. 5.6. Sectional view of Tianyi Zhenqing Palace, Mount Wudang, Hubei, 1314. (Drawing by author. Photo courtesy of Zhang Jianwei.)

one-rafter beam and along-beam tie are found in Yuan timber buildings in the Lower Yangzi—the main halls of Yanfu Monastery and Tianning Monastery in Zhejiang, and the main hall of Zhenru Monastery in Shanghai (see chapter 4). The cicada's abdomen beam under an interior tie beam can also be found in Yuan timber-framed buildings in Sichuan. These interior beams and tie beams, in contrast to the bracket sets that are purely decorative, are structural members that support the load of the roof. They may not be structurally reasonable in all aspects but are supposed to bear the load or to tie the columns according to the mechanism in a timber-framed building. Since there are no columns built in the front, however, the wall on the elevation is clearly load-bearing. This factor slightly differentiates Zhenqing Palace from real timber-framed buildings where walls are never load-bearing.

With regard to most non-timber-framed monuments, such as pagodas and tomb chambers, the imitation of timber elements is merely symbolic rather than structural, and it does not always follow the proportionality of a real timber-framed building. The most frequently imitated objects, such as the bracket sets, roof styles, architraves, and tie beams, are structural in a timber-framed building. In a non-timber-framed monument, however, they usually are decorative and not necessarily structural. In contrast to the existing tradition of timber imitation in tombs and pagodas, the elements imitating timber in Zhenqing Palace, on the other hand, are structural. Those structural members—beams, columns, and tie beams—are made exactly like those in contemporary timber-framed buildings. It seems that, regardless of the differences between the nature of stone and timber, the craftsmen adopted the design of a timber-framed building and precisely applied it to this stone building. When building Zhenqing Palace, each stone was carved exactly like the corresponding timber members with mortises and tenons. The stone building was assembled just like a timber-framed building, which may explain the twenty-eight years of time-consuming construction. The next example of a stone building, however, is along different guidelines in terms of timber imitation.

THE TEMPLE OF WESTERN PARADISE

The Temple of Western Paradise (Xitiansi 西天寺), also known as the Stone Hall (Shidian 石殿) at Jijian (Desolate Reflection) Monastery 寂鑑寺, represents a different type of stone building. Jijian Monastery, located in the suburb of Suzhou in southeast China, is built on the Mountain of Heavenly Pond (Tianchishan 天池山), which is fifteen kilometers away from downtown Suzhou. This monastery is known for three stone monuments that are dated to the Yuan dynasty— the Temple of Western Paradise, which is a three-bay worship hall, and two house-shaped stone altars. The remaining architecture in the complex of Jijian Monastery generally was constructed in recent decades as part of the landscape of the Tianchishan Park.

Jijian Monastery was once a private residence of a local official named Zhang Yu 張裕, who was the prefect of Kuaiji 會稽 Prefecture during the Liu-Song dynasty (420–479). During the Qiandao reign (1165–1175) of the Southern Song, another official, Zhang Tingjie 張廷傑, expanded the residential complex into his own villa and added some Buddhist sculptures on the mountain. It was not until the seventeenth year of the Zhizheng reign (1357) of the Yuan dynasty that Monk Daozai 僧道在 developed it into a Buddhist monastery. In 1369, the second year of the Hongwu reign of the Ming dynasty, a Buddhist monk, Shi Kexin 釋克新, wrote an account entitled *Tianchi Jijian chan'anji* 天池寂鑒禪庵記 (An account of Jijian Zen Nunnery at Tianchi). It records the course of the construction in 1357 as follows:

> A three-bay stone hall was built. Statues of Śākyamuni, Bhaiṣajyaguru (the Buddha of Medicine), and Amitābha were carved out of rocks. Statues of bodhisattvas and guardians, as well as offering vessels, were all carved in stone. Stones were piled as an outer gate. The gate was covered by a double-eave roof. Oil lamps were placed inside at night. The gate was called Tower of the Heavenly Lantern. Thirty-five names of the Buddha were carved on the cliff, flanked by two chiseled pools. Two house-shaped altars were built of stone to enshrine [the statues of] Maitreya and Amitābha respectively. One was called the Palace of Tuṣita Heaven and the other was called the Garden of Sukhāvatī. A Buddhist pagoda was built in the front, grandly facing the stone house-shaped altars. As to the other buildings, such as the recitation room, kitchen, bathroom, and guest house: all were constructed as standard.[8]

In this account, the construction of the three Yuan stone monuments at Jijian Monastery—the Temple of Western Paradise (the Stone Hall), the Palace of Tuṣita Heaven (house-shaped altar), and the Garden of Sukhāvatī (house-shaped altar) as well as other accessory buildings in the monastery—are introduced briefly. None of the accessory buildings mentioned in the account survives from the Yuan dynasty, probably because they were built of timber.

Different from the two house-shaped altars that are miniatures, the Temple of Western Paradise, as the main hall of Jijian Monastery, is a life-size building. The building has a nine-ridged roof with single eave, and its facade, facing south, is three bays wide (fig. 5.7). An architrave (*lan'e* 闌額) is built on top of the columns, and the bracket sets are replaced by simple beams. In the central bay, two accessory pillars are installed to decrease the span of the tie beam. The total width of the facade is 7.64 m. The ratio of the central bay to the side bay is close to 3:2, similar to the second gatehouse of Yunyan Monastery that is also located in Suzhou.

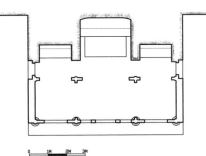

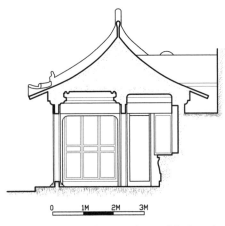

The plan of the Temple of Western Paradise is divided into two areas by the interior pillars (fig. 5.8). The front three bays serve the worshippers; the three rear bays are actually three niches enshrining Buddhist statues. The middle niche, which is much deeper than the side ones, hosts the statue of Avalokiteśvara. Notably, this building has two exits chiseled into the side wall; most Yuan timber-framed halls have rear exits instead of side ones. It is evident that the Temple of Western Paradise is attached to the mountain and is not separated from the hillside (fig. 5.9). The original idea to build this structure probably was inherited from the design of Buddhist caves, which will be discussed further.

Inside the building, each bay is decorated with a coffered ceiling (*zaojing* 藻井). There are four kinds of coffered ceilings (fig. 5.10): (1) each of the back side bays has a flat and plain rectangular ceiling panel; (2) each of the front side bays has a flat octagonal ceiling panel with sixteen rafter-end-like ornaments; (3) the front central bay is canopied by a recessed rectangular coffered ceiling with a relief of a Chinese dragon intertwining with clouds; and (4) the back center bay that hosts a statue of Avalokiteśvara is canopied by a

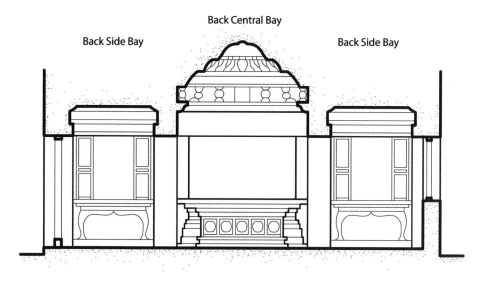

Back Central Bay

Back Side Bay

Back Side Bay

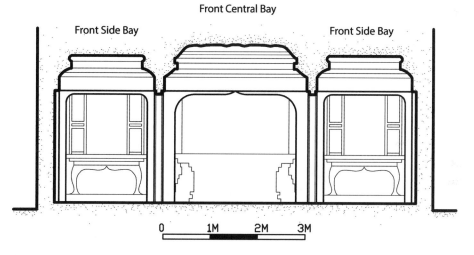

Front Central Bay

Front Side Bay

Front Side Bay

0   1M   2M   3M

Fig. 5.10. East-west sectional views of the Temple of Western Paradise, Suzhou, Jiangsu, 1357. (Redrawn by author after Liu Xujie and Qi Deyao, "Jiangsu Wuxian Jijiansi Yuandai shidianwu," 44–45.)

decagonal recessed coffer. This decagonal coffer is decorated by, from outer rings to inner rings, *ruyi* 如意 patterns, lotus buds, rafter-end-like ornaments, unidentified floral patterns, and a *taiji*-like 太極 pattern (fig. 5.11).[9]

A surprising iconographic connection is found between the coffered ceilings in Xitiansi and the coffered ceilings in a Lamaist temple in Lhasa, thousands of miles away. The coffered ceiling, dated to the period of Tibetan Empire (seventh to eighth century), in the main hall of Jokhang Temple (Dazhaosi 大昭寺) is similar to the coffered ceilings in the Temple of Western Paradise; they both have a rafter-end-like ornament, with a floral pattern in the center

Fig. 5.11. Coffered ceiling in the back central bay of the Temple of Western Paradise, Suzhou, Jiangsu, 1357. (Drawing by author.)

and a unique *taiji* pattern in the center of this floral pattern (fig. 5.12).[10] The only difference is that the coffered ceiling in Jokhang Temple is carved in wood, whereas at the Temple of Western Paradise it is carved of stone.

On the one hand, the stone coffered ceilings of the Temple of Western Paradise share some iconographic features with the wooden coffered ceiling in the far-off Jokhang Temple in Lhasa; on the other hand, it is quite unique if compared to other local monuments in Suzhou. The brick pagodas of Yunyan Monastery and Bao'en Monastery 報恩寺 in Suzhou, one dated to the Northern Song and the other to the Southern Song, both have circular domelike coffered ceilings with bracket sets and curved rafters. They look quite similar to the timber domelike coffered ceilings in the main hall of Baoguo Monastery 保國寺 (fig. 5.13), dated to the Northern Song. The brick coffered ceilings in these two pagodas faithfully imitate the timber one by retaining the most characteristic feature of timber-framed architecture—the bracket sets and curved rafters. The Temple of Western Paradise, however, did not follow the local tradition of timber imitation by copying the prototype of the coffered ceiling in local timber-framed buildings.

Fig. 5.12. Coffered ceiling in Jokhang Temple, Lhasa, Tibet, seventh to ninth centuries. (Photo courtesy of Gao Feng.)

The contrast between the Temple of Western Paradise and other local Song-Yuan buildings and the similarity between it and Tibet's Jokhang Temple are explainable. Early in the Yuan dynasty, when the Southern Song court surrendered to the Mongols, the Mongol-Yuan rulers, who were sponsors of Lamaist Buddhism, immediately sent monks to Hangzhou to convert both Daoist monasteries and Chinese Buddhist monasteries into Lamaist temples. As Suzhou and Hangzhou are relatively close to each other, the Temple of Western Paradise might have been influenced largely by Lamaist Buddhism in Hangzhou. In today's Hangzhou, the

Fig. 5.13. Domelike coffered ceiling in the main hall of Baoguo Monastery, Ningbo, Zhejiang, 1013. (Photo courtesy of Luo Dengke.)

Lamaist caves on Feilaifeng 飛來峰 (Peak of the Flying Arrivals) and in Baocheng Monastery 寶成寺 still exist.[11] Jijian Monastery, the temple complex where the Temple of Western Paradise is located, was expanded into a Buddhist monastery during the Yuan dynasty. Given its location close to Hangzhou, it is reasonable that lamas, rather than monks from local Chinese Buddhist monasteries, oversaw the construction of the main hall. Moreover, similar to those Lamaist caves constructed in Hangzhou during the Yuan, Jijian Monastery was indeed constructed as a cave temple rather than a Chinese Buddhist monastery with symmetrical plan and courtyards.

In sum, The Temple of Western Paradise is a stone building that imitates the appearance of a traditional Chinese timber-framed building but was constructed as a rock-cut Buddhist cave temple. The new material of stone was no longer treated as timber; characteristic timber components, such as bracket sets, are no longer found here. Instead of imitating local timber-framed buildings that represent Han Chinese Buddhism, the builders of the Temple of Western Paradise intentionally borrowed motifs from the non-Han Lamaist temples and avoided copying local Han Chinese Buddhist architecture. This clearly displays the influence of Lamaist Buddhism in the heartland of Chinese culture.

THE MAIN HALL OF BAOSHAN MONASTERY

Another example that is more similar to Zhenqing Palace than to the Temple of Western Paradise is the main hall of Baoshan (Treasure Mountain) Monastery 寶山寺 located in Shunchang 順昌, Fujian province. Baoshan Monastery was named after the mountain Baoshan (Treasure Mountain) where it is located. The monastery is built on top of the Treasure Mountain, overlooking surrounding hills and valleys. Compared to the courtyard-style temples and monasteries that are usually built on flat ground in China, Baoshan Monastery is castle-like, fortressed by thick brick walls. Today, the monastery is composed of east, west, and residential precincts. Only the main hall in the west precinct was built during the Yuan; all the other buildings are of timber and were built in the twentieth century. The main hall of Baoshan Monastery is built completely of stone. Some scholars explain that Treasure Mountain's peak is foggy and humid all year, and probably this is why people used stone: it is more durable in such an environment.[12] For this reason, the main hall is the only structure in the monastery that survives from the Yuan dynasty.

Although there are no historical records mentioning the main hall of Baoshan Monastery in local gazetteers or other literature, the inscriptions carved on the beams relate much history. The earliest inscription is the one at the bottom of the ridge purlin. The inscription reads: "Celebration of the accomplishment of the construction with the funds raised from the populace, at the *jimao* hour (5–7 p.m.) on the auspicious day, [that is] the 28th day in the seventh month in the 23rd year of Zhizheng reign, the year of *guimao,* of the Great Yuan."[13] The inscription clearly states that the building was first constructed in the twenty-third year of the Zhizheng reign (1363). Given that the ridge purlin bearing this inscription is still intact, it is clear that the main structure of the building has not been altered significantly since then. In addition to the Yuan inscription, other inscriptions record later restorations or repairs from the Hongzhi reign (1488–1505) of the Ming dynasty (1368–1644) to the Guangxu reign (1875–1908) of the Qing (1616–1912). Later repairs, however, only involved replacement of a few members or roof tiles. The main structure of the building has not been altered since the original construction in the Yuan dynasty.[14]

The main hall of Baoshan Monastery has a rectangular plan, measuring 14.40 m by 9.87 m, and faces northwest (fig. 5.14). This can be considered a midsize building; it is larger than Zhenqing Palace in Mount Wudang. The elevation of the building is divided into five bays by four columns and is covered by a two-slope roof

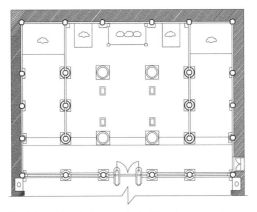

Fig. 5.14. Plan of the main hall of Baoshan Monastery, Shunchang, Fujian, 1363. (Redrawn by author after Lou Jianlong and Wang Yimin, "Fujian Shunchang Baoshansi dadian," 69.)

(*xuanshan* 悬山) that is relatively low-ranking (fig. 5.15).[15]

The structure of the building is a hybrid of "the lifting-beams style" (*tailiang* 抬梁) and "the post-and-tie construction style" (*chuandou* 穿斗), which was common among the timber-framed buildings of the Song and Yuan dynasties in southeast China, especially in low-ranking buildings. The middle bay of the building is constructed in the lifting-beams style, where the central top two-rafter beam is lifted (*tai*) in order to be installed over the longer four-rafter beam (fig. 5.16, top). On the other hand, the end bay is built in the post-and-tie construction style. The central column goes all the way to the top, and beams pass through (*chuan*) the shaft of the central column (fig. 5.16, bottom).

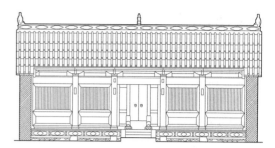

Fig. 5.15. Front elevation of the main hall of Baoshan Monastery, Shunchang, Fujian, 1363. (Redrawn by author after Lou Jianlong and Wang Yimin, "Fujian Shunchang Baoshansi dadian," 69.)

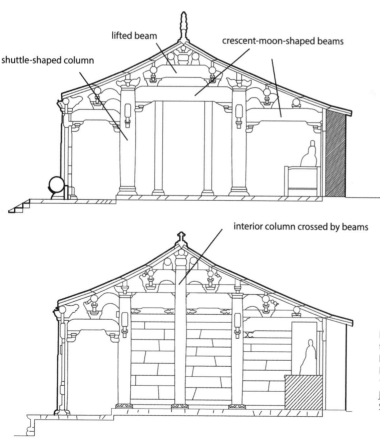

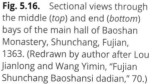

Fig. 5.16. Sectional views through the middle (*top*) and end (*bottom*) bays of the main hall of Baoshan Monastery, Shunchang, Fujian, 1363. (Redrawn by author after Lou Jianlong and Wang Yimin, "Fujian Shunchang Baoshansi dadian," 70.)

As no ceiling was installed, the entire roof structure is visible. The huge load of the stone roof structure is carried by the stone columns, and the columns are tied by stone tie beams or stone crossing beams. This is just how a timber-framed structure works. In addition, the builder or later repairers had all inscriptions inscribed on the bottoms of beams. This method of documenting the construction history of architecture often is seen in timber-framed buildings. Although the walls of the buildings are between 70 and 83 cm thick according to the structural frame, this is not a wall-bearing building. The walls are used only as room dividers. It is basically a stone building based on the design and principles of a typical timber-framed structure building.

Major structural members in this building honestly reflect certain characteristic details of timber-framed architecture. For example, the bulging stone columns, called shuttle-shaped columns (*suozhu* 梭柱), reflect how a timber column should be made according to the YZFS. Similar bulging columns are utilized in the main hall of Hualin Monastery 華林寺, a Northern Song timber-framed building also located in Fujian. Moreover, rafter beams in the main hall of Baoshan Monastery are made as crescent-moon beams alike in other timber-framed buildings dated to the Song and Yuan in southeast China, and they also echo the crescent-moon beam mentioned in the YZFS.

Although the main hall of Baoshan Monastery basically was constructed in imitation of a timber-framed building, the builders sometimes were flexible in accommodating the nature of the stone. For example, in contrast to Zhenqing Palace at Mount Wudang, where bracket sets are installed under the curved front eave, in the main hall of Baoshan Monastery there is no projected bracket arm built under the front eave. The frontal eave is less than 10 cm wide and is no longer curved and outstretching. Since the main hall of Baoshan Monastery is larger than Zhenqing Palace, and stone is not as ductile as timber, it may not have been safe to build outreaching curved eaves supported by complicated bracket sets.

Nonetheless, in order to preserve the aspect of timber-framed architecture, bracket sets still were used on the interior structure of the main hall of Baoshan Monastery. Beams and columns all are connected by joints that consist of bracket arms and blocks. Those bracket arms and blocks, however, are no longer single pieces. They are carved and integrated as part of the beams or tie beams to increase the stability and integrity of the structure of the building. The main function of the bracket sets is decorative and representative of the characteristic details of a timber-framed building.

Another important example that supports the flexibility of the builders is the modular unit they used for this building. Unlike most timber-framed buildings that are based on a single modular unit, the builders of this stone building actually adopted a bi-unit modular system. For the decorative members, such as bracket sets, the builders used the seventh-grade modular unit; for structural members, such as columns, beams, and tie beams, however, they used the fifth-grade unit.[16] Therefore, those structural members are proportionally thicker and stronger than those nonstructural members. The roof load is reduced reasonably by using smaller decorative members, and the structure is reinforced by using larger structural members.

To summarize the significance of the main hall of Baoshan Monastery, first of all it is a stone building that was constructed based on timber-framed architectural principles. Due to its faithful imitation of timber-framed buildings, the stone building shared many features with local, real timber-framed buildings in Fujian province. As stone is not perishable, the main hall of Baoshan Monastery has become a textbook for people to study timber-framed architecture in Fujian in the Song, Yuan, and Ming periods. Second, although they followed some designs in a timber-framed building, the builders did adapt timber-framed architectural principles to accommodate the nature of the new material. It is appreciable that the builders tried to balance faithfulness to timber-framed architecture with the capacities of a stone structure.

THE STONE TEMPLE OF AMITĀBHA

The last stone building introduced in this chapter is the Stone Temple of Amitābha 彌陀巖 (Mituoyan) located on Qingyuan (Clear Fountainhead) Mountain 清源山, which is close to the city of Quanzhou in Fujian province.[17] It is located at the south side of Qingyuan Mountain, leaning toward the cliff of the mountain. The Stone Temple of Amitābha, as its name suggests, enshrined a statue of Amitābha Buddha. The history of the Stone Temple of Amitābha can be learned from a stele embedded in the cliff next to the stone building. The inscription on the stele is entitled *Xiu Mituoyan ji* 修彌陀岩記 (the Record of the construction of the Stone Temple of Amitābha) and reads:

> The Stone Temple of Amitābha has become dilapidated. A monk from Jinling (modern Nanjing), named Juecheng, travelled to Quanzhou. He met with Administrator San-dan-ba, Censor Tiemuer Buhua (Timur Buga), Investigating Censor Sun Sanbao, and his assistant Shijianu. They donated their properties and initiated the fundraising. They raised funds from the populace and rebuilt the building with stone. They built terraces and pagodas, altered the roofs of the halls, and moreover, finely carved the statues of the Buddha and pasted them with gold. It took four years in total. Sun Shijue, a gentleman from the local commandery, donated the profit of his land to fund the monastic practice and the incense burners. He uses this merit to benefit all beings. The people who demonstrate [the miracle of] Bodhi are capable and intelligent. . . . We erected a stele to announce the accomplishment [of the construction of the building] on the first day of the second month in the twenty-fourth year of Zhizheng reign, the *jiachen* year of the Great Yuan.[18]

Fig. 5.17. Front elevation of the Stone Temple of Amitābha, Qingyuan Mountain, Fujian, 1364. (Redrawn by author after Cao Chunping, "Quanzhou Qingyuanshan Mituoyan yu Ruixiangyan," 94.)

Fig. 5.18. Bracket sets of the Stone Temple of Amitābha, Qingyuan Mountain, Fujian, 1364. (Photo courtesy of Li Xinjian.)

The inscription suggests that an older version of the Stone Temple of Amitābha existed before the Zhizheng reign, probably a timber-framed building. The current stone building is a newer version that was rebuilt in 1364.

The Stone Temple of Amitābha is a small stone hall only one bay wide (fig. 5.17). It is oriented toward the east, and the plan is square. It looks very similar to a uni-storied pagoda, such as the Sui dynasty pagoda in Shentong Monastery, Shandong province.[19] Judging from the facade of the Stone Temple of Amitābha, the building bears many features of a timber-framed building: columns, tie beams, and bracket sets. The bracket sets were simplified by replacing transversal arms that are parallel to the wall plane with a one-piece tie beam (fig. 5.18). Nevertheless, they still are considered functional as the eaves are supported by projected bracket arms. In contrast to the exterior of the building that bears many features of timber-framed architecture, the interior of the hall was designed otherwise. The recessed coffered ceiling merely is constructed with tiers of stone pieces. There is no sign of imitation bracket sets, beams, purlins, or rafters of timber-framed architecture.

It is remarkable that the arch of the entrance is pointed like an ogee arch, and such a pattern is also repeated on the finial at the top of the building (fig. 5.17). An ogee arch is a characteristic feature in Islamic architecture, and a connection between the Stone Temple of Amitābha and Islamic architecture is feasible. The city of Quanzhou, only a few miles away from Qingyuan Mountain, was largely populated by Muslim communities during the Song and Yuan dynasties. Shengyou Mosque 聖友寺 (Mosque of the Companions), one of the oldest mosques extant in China, is located in Quanzhou.[20] This mosque is built of stone, and an ogee arch very similar to that of the Stone Temple of Amitābha still can be seen there. So, we might plausibly accept the deduction that the Stone Temple of Amitābha was influenced by such mosques, which also may partially explain why people chose stone over timber when rebuilding this structure in 1364.

In addition to learning from the mosques, the builders of the Stone Temple of Amitābha also borrowed a few designs from the twin pagodas of Kaiyuan Monastery 開元寺 in Quanzhou (fig. 5.19).[21] The facade of the Stone Temple of Amitābha is comparable to one of the twin pagodas, having similar sparrow braces (*queti*

雀替, a right-triangle piece used to support a column and beam joint), tie beams, and bracket sets where transversal arms are replaced by a one-piece tie beam. On top of the Stone Temple of Amitābha there is also a miniature stupa placed as a pagoda finial.

In summary, the Stone Temple of Amitābha is neither a pure imitation of a timber-framed building nor a transformed cave temple, but rather a transformation of a pagoda influenced by mosques. According to the historical record, the structure was rebuilt during the Yuan due to its poor condition. Before then, it was a dilapidated timber-framed building. Due to the similarities between the Stone Temple and the twin pagodas of Kaiyuansi, this stone building also may be considered an altered version of a stone pagoda. It is interesting to note that, although both it and the main hall of Baoshan Monastery are located in Fujian province, and the Stone Temple was built only one year after the monastery, the construction principles of these two buildings are completely different. The main hall of Baoshan Monastery is mainly a true replica of a timber-framed building, while the design of the Stone Temple of Amitābha has been infused with features from pagodas and mosques.

Fig. 5.19. Detail of Zhenguo Pagoda at Kaiyuan Monastery, Quanzhou, Fujian, 1238–1250. (Photo courtesy of Cai Yukun.)

These four examples of stone buildings can be categorized into three generic styles that accord with the structural characteristics of each building:[22]

1. Imitation-timber style, represented by Zhenqing Palace and the main hall of Baoshan Monastery, is characterized by the faithful representation of timber-framed architecture: stone pieces are prefabricated as different architectural members with mortise and tenon joints, and assembled together later. In both buildings, the beams, bracket sets, and many other characteristic features of timber-framed architecture were copied in stone. It seems, however, that the builders were not completely unaware of the nature of the new material. In fact, the builders also adapted the timber-framed architecture design to accommodate the stone. In Zhenqing Palace, the front wall is load-bearing; in the main hall of Baoshan Monastery, the builder used a bi-unit modular system to lessen the burden of the stone-frame roof structure.

2. Cave-temple style is represented by the Temple of Western Paradise of Jijian Monastery, a rock-cut building chiseled into the stone. This type

derives from the construction of Buddhist cave temples in China and India; the stone building was carved as a cave temple instead of being built as a timber-framed building. Typical timber members, especially load-bearing members, are no longer copied in stone. Although there is still visual representation of timber-framed architecture—such as the roof, columns, lintels—they are not "built" but "carved." Moreover, characteristic timber members, such as bracket sets and crescent-moon-shaped beams that have been found in stone buildings of the imitation-timber style, are not found in this type. The cave-temple style, though it retains the appearance of a timber-framed building, represents a technical departure from the tradition of timber-framed architecture in China and was in some sense influenced by Lamaist Buddhism.

3. Uni-storied-pagoda style, represented by the Stone Temple of Amitābha, defines a structure that is similar to a uni-storied pagoda but does not function as a pagoda. In terms of timber imitation, this style is between the imitation-timber style and the cave-temple style. The Stone Temple of Amitābha is an altered version of the stone pagoda of the Song dynasty with added influence from Islamic architecture.

The reason for choosing stone or copper over timber varied from case to case. In the main hall of Baoshan Monastery, lessons learned from earlier timber-framed buildings were adapted to the later stone building. It is probably for this reason that more durable and long-lasting projects to enshrine the deity, such as the Little Copper Hall and Zhenqing Palace at Mount Wudang, were possible. It also may be an intentional departure from the Chinese tradition of timber-framed architecture, such as in the case of the Temple of Western Paradise. Inspired by Buddhist caves, pagodas, and the exotic Islamic architecture, people in the Yuan dynasty began to accept the idea of building a worship space out of stone or copper.

The five cases introduced in this chapter present a diversity in architectural materials, spatial design, and construction method. The extant non-timber-framed Yuan architecture, mostly stone, was unique in the history of Chinese architecture, which mainly consisted of wooden constructions. The varieties of Yuan architecture exemplified in this chapter, with their different designs and stories, clearly footnote the religious diversity of the Yuan dynasty.

Yuan emperors primarily were patrons of Tibetan Buddhism. Khubilai Khan held to some of the primitive shamanic practices of the Mongols and later inclined toward Tibetan Buddhism. In the second half of the thirteenth century, Tibetan Buddhism received a great stimulus, and the succeeding Mongol emperors maintained the political supremacy of Tibetan Buddhism until 1368, the last year of the Yuan dynasty.[23]

Generally speaking, the Mongol rulers' own preference for Tibetan Buddhism did not interfere much with their endorsement of other practices. Ever since Chinggis Khan (r. 1206–1227), the Mongol rulers had been well known for their religious tolerance.[24] Evidence has shown that Buddhist monks, Christian priests, Daoist priests, and Muslim clerics all were exempt from tax duties or payment. Such a policy was believed to date back to the time of Chinggis Khan[25] and repeatedly appeared in decrees from the reigns of Khubilai Khan (r. 1260–1294) to the last Yuan ruler, Toghon Temür (r. 1333–1370).[26] Confucianism, though initially excluded from the policy during Chinggis Khan's time, was later granted somewhat similar privileges during the reign of Ögedei Khan (r. 1229–1241).[27] Although Jewish clergy rarely received the same privilege and state patronage, the practice of Judaism never was prohibited.[28] Admittedly, there was a brief reversal of this policy during the late stages of Khubilai Khan's reign when he tried to restrict the religious privileges of all religions except Tibetan Buddhism; his decrees were all revoked after his death.[29] The motive for allowing such diverse practices of Chinese and non-Chinese religions in the Yuan was certainly political—namely, to assure compliance from the native Chinese and, of equal importance, the non-native Muslims, Jews, and Christians (the Semu people) whom the Mongols had conquered and brought from Eurasia.

The diversity of religious practices, especially the non-Chinese ones, of the Yuan was evident in the architectural remains and textual records of Tibetan Buddhist temples, mosques, synagogues, and Christian churches that existed during the Yuan dynasty. Examples are the Miaoying Monastery 妙應寺 and its White Pagoda; a Tibetan Buddhist temple in Beijing;[30] the Mosque of the Companions in Quanzhou, Fujian province; the Kaifeng Synagogue in Kaifeng, Henan province;[31] and the Temple of the Cross 十字寺, a Christian church at Fangshan, Beijing.[32] As a handful of Yuan mosques survive, we have learned that the architectural form of the Yuan mosque was still original when compared to Islamic architecture. It was not yet as sinicized as it was in the Ming dynasty.[33]

Although this traditionally non-Chinese architecture was not the central subject of this chapter, the technology of constructing these "alien" non-timber-framed buildings influenced the Chinese. As shown here, the emergence of a number of non-timber-framed buildings in the Yuan probably was related to the imported influences of foreign architecture. New materials and new ideas then became more acceptable and possible to the native Chinese craftsmen.

Besides the cultural and religious influence from non-native sources, the non-timber-framed architecture introduced in this chapter also testifies to the availability of skilled stonemasons at that time. Although the names of the stonemasons who built these buildings are still unknown, the name of one Chinese stonemason was repeatedly mentioned in the historic literature of the Yuan dynasty. Yang Qiong 楊瓊, a Han Chinese, was a native of Quyang in modern Hebei province; he came from a family who had been in masonry for generations.[34] In 1260, Yang was summoned to serve Khubilai Khan due to his already established fame. He was known to have built numerous stone projects in Dadu, Shangdu, and Kaiping, including pavilions, baths, and gates. During the 1270s, Yang was a governmental official supervising offices and agencies related to masonry. Khubilai Khan himself conferred a title of nobility on him because of his outstanding performance and contributions.[35] Yang's example was used as evidence that "Khubilai Khan heavily relied on his stonemasons."[36] The masonry work done in his palace in Dadu was praised as "one of the best characteristics of the architecture."[37] Yang was favored by the emperor and attained high social status.

The reason Khubilai Khan relied on his stonemasons probably was his desire to build a luxurious palace. Zhu Qiqian (1871–1964) described that palace thusly:

> If we look at the layout [of the palace in Dadu], there is no mistake according to the ritual classics, which means if we compare the names of the palaces in Dadu to those in Bianliang (capital of the Northern Song), more than half are called by the same names. The difference is that the order [of palatial architecture] of the Song dynasty was simplistic. Even in the palatial city, people could appreciate the natural landscape of mountain and/or forest. While in the Yuan palace, only luxury and elaboration were favored. Every palace is splendid in green and gold. . . . This is where the Mongols are not completely sinicized.[38]

Therefore, masonry projects fulfilled the need for luxury, something not rooted in the Song architectural tradition.

The trend in Dadu might have influenced other places. As we can see from examples outside Dadu, stone architecture did become popular, and even Chinese building projects, such as the Daoist temple of Zhenqing Palace on Mount Wudang, were built in stone. Nevertheless, the non-timber-framed buildings of the Yuan dynasty do not suggest a revolution in Chinese architectural history. It is more probable that people built them to carry on older traditions. Even though they were using a nontraditional material, the architects of the Yuan period were still limited by the timber-imitation tradition that was dominant in non-timber monuments for a long time. In terms of stone technique, the Yuan buildings were likely to have been experimental. Judging from the non-timber-framed buildings discussed here, it seems that even during the Yuan there were no specific rules to follow; the craftsmen could choose whether to be faithful to timber models, to expand the idea of Buddhist caves, or to alter a stone pagoda.

CONCLUSION

In a broader context, Yuan architecture was the key to understanding the Song-to-Ming transition in architecture. That architecture retains all the architectural features related to pre-Yuan regimes such as the Northern Song, Southern Song, and Jin dynasties. When it comes to the Ming dynasty, a new dynastic style was formed on the basis of the remains of Yuan architecture. The new style was developed through a process of careful and deliberate selection in order to cater to two needs of the early Ming emperors: (1) to revive the regularity of Song/Chinese tradition, and (2) to economize on the costs of construction as much as possible.

As we further explored Yuan architecture on a regional level, we found different features from pre-Yuan regimes preserved in various regional traditions in the Yuan. In the region of north China, timber-framed buildings basically fell into two distinct styles—the conventional and the big-architrave—that were different in terms of the roof framing, the principles of the bearing system, and the artistic presentation. The conventional style, represented by Dening Hall of the Temple of the Northern Peak, is a continuum of Northern Song architecture, which resulted from Khubilai Khan's intention, probably on the advice of his Chinese counselors, to legitimize his sovereignty by constructing imperial architecture in an orthodox Chinese style, as he did in Dadu.

The big-architrave style, on the other hand, was a more organic development coping with the realities of the time: given the limited resources and devastated economy in north China, architecture had to adapt as well. The big-architrave style was revolutionary compared to the conventional style, including many simplifications and experimentations. The Lower Yangzi tradition was a continuation of the Song tradition in south China. It retains the regularity recorded by the YZFS and the "elegant appearance" often noted by modern scholars and used to describe Song architecture. The Upper Yangzi tradition, on the other hand, was unique: each building combined new features from the north, especially those that were developed fully during the Jin dynasty. In other words, the Upper Yangzi tradition was a hybrid of the conventional style and the big-architrave style in north China and likely incorporated the changes that had occurred since the Jin dynasty. In general, architecture in these three regions was quite diversified. Hardly any "dynastic style" or "official style" was observed.

The development of architecture follows a trajectory that runs parallel to the arts and crafts of the Yuan dynasty. In the introductory section of *The World of Khubilai Khan: Chinese Art in the Yuan Dynasty* (2010), James Watt presents two perspectives from which to view Chinese art. One is to observe its history as "a single, continuous line of development that revitalizes itself from time to time by going back to ancient models"; the other, as "a continual integration of cultural influence across borders into the mainstream of Chinese culture." Accordingly, Watt argues that the relatively short-lived Yuan dynasty represents the second perspective.[1] As for the convergence of various pre-Yuan cultural and artistic traditions, he notes that the arts of the Xixia (1038–1227), Liao (907–1125), and Jin (1115–1234) dynasties "were themselves all hybrids, and also strongly influenced by the culture of the Northern Song." As for the arts of the Southern Song, Watt notes that "they can be regarded as a continuum with those of the Northern Song."[2]

Based on Watt's theory, what is analogous between the architecture and arts of the Yuan dynasty is that both developed on the basis of the divided traditions of pre-Yuan regimes, and each distinctive tradition was more or less influenced by the Northern Song. Moreover, given the innovative usage of new building materials—stone and metal—and the adventurous and revolutionary timber-framed structures found in north China, Yuan architecture and arts did not merely go back to the ancient models, Watt's first perspective, but display a continual integration of cultural influence across borders that falls into Watt's second perspective.[3]

However, there were still differences between the architecture and arts of the Yuan. Watt calls the Yuan style in Chinese art "the result of the *amalgamation* of artistic traditions current in North and South China before the conquest of the Southern Song by the Mongols."[4] From a close study of Yuan architecture beyond the capital Dadu, it becomes evident that the architecture in general was neither an "amalgamation" nor "synthesized." Various regional traditions of Yuan demonstrate a coexistence of pre-Yuan traditions that were divided in the architecture.

The different trajectories taken by Yuan architecture and art were the result of the diverse natures of producing architecture and art. The architecture examined in this study has mainly been that of temples, shrines, and monasteries, as well as civic buildings. These were likely large projects that demanded more natural resources and manpower than do paintings and handicrafts. Further, designing and constructing a building were dependent on local resources and manpower. It was easier for local craftsmen to rely on the methods and techniques that were most familiar to them than to quickly adopt a new fashion, unless mandated by regulations. Therefore, the distinct timber structural designs of pre-Yuan regimes were not assimilated until the early Ming dynasty, when the construction of Nanjing and Beijing made it possible.

Probably on account of the nature of Chinese premodern architecture as an institutional tool that, ideally, was intended to conform to the order of a hierarchic Confucian society, the history of Chinese architecture is often discussed and labeled by dynasties. This has been an effective approach when enough consistency can be observed in the architectural remains, visual representations, or literal records. It is, however, a less effective approach for the study of Yuan architecture, extant examples of which demonstrate a lack of a "dynastic style" or an "official style" outside of Dadu. This may also suggest a lack of political authority, at least Chinese-style authority, over architecture beyond the capital, quite a unique and remarkable phenomenon in Chinese history considering that the Yuan was a unified empire.

In sum, the reasons behind the diversity of Yuan architecture vary. First, it resides in the division among the pre-Yuan regimes, Chinese and non-Chinese. Second, diversity arose from the foreign cultures and religions that entered China along with the Mongol conquerors. Last, the diversity in the refinement of architecture mirrored the unbalanced economic and political realities in different regions from the time of the Song-Yuan war through the Yuan. Here, architecture has served as a microcosm of the social and cultural changes that took place both before and during the Yuan.

APPENDIX
Glossary of Chinese Architectural Terms

Chinese	English	Note
ang 昂	inclined cantilever	Available in two types: downward cantilever (see *xia'ang*) and upward cantilever (see *shang'ang*); if not noted, always refers to downward cantilever
angting tiaowo 昂桯挑斡		Type of inclined cantilever that does not project toward the outside of the building, and its inner end is inclined upward to carry the lower purlin
angwei tiaowo 昂尾挑斡		Type of inclined cantilever that projects toward the outside of the building, and its inner end is inclined upward to carry the lower purlin; also known as *tiaogan* 挑桿 in Qing architecture
bajia chuanwu 八架椽屋	eight-rafter building	Building with a transverse span of eight rafters
ban 瓣	segment	Segment of a curved profile
bujian puzuo 補間鋪作	intercolumnar bracket set	Bracket sets that are built between the columns instead of atop columns; usually sit on top of the railing architrave (*lan'e*) and the flat architrave (*pupaifang*)
cai 材	(modular) unit	A *cai* is a modular unit recorded in the *YZFS* of the Northern Song; the measurement of a *cai* equals the sectional area of a single-unit (see *dancai*) bracket arm; there are eight grades of *cai* in accordance with architecture of different sizes and functions.
cai-fen zhi 材份制	*cai-fen* modular system	Modular system recorded in the *YZFS* and adopted in Song carpentry; *cai* is the major unit and *fen* is the sub-unit; 1 *cai* = 15 *fen*
cao 槽	trough	Structural frame composed of a row of columns

Chinese	English	Note
caofu 草栿	rough beam	Rafter beam with no decorative treatment
caojia 草架	rough roof framing	Roof framing above ceiling level with no decorative treatment
cejiao 側腳	batter	Column with a top leaning slightly inward and bottom outward
cha'ang 插昂	inserting cantilever	Structurally a projecting bracket but appears like a cantilever
chandu chuomu 蟬肚綽幕	cicada's abdomen joist	Curtain-mounting joist (see *chuomufang*) with its bottom profile shaped like a cicada's abdomen
chanlongzhu 纏龍柱	dragon column	"A column entwined by a sculptured dragon"[1]
chanzhuzao 纏柱造	wound-column built	Construction method used for multistory buildings, whereby each column of the upper story is set on a beam and is wound round by three capital blocks at each corner
chashou 叉手	forking-hand	Slanting struts used to support and stabilize the ridge purlin
chazhuzao 叉柱造	forking-column built	Construction method for multistory buildings, whereby each column of the upper story stands on the capital block of the lower story
chengchuanfang 承橡方	rafter bearer	Square purlin to support eave rafters
cheshang mingzao 徹上明造	exposed roof	"A roof frame without a ceiling in which beams, struts, purlins, and rafters are exposed from below; all members are planed smoothly and often artistically treated"[2]
chi 尺	Chinese feet	Unit of length; in the Song dynasty, one *chi* varied between 31.6 and 32.9 cm (Yuan *chi* is the same as Song *chi*)[3]
chonggong 重栱	double bracket	Double-tier bracket set, parallel to the elevation of a building and composed of a long bracket (see *mangong*) placed above a short bracket (see *guazigong*)
chuan 橡	rafter	

Chinese	English	Note
chuandou 穿斗	post-and-tie construction	Type of building structure with purlins resting directly on columns and with tie beams tying the columns together in the transverse direction
chuban 出瓣	outward petal	Convex segment of a profile (also see *ban*)
chuomufang 綽幕方	curtain- mounting joist	Short supporting timber for additional abutment of architraves, immediately under and parallel to an eave architrave (see *yan'e*), forerunner of *queti* (see *queti*).
cijian 次間	side bay	The bay next to the central bay
da'e 大額	big architrave	Lateral column-top tie beam parallel to the facade of the building; it supports the main load of the roof structure; it has to be considerably thicker than the railing architrave (*lan'e*)
da'efang 大額枋	big-architrave tie	Qing term; major architrave used in Ming-Qing architecture
da'eshi 大額式	big-architrave style	Building style that is identified by the usage of a big architrave
damuzuo 大木作	large-scale carpentry	Type of building work regarding cutting, shaping, and joining structural members, and framing buildings
dancai 單材	single-unit	Width of a bracket arm that is equal to one unit of *cai*
dangong 單栱	single bracket	Single bracket arm that is parallel to the elevation of a building
dangxinjian 當心間	central bay	Bay along the central axis of a building plane usually wider than the others
dianban 墊板	filler board	Board used to fill between a purlin and a tie beam or between beams; Qing term
diange 殿阁	palatial style	Type of timber structure in Song architecture; from bottom to top, it consists of three parts: uni-height columniation, a bracketing layer, and a roof frame; its columns are arranged in a certain pattern of trough (see *cao*)

Chinese	English	Note
dingfu 丁栿	T-beam	Beam spanning between gable and interior columns; it intersects a transverse beam forming a T-shaped plan; supports the gable structure of a gable-on-hip roof or a hip roof[4]
dingtougong 丁頭栱	T-bracket	Half-projecting bracket, with its tenon at the rear, mortised into a column
dou 枓	bearing block	Block in a bracket set with an opening in either one way or both ways to receive brackets above
dougong 枓栱	bracket set	Qing's equivalent term to *puzuo* (see *puzuo*)
doukoutiao 枓口跳	block-mouth tier	Connection between a column and a beam wherein the projecting end of the beam is made as a half-projecting bracket received by a capital block on top of the column
e'jiaodou 訛角斗	rounded-off block	Capital block with rounded-off angles
er 耳	ear (of block)	Upper part of a block with an opening cut either one way or both ways to receive brackets above; also known as the "ear of block" (*dou'er*枓耳)
fang 方	lintel	Horizontal structural member under and parallel to purlins
fen 份		Subsidiary modular unit; 15 *fen* = 1 *cai*
fu 栿	transversal beam	Beam laid perpendicular to the longitudinal side of a building
fubigong 扶壁栱	buttress-bracket	Longitudinal frame of a bracket set directly above a row of columns that is composed of lintels, brackets, and blocks, with various configurations
fulian 覆蓮	upside-down lotus	Carving of downward lotus petals; also known as *pudi lianhua* 鋪地蓮華
fupen 覆盆	overturned bowl	Ovolo molding, the upper part of a stone column base shaped as an overturned bowl, sometimes enriched with upside-down lotus or other decorative patterns
gong 栱	(bow-shaped) bracket arm	Major component of bracket sets; either perpendicular to the wall plane (see *huagong*) or parallel to it (see *guazigong, mangong, linggong*, etc.)

Chinese	English	Note
guazigong 瓜子栱	short bracket	Shortest bracket in a bracket set, parallel to the elevation of a building; it is usually beneath a long bracket (see *mangong*) in a double-bracket structure
heta 合踏	foot bearer[5]	Two plain blocks that support the king post
huagong 華栱	projecting bracket	Bracket placed at a right angle to the elevation of a building
huatouzi 華頭子	bracket arm with two-scroll profile	Variety of projecting bracket with a two-scroll profile projecting from a block to support a downward cantilever
jia'ang 假昂	pseudo-cantilever	Qing equivalent to *cha'ang* (see *cha'ang*)
jian 間	bay	Basic spatial unit defined by four columns
jianzhuzao 減柱造	eliminated-column structure	Structure used in a mansion-style building comprising two or three different structural frames so that the columns are placed without strict symmetry, and some columns are eliminated
jiaohudou 交互枓	cross block	Block in a bracket set placed on top of a projecting bracket or an inclined cantilever
jiaozhu 角柱	corner column	Column placed at the corner of a timber structure
jinjian 盡間	end bay	Corner bay of a building
jituan 脊槫	ridge purlin	Purlin on top of a roof frame
jixinzao 計心造	crisscross-heart structure	Use of either a double bracket or a single bracket added above a projecting bracket
juansha 卷殺	entasis	"An artistic treatment of rounding off the ends of a bracket, beam, or tapered column to create an elliptic or convex profile"[6]
juetou 爵頭	locust head	Overhanging bracket-end; the topmost member parallel to and above projecting bracket and inclined cantilever; also called *shuatou* 耍頭

Chinese	English	Note
jugao 舉高	raising roof	Method of determining the height of the ridge
juzhe 舉折	folding roof	Method of determining the roof curve
lan'e 闌額	railing architrave	Major beam spanning between eave columns; it is as wide as the facade of the building, and its ends do not project beyond the eave columns
liangchuanfu 兩椽栿	two-rafter beam	Beam with a span of two rafters
lianzhudou 連珠枓	piled blocks	Two blocks piled to sit on a projecting bracket to support an upward cantilever above
liaoyanfang 撩檐方	square eave purlin	Eave purlin square in section
linggong 令栱	outermost bracket	Outermost bracket arm in a bracket set parallel to a building elevation
litiao 裏跳	inner projection	Part of a bracket set that projects from the center line of columns toward the interior
liuchuanfu 六椽栿	six-rafter beam	Beam that has a span of six rafters
liujia chuanwu 六架椽屋	six-rafter building	Building with a transverse span of six rafters
ludou 櫨枓	capital block	Big block in the shape of a column capital to support a bracket set above
mangong 慢栱	long bracket	Longer bracket used in a double bracket; placed above a short bracket (see *guazigong*)
mantangzhu 满堂柱	full-house column style	Style used in a mansion-style building by placing columns on each crossing of the axes of colonnade
mingfu 明栿	exposed beam	Main beam visible inside a building; artistically finished and usually in a slightly arched shape
mingjian 明間	central bay	Qing equivalent term of *dangxinjian*
nidaogong 泥道栱	short bracket arm	Short bracket arm parallel to the elevation of the building on a capital block and cross fixed with a projecting bracket

Chinese	English	Note
niujituan 牛脊槫	buffalo-spine purlin	Purlin placed directly above the center line of the row of eave columns
panjian 襻間	straining tie	Purlin tie allocated for every other bay to hold a purlin; usually each end is trimmed as a half-bracket
ping 平	flat	Middle part of a block
ping'an 平闇	plain lattice ceiling	Ceiling composed of a small, square, grid framework covered by thin plates, neither painted nor decorated
pingbanfang 平板枋	flat architrave	Qing equivalent term to *pupaifang* (see *pupaifang*)
pingliang 平梁	upmost beam	Uppermost beam of a roof frame, two rafters in length, that supports a dwarf pillar on its center to hold a ridge purlin above
pingqi 平棊	decorated lattice ceiling	Ceiling composed of a square, grid framework; square grid of *pingqi* is much larger than those of *ping'an*
pingqifang 平棊方	ceiling joist	One of a pair of beams to support a ceiling above
pupaifang 普拍方	flat architrave	Flat beam resting directly on top of the eave columns
puzuo 鋪作	(layers of) bracket sets	Interface between vertical members (such as columns and pillars) and horizontal members (such as beams, architraves, and tie beams); mainly are composed of bracket arm and blocks. In the *YZFS*, *puzuo* is numbered by the layers of its horizontal members. The smallest *puzuo* that has only one projecting bracket (*huagong* 華栱) is numbered four. The more projecting brackets it has, the higher the number (also see *dou* and *gong*)
qi 敧	apophyge	Lower inclined part of a block; also pronounced *yi*
qixindou 齊心枓	central block	Block placed at the center of a bracket
queti 雀替	sparrow brace	Bracket-like timber used to support a column and beam joint; Qing term

Chinese	English	Note
rufu 乳栿	two-rafter eaves beam	Two-rafter beam with its outer end laid on the bracket set of an eave column and its inner end on the set of an interior column or tenoned into the column
sanchuanfu 三椽栿	three-rafter beam	Beam that has a span of three rafters
sandou 散枓	end block	Block placed on each end of a bracket that is parallel to the elevation of a building
shang'ang 上昂	upward cantilever	Transverse arm of a bracket set projecting from the first step of the inner projection with its head raised to adjust the height of the bracket set
shangpingtuan 上平榑	upper purlin	Purlin next to the ridge purlin
shanmen 山門	gatehouse	Gate of a Buddhist or Daoist temple
shanzhu 山柱	gable column	Column at the center of a gable that supports the ridge; Qing term
shaojian 稍間	next-to-the end bay	Bay next to the end bay in a building with seven or more bays
shengqi 生起	raising-up	When the height of both interior and perimeter columns slightly and gradually increases from the center bay of a building toward the corners. The number of bays determines the increasing height for the corner column.
shipaigong 實拍栱	immediate bracket	Projecting bracket immediately below a lintel or another projecting bracket without any bearing block in between
shoufen 收分	batter	Inclined from the vertical as in a walling construction; it is so constructed that its thickness is gradually decreased with its height.
shunfuchuan 順栿串	along-beam tie	Horizontal timber connecting a pair of columns; located below and parallel to the main beam to provide additional resistance to the movement of columns
shunjichuan 順脊串	along-ridge tie	Tie beam below the ridge purlin to reinforce the roof frame

Chinese	English	Note
shunshenchuan 順身串	along-purlin tie	Structural member of wood connecting two columns under the middle or lower purlin
shuzhu 蜀柱	dwarf pillar	Vertical strut situated on a beam to support a ridge or a purlin
sichuanfu 四椽栿	four-rafter beam	Beam that has a span of four rafters
sijia chuanwu 四架椽屋	four-rafter building	Building with a transverse span of four rafters
sufang 素方	plain beam	Collective name for long timber beams used in a bracket-set unit
sufupen 素覆盆	plain overturned bowl	Overturned bowl with no decoration
suozhu 梭柱	shuttle-shaped column	Tapered column with a slightly convex curving profile, usually only at the upper third of the shaft
tailiang 抬梁	lifting beams	Type of building structure characterized by the placement of beams on columns repeatedly until a ridge is formed
tatou 楂头	cut-off timber end	End of a rectangular timber cut off diagonally and further trimmed into a folding line
tiao 跳	step	Any overhanging member in a bracket set, either a bracket arm or an inclined cantilever, transversally projecting from a capital block is considered one step.
timu 替木	wooden strip	"A bracket-like timber used to hold two abutted purlins together, or to provide support to the end of a purlin"[7]
tingtang 廳堂	mansion style	Type of building that is smaller in size and lower in rank than the palatial style, does not have a layer of bracket sets but may have bracket sets. The building is formed by parallel transverse frameworks connected by longitudinal purlins and ties.
touxinzao 偷心造	stolen-heart structure	In all brackets, only transverse members are used, without any bracket parallel to the elevation of the building; literally "stolen-heart."

Chinese	English	Note
tuofeng 駝峰	camel hump	Solid block or plank curved at the top in the shape of a camel's hump, placed above a beam to receive the end of a higher-level beam
tuojiao 托腳	support footing	Inclined strut resting on the end of a beam to support and strengthen a purlin above
waitiao 外跳	outward projecting	Part of a bracket set projecting toward the outside from the central line of eave columns
wuchuanfu 五椽栿	five-rafter beam	Beam with a span of five rafters
wunei'e 屋內額	interior architrave	Beam that spans between adjacent interior columns with its ends inserted into the columns, or resting directly upon a camel hump (see *tuofeng*)
wuneizhu 屋內柱	interior column	Columns situated inside a building, to the eave columns
xia'ang 下昂	downward cantilever	Transverse arm of a bracket set, of which the head is inclined down toward the outside and its tails up against the bottom of a lower purlin to adjust the slope and increase the projection length of the eaves; usually just called *ang*
xianglun 相輪	transmigration wheel	Number of tiers of wheel-like elements in the middle part of a pagoda finial, usually thirteen tiers
xiao'efang 小額方	small-architrave tie	Qing equivalent term of *you'e* (also see *you'e*)
xiaomuzuo 小木作	small-scale carpentry	One of thirteen types of building work specified in the *YZFS* that include internal furnishing, external joinery, minor carpentry, and gigantic furniture
xiapingtuan 下平槫	lower purlin	Purlin next to the purlin along the line of eave columns
xiefu 斜栿	diagonal beam	Diagonal strut connecting the purlins
xiegong 斜栱	oblique arm	Oblique projecting bracket of a 45° or 30° angle
xuanshan 悬山	overhanging-gable roof	Two-sloped roof projecting beyond the gable walls at both ends; Qing term; also known in Song as *busha liangtouzao* 不厦两头造

Chinese	English	Note
xuexie 鞾楔	boot-shaped wedge	Wedge as a transitional member to hold an upward cantilever
yacaofang 壓槽方	axial beam	Horizontal beam at the bottom of a roof frame, and right over the eave columns and the bracket sets
yan'e 檐額	eave architrave	Architrave similar to a railing architrave (*lan'e*) that spans eave columns; thicker than a railing architrave, its ends project beyond the eave columns
yanzhu 檐柱	eave column	Columns right under the eave
yatiao 壓跳	press-projection	If the inner part of a projecting bracket is trimmed into a folding line (see *tatou*) instead of a regular bracket to support a beam in a capital bracket set, it is called *yatiao*.
yixinggong 翼形栱	wing-shaped bracket	Decorative bracket parallel to the elevation of the building
yizhuzao 移柱造	displaced-column structure	Style used in a mansion-style building by comprising two or three different structural frames so that the columns are placed without strict symmetry, and some columns are displaced
yongdingzhu 永定柱	permanent-column	Columns rising from the ground to support the upper structure in a multistory building
you'e 由額	associate architrave	Subsidiary beam, situated at a proper height under a railing architrave (*lan'e*)
yueliang 月梁	crescent-moon-shaped-beam	Type of artistically crafted beam with both its top and bottom profiles curved slightly downward
zaojing 藻井	coffer	Decorated and recessed ceiling
zhaqian 劄牽	one-rafter beam	Beam spanning one rafter, its outer end supporting a purlin and its inner end mortised into a column
zhi 栔	subsidiary module	Subsidiary modular unit; 1 *zhi* = 6 *fen*
zhiliang 直梁	straight beam	Beam with flat surfaces

Chinese	English	Note
zhongpingtuan 中平槫	middle purlin	All purlins between the lower and the upper purlins
zhuchu 柱礎	column base	Plinth; a square stone base for a column; its lower part is buried in the platform and the upper part exposed and decorated
zhuliangshi 柱梁式	column-and-beam-style	Timber structure consisting of only columns and beams, without any bracket set
zhutou puzuo 柱頭鋪作	capital bracket set	Bracket set atop a column
zhuzhi 柱櫍	column foot	Round wooden molding separating the column shaft from its stone base; by the time of the YZFS, made of stone instead of wood
zucai 足材	full-unit	Measurement of the width of a bracket arm that is equal to one unit of *cai* plus one unit of *zhi*

NOTES

INTRODUCTION

1 Jiren Feng, *Chinese Architecture and Metaphor*, 26.

2 The *Yingshanling* is an official document enacted during the Kaiyuan 開元 reign (713–741) of the Tang dyansty. The original document no long exists. Excerpts of the *Yingshanling* are found in annotations and citations of other works from the Tang, Song, and Yuan dynasties. By citing an excerpt discovered in *Tang huiyao* 唐會要, an early Song book on important documents of the Tang dynasty, Jiren Feng indicates that the *Yingshanling*, "for the first time in Chinese architectural literature," shows the association between "almost every aspect of the Chinese architectural systyem" and the status of the owner of the building. For more discussion on the *Yingshanling*, see Jiren Feng, *Chinese Architecture and Metaphor*, 54–59.

3 The *YZFS* is the oldest and most complete extant textual record of Chinese architecture and building techniques published during the Northern Song. Unless otherwise noted, all terms used in this book to describe Yuan architecture are the Song dynasty ones used in the *YZFS*. For studies on the *YZFS*, see Qinghua Guo, "*Yingzao fashi*: The Twelfth Century Chinese Building Manual," and J. Feng, *Chinese Architecture and Metaphor*. Also, see chapter 1 for more discussion on the *YZFS*.

4 Jiren Feng, *Chinese Architecture and Metaphor*, 29.

5 Steinhardt, "Standard Architecture in a Multi-centered, Multi-cultural Age," 60.

6 According to an imperial edict recorded in *juan* 47 of *Yuanshi* (The history of Yuan), it is said, "The empire is named 'grand *yuan*,' referring to the term, *qianyuan*, from the *I ching*." (The original text reads 可建國號曰大元, 盖取易經 "乾元" 之義; see *Yuanshi*, *juan* 47, 138). The *I ching* (The book of changes) is a divination text of ancient China. *Qian* 乾 is the name of hexagram 1 in the *I ching* and means heaven, while *yuan* means the primal or the origin. For more details of the *I ching*, see Nielsen, *A Companion to Yi jing Numerology and Cosmology*.

7 Steinhardt, "Towards the Definition of a Yuan Dynasty Hall," 58.

8 See Zhu and Kan, "Yuan Dadu gongyuan tukao," 98, and more discussion in chapter 5.

9 "Yuan architecture" here means architecture that was built during the Yuan dynasty (1271–1368) and in the territory of Khubilai Khan's empire of Yuan. Most examples of architecture discussed in this book were built by the Han-Chinese and in the areas previously occupied by the Song dynasty. "Yuan architecture" discussed here still is considered part of "Chinese architecture." Architecture such as Lama temples, mosques, and synagogues that was not attached to the Han-Chinese tradition, will not be covered in this book in detail.

10 Both Song and Ming architecture had international influence in Japan and Korea. Architecture of *Zenshōyō* 禅宗様 and *Ōbakuyō* 黄檗様 in Japan is known to

have prototypes in Song and Ming architecture respectively. Influence of Yuan architecture, however, has not yet been found in Japan or Korea. This probably is due to the Mongols' destructive subjugation of Korea and, later, the invasion of Japan in the late thirteenth century when they demanded that Korea provide them with assistance; see Rossabi, "The Reign of Khubilai Khan," 436–442. More likely, the absence of a dynastic style in Yuan architecture itself also explains the death of international influence.

11 Steinhardt's articles "The Plan of Khubilai Khan's Imperial City" (1983) and "Imperial Architecture along the Mongolian Road to Dadu" (1988) respectively survey the course of the construction of Shangdu, Dadu, and other imperial projects by Mongol conquerors. Another article by Cary Liu, "The Yüan Dynasty Capital, Ta-tu: Imperial Building Program and Bureaucracy" (1992), discusses the bureaucratic system and the people involved in constructing Dadu. Chen Gaohua's monograph on Yuan capital studies, *Yuandai Dadu Shangdu yanjiu* 元代大都上都研究 (1982), originally in Chinese, was recently translated into English and published as *The Capital of the Yuan Dynasty* (2014).

12 See Fu's reconstruction in "Yuan Dadu danei gongdian de fuyuan yanjiu," 326–356.

13 The phrase "architectural style" is translated from the Chinese term *jianzhu xingshi* 建築形式. *Jianzhu* is "architecture" and *xingshi* is "form" or "style." When the term *jianzhu xingshi* is used in scholarly writings on traditional Chinese architecture, it often refers to a collection of features in architecture, including the timber-framed structure, the proportion and dimension of the building, the plan configuration, and sometimes the nonstructural part, such as decorations and small carpentry.

14 Fu Xinian, "Yuan Dadu danei gongdian de fuyuan yanjiu," 327.

15 Steinhardt, "Temple to the North Peak," 72.

16 A recent article on Yuan timber structure as a transitional stage between Song and Qing was written by Zhao Xiangdong and published in 2013. This article focuses on two examples of Yuan buildings in Zhengding, Hebei province. See Zhao Xiangdong. "Chengqi bianyi," 124–128.

17 Unless noted otherwise, the line drawings of plans, elevations, sectional views, and enlarged details of the buildings are by the author. Most measured line drawings are reproduced by the author using computer-aided design (CAD) software based on drawings and measurements provided by the administrators of respective buildings. Some of the early drawings were produced decades ago, and others are flawed. Therefore, the drawings were corrected on the computer whenever necessary, and the measurements of these buildings in the drawings are believed to be accurate. For some line drawings, if there is no scale, that means it is only a sketch rather than a measured drawing and merely indicates the composition of the members, not the real measurements.

CHAPTER 1: YUAN ARCHITECTURE

1 Liang, *Chinese Architecture*, 72.
2 Liang, *Chinese Architecture*, 103.
3 Fu et al., *Chinese Architecture*, p. 136.
4 Liang, *Chinese Architecture*, 103.
5 Yang Zirong, "Lun Shanxi Yuandai yiqian mugou jianzhu de baohu," 62.

6 Zhongguo guojia wenwuju, "Diqipi quanguo zhongdian wenwu baohu danwei mingdan" (2013).

7 The four Northern Song buildings are the main hall of Hualin Monastery 華林寺大殿 in Fuzhou, Fujian province, dated to 964; the Daxiongbao Hall of Mei Nunnery 梅庵大雄寶殿 in Zhaoqing, Guangdong province, dated to 996; the main hall of Baoguo Monastery 保國寺大殿 in Ningbo, Zhejiang province, dated to 1013; and the Sanqing Hall of Yuanmiao Daoist Temple 元妙觀三清殿 in Putian, Fujian province, dated to 1015. The three Southern Song buildings are the Sanqing Hall of Xuanmiao Daoist Temple 玄妙觀三清殿 in Suzhou, Jiangsu province, dated to 1179; the main hall of Guangxiao Monastery 光孝寺大殿 in Guangzhou, Guangdong, dated to 1241–1252; and the Feitianzang Hall of Yunyan Monastery 雲巖寺飛天藏殿 in Jiangyou, Sichuan province.

8 Guo Qinghua, "*Yingzao fashi*," 5.

9 Pan Guxi and He Jianzhong, *Yingzao fashi jiedu*, 2.

10 Guo Qinghua, "*Yingzao fashi*," 3.

11 For more about Wang Anshi's reform, see James T. C. Liu, *Reform in Sung China: Wang An-Shih (1021–1086) and His New Policies* (1950).

12 Pan Guxi and He Jianzhong, *Yingzao fashi jiedu*, 2.

13 J. Feng, *Chinese Architecture and Metaphor*, 106.

14 J. Feng, *Chinese Architecture and Metaphor*, 137.

15 J. Feng, *Chinese Architecture and Metaphor*, 14.

16 See Pan Guxi and He Jianzhong, *Yingzao fashi jiedu*, p. 5. For a discussion about the *Mujing*, see J. Feng, *Chinese Architecture and Metaphor*, 61–75.

17 Needham et al., *Science and Civilisation in China*, 82.

18 Guo Daiheng, *Zhongguo gudai jianzhushi*, 3:753.

19 The Moni Hall of Longxing Monastery is dated to 1052. The building has a square plan with four porches extended on each side. It has a hip-and-gable roof with two layers of eaves. Moreover, each porch was built with a hip-and-gable roof, which rendered the building with multilayers of eaves that form a contour of variations.

20 According to the *YZFS*, the arrangement of columns in a palatial-style building should be in accordance with the regulation of *cao* (trough), and no column should be skipped or displaced. Compared to a standard *cao*, if a number of columns are skipped, such a design is called the "eliminated-column structure"; if a number of columns are displaced, such a design is called the "displaced-column structure."

21 The Sage Mother Hall is a finely built timber building dated to 1102, the first year of Chongning reign of the Northern Song. It is located at the Jin Shrine near Taiyuan, Shanxi. For a monographic study, see Miller, *The Divine Nature of Power Chinese Ritual Architecture at the Sacred Site of Jinci* (2007).

22 The Amitābha Hall of Chongfu Monastery is dated to 1143, Huangtong 皇統 reign of the Jin dynasty. For a monographic study on Chongfu Monastery, see Chai Zejun, *Shuozhou chongfusi* (2000).

23 The so-called trough means a certain array of columns. The four types of trough (*cao* 槽) are *shennei fenxin doudicao* 身內分心斗底槽, *shennei dancao* 身內單槽, *shennei shuangcao* 身內雙槽, and *jinxiang doudicao* 金箱斗底槽. All four types are designed for large buildings.

24 Wang Yuan, "Zhongguo de fodian jianzhu yu foxiang," 90.

25 Both the Great East Hall of Foguang Monastery and the Amitābha Hall of Chongfu Monastery have seven bays. The Great East Hall is 34 m wide and the Amitābha Hall is around 40 m wide.

26 Wright, *Buddhism in Chinese History*, 96–98.

27 The palatial style and the mansion style are described in the *YZFS* as two theoretical types of timber-frame buildings. Nevertheless, there are more varieties in reality than the author of the *YZFS* could ever have predicted. Modern scholars such as Chen Mingda and Zhang Shiqing tried to develop the theory and attempted to define a new style that was in between the palatial style and the mansion style. Chen Mingda calls this in between style "Fengguo Monastery style 奉國寺式," a style represented by the main hall of Fengguo Monastery, dated 1019. Based on his research on timber buildings in the Lower Yangzi, Zhang Shiqing names the in-between one "mansion structure of palatial style" (*dianshi tingtang zao* 殿式廳堂造). Furthermore, Chen's in-between style was not exactly the same as Zhang Shiqing's. See more discussion on this issue in chapter 2.

28 1 *cun* = 3.2 cm.

29 Pan Guxi and He Jianzhong, *Yingzao fashi jiedu*, 53.

30 Pan Guxi and He Jianzhong, *Yingzao fashi jiedu*, 50.

31 Pan Guxi and He Jianzhong, *Yingzao fashi jiedu*, 83.

32 Fu Xinian, *Fu Xinian jianzhushi lunwenji*, 104.

33 Liang, *Chinese Architecture*, 21.

34 For more information about Liao architecture, see Steinhardt, *Liao Architecture* (1997).

35 Steinhardt, "A Jin Hall at Jingtusi," 108.

36 Wang Qiheng, "Jin ke *Chong jiaozheng dili xinshu*," 4.

37 Liang, *Chinese Architecture*, 103.

38 Guo Huayu, *Mingdai guanshi jianzhu damuzuo*, preface.

39 Pan Guxi, *Zhongguo gudai jianzhushi*, 4:428.

40 For an annotated list of important Ming buildings, see Guo Huayu, *Mingdai guanshi jianzhu damuzuo*, 190–201.

41 Pan Guxi, *Zhongguo gudai jianzhushi*, 4:428.

42 Pan Guxi, *Zhongguo gudai jianzhushi*, 4:236.

43 Guo Huayu, *Mingdai guanshi jianzhu damuzuo*, 1.

44 Ruitenbeek, *Carpentry and Building in Late Imperial China*, 7.

45 See J. Feng, *Chinese Architecture and Metaphor*, 54. Although the excerpt that Feng used in his book concerns only "the residences of princes and dukes and those whose ranks are lower" (Feng 2012, 55), it does not mean that those rules applied only to domestic architecture. The residences of princes and dukes and those who have (lower) official ranks are equivalent to the imperial palaces of the emperor. As these so-called residences are associated with official ranks, they are certainly part of the official architecture system. In other words, the excerpt of the *Yingshanling* shows a general rule about the buildings that were supervised by the court. Zhang Shiqing also indicates that the (same) excerpt from the *Yingshanling* about *zhaidi* 宅第 (residence) was in fact about social hierarchy as represented by architecture (Zhang Shiqing 2010, 144). In addition, the excerpt indicates that decorative features, such as tile decorations, are also related to the official ranks. Similar to the *YZFS* as a court-enforced building code, the *Yingshanling* also did not mention any regional variations.

46 See Guo Qinghua, "*Yingzao fashi*," 1. We have not yet found any documentation from extant literature on Chinese architecture to suggest in particular that the rank of a divinity would have an impact on the size/details of religious architecture. In many cases, the size and the design of a temple is related to the official rank of the patron(s) of the temple.

47 Guo Huayu, *Mingdai guanshi jianzhu damuzuo*, 19.

48 Guo Huayu, *Mingdai guanshi jianzhu damuzuo*, 14.

49 Guo Huayu, *Mingdai guanshi jianzhu damuzuo*, 16.

50 Guo Huayu, *Mingdai guanshi jianzhu damuzuo*, 11.

51 Guo Huayu, *Mingdai guanshi jianzhu damuzuo*, 173.

52 Guo Huayu, *Mingdai guanshi jianzhu damuzuo*, 52.

53 Guo Huayu, *Mingdai guanshi jianzhu damuzuo*, 25.

54 Guo Huayu, *Mingdai guanshi jianzhu damuzuo*, 40.

55 Guo Huayu, *Mingdai guanshi jianzhu damuzuo*, 45.

56 The so-called camel hump is a solid block or plank curved at the top in the shape of a camel hump. It is placed above a beam to receive the end of a higher-level beam.

57 The flat architrave (*pupaifang*) is mentioned in the YZFS only with the entry of the balcony substructure (*pingzuo* 平坐); see *juan* 4 of the YZFS. For a modern citation, see Liang Sicheng, *Liang Sicheng quanji*, 7:116. Therefore, the flat architrave is not a standard column-top tie beam.

58 Guo Huayu, *Mingdai guanshi jianzhu damuzuo*, 175.

59 Zhang Yuhuan, "Shanxi Yuandai diantang de damu jiegou," 89.

60 Liang Sicheng, *Liang Sicheng quanji*, 7:135.

61 Pan Guxi and He Jianzhong, *Yingzao fashi jiedu*, 72.

62 Pan Guxi and He Jianzhong, *Yingzao fashi jiedu*, 73.

63 The measurements are from Guo Daiheng, *Donglai diyishan*, 84. There are two standards of *cai* in the main hall of Baoguo Monastery. The larger one, used for regular bracket sets, measures 21.75 cm, and the smaller one, used for bracket sets in the coffer (*zaojing* 藻井) measures 17 cm (Guo Daiheng 2003, 88) I use the smaller one as the railing architrave would measure exactly 2C. Either way, the ratio between the railing architrave and the eave architrave matched the YZFS.

64 Sichuansheng wenwu kaogu yanjiuyuan, *Huaying Anbing mu*, 153.

65 See chapter 2 for more discussions on local features of Yuan buildings in Sichuan. See chapter 3 for a detailed study about Feilai Hall in the Temple of the Eastern Peak.

66 Wang, "Shanxi Dingxiang Guanwangmiao kaocha zhaji," 26. The main hall of Guanwang Temple is a small Yuan building of three bays' width. It is located at Dingxiang, a county not far from Mount Wutai.

67 Guo Huayu, *Mingdai guanshi jianzhu damuzuo*, 173.

68 Liang, *Chinese Architecture*, 103.

69 The definition and function of the "big-architrave-style" will be discussed with details in the next chapter.

70 Oblique arm is found often in nonofficial Ming architecture outside the capital and, in rare cases, in official projects that might have been influenced by the local tradition, such as the complex of Bao'ensi in Pingwu, Sichuan province.

71 The oldest extant oblique arm discovered so far is at the middle hall (*zhongdian*) of South Jixiang Monastery 南吉祥寺 dated to 1023–1031, in Linchuan, Shanxi province. It became very popular, however, during the Jin dynasty in the modern provinces of Shanxi and Hebei. The oblique arm also is considered a signature of Jin architecture due to its popularity during the Jin dynasty. See more discussion on this topic in Harrer, "Fan-Shaped Bracket Sets and Their Application in Religious Timber Architecture of Shanxi Province" (2010).

72 Guo Huayu, *Mingdai guanshi jianzhu damuzuo*, 157.

73 Pan Guxi, *Zhongguo gudai jianzhushi*, 4:438.

74 *Mingshi, juan* 59, pp. 1455, 1470.

75 *Mingshi, juan* 68, p. 1667. The original quote reads: 敦崇儉樸, 猶恐習於奢華, 爾乃導予奢麗乎？

CHAPTER 2: REGIONAL TRADITIONS

1 Pan Guxi, *Zhongguo gudai jianzhushi,* 4:428.

2 Nine out of ten buildings studied in the Upper Yangzi region are located in today's Sichuan province, and all were within the Sichuan Xingsheng 四川行省 (Sichuan Branch Secretariat) during the Yuan dynasty.

3 The Lower Yangzi region customarily is called Jiangnan. "Jiangnan" is not only a geographical term but also represents a specific culture in Chinese history and today. In a narrow sense, "Jiangnan" culturally means the Lower Yangzi delta, including Zhejiang province, south Jiangsu and Anhui provinces, and the metropolis of Shanghai.

4 Yongle Palace is currently located in Yuncheng, Shanxi province. It is a major Yuan Daoist monastery related to the Quanzhen sect 全真教. It is significant not only for its well-preserved Yuan architecture but also for its precious Daoist wall paintings. For architecture of Yongle Palace, see Du Xianzhou, "Yonglegong de jianzhu" (1963).

5 The complex of Guangsheng Monastery, including Upper Guangsheng Monastery 上廣勝寺, Lower Guangsheng Monastery 下廣勝寺, and Shuishen (Water God) Temple 水神廟, is located in Hongdong County in south Shanxi province. For a complete study of Guangsheng Monastery, see Chai and Ren, *Hongdong Guangshengsi* (2006).

6 The Society was founded by Zhu Qiqian 朱啓鈐, a retired official of the Beiyang Government, in July 1930. It was the first modern entity that investigated and studied historic sites and monuments in China. Although it was a small and privately funded organization, the Society and its major publication, *Zhongguo yingzao xueshe huikan* 中國營造學社彙刊, the *Bulletin of the Society for Research in Chinese Architecture,* are recognized as the cornerstone of modern scholarship on Chinese architectural history, with many valuable publications and prestigious core members.

7 Zhang Yuhuan, "Shanxi Yuandai diantang de damu jiegou," 72.

8 Zhang Yuhuan, "Shanxi Yuandai diantang de damu jiegou," 72.

9 The only two comprehensive studies on regional traditions of Yuan architecture in north China that the author has found so far are two master's theses in Chinese: one by Liu Rui on Yuan timber architecture in Shaanxi province, published in 2009, and one by Qu Yuxuan on Yuan architecture in the southeast Shanxi province, published in 2014. See Liu Rui, "Shanxi Yuandai jianzhu," and Qu Yuxuan, "Song Jin jianzhu yingzao jishu."

10 "Rectangular plan" hereafter suggests a plan with a distinct length and width of different sizes; while, on the other hand, "squarish plan" indicates a rectangular plan with four equal or near-equal sides.

11 Mingyingwang Hall, dated to the second year of Yanyou 延祐 reign (1315), is the main building of Shuishen Temple in Guangsheng Monastery. It is well known for its Yuan wall paintings; see Chai Zejun and Ren Yimin, *Hongdong guangshengsi,* 68. The main hall of Erlang Temple is located at Pingyao, Shanxi. The main hall of

Longtian Temple is dated to the sixth year of Yanyou 延祐 reign (1319) of the Yuan dynasty. It is located at Jiexiu County, Shanxi. See Zhang Yuhuan, "Shanxi Yuandai diantang de damu jiegou," 81.

12 Guangji Monastery is located at the county seat of Wutai, Shanxi province. Only the main hall was built in the Yuan dynasty.

13 According to Zhang Yuhuan, both the eliminated-column structure and the displaced-column structure originated during the Song, Liao, and Jin periods but did not become popular until the Yuan dynasty, especially in north China; see Zhang Yuhuan, "Shanxi Yuandai diantang de damu jiegou," 86–87. Pan Guxi also verifies that the eliminated-column structure and the displaced-column structure were developed fully during the Yuan in the north; see Pan Guxi, *Zhongguo gudai jianzhushi,* 4:345.

14 For a monographic study on Yanshan Monastery, see Chai Zejun, *Fanshi Yanshansi* (1990).

15 Chuanfa Zhengzong Hall of Yong'an Monastery, located in Hunyuan 渾源 of northern Shanxi, is a large-scale Yuan building. Its facade is five bays wide, its side three bays wide.

16 Zhang Yuhuan, "Shanxi Yuandai diantang de damu jiegou," 99. A personal comment made by Alexandria Harrar suggests that the wing-shaped bracket is a feature that was inherited from the Tang dynasty because it is found in the Great East Hall of Foguang Monastery, dated 857.

17 Zhang Yuhuan, "Shanxi Yuandai diantang de damu jiegou," 72.

18 The Municipal Hall of Huo Prefecture in Huo County, Shanxi, is a well-preserved government building of its kind. Extant are the gateway, the inner gateway, the memorial archway, the first hall, and the second hall. The first hall was built in the Yuan dynasty. See Li Yuming, *Shanxi gujianzhu tonglan,* 262.

19 The flat architrave was a flat board that usually lay in the same position in a "conventional-style" building.

20 See Fu Xinian, *Zhongguo kexue jishushi,* 230–257. I believe that such a shift is possibly related to the development of the bracket sets since the fifth century.

21 Zhang Yuhuan, "Shanxi Yuandai diantang de damu jiegou," 72.

22 Zhang Yuhuan, "Shanxi Yuandai diantang de damu jiegou," 80–85.

23 Shousheng Monastery is located in Xinjiang County, Shanxi province. The main hall was first built in Yuan and reconstructed in Ming. Zhang Yuhuan believes that many Yuan features still remain in this building. See Zhang Yuhuan, "Shanxi Yuandai diantang de damu jiegou," 80.

24 These five buildings are the main hall of Lifeng Temple (fig. 3.1), Lord Wenchang Hall of Wulong Temple (fig. 3.26), Pantuoshi Hall of the Grand Temple at Mount Qiqu (fig. 3.46), the main hall of Dubai Monastery (fig. 3.52), and Yong'an Temple (fig. 3.56).

25 Although Pantuoshi Hall seems to have three "inter"columnar sets on the facade, however, two would have been capital sets if the two front eave columns had not been removed. Therefore, Pantuoshi Hall still is considered to have only one intercolumnar set in the central bay on its facade.

26 For a study of the buttress-bracket, see Xu Yitao, "Gongyuan qi zhi shisi shiji Zhongguo fubigong xingzhi liubian yanjiu" (2005).

27 Zhang Shiqing divides the cantilever-relevant members into three groups: downward cantilever (*xia'ang* 下昂), upward cantilever (*shang'ang* 上昂), and *tiaowo*

挑幹, based on their different bearing structures. See Zhang Shiqing, *Zhongguo Jiangnan Chanzong siyuan jianzhu yanjiu,* 179–194.

28 See a modern reference in Liang Sicheng, *Liang Sicheng quanji,* 7:81.

29 Liang Sicheng, *Liang Sicheng quanji,* 7:121–124.

30 The bracket sets of the main halls of Zhenru Monastery and Xuanyuan Palace will not be included in this section since they were later additions of the Ming dynasty.

31 Liang Sicheng, *Liang Sicheng quanji,* 7:103.

32 Another big boot-shaped wedge of the Yuan dynasty is also found in the main hall of Yong'an Monastery in the Upper Yangzi.

33 Liang Sicheng, *Liang Sicheng quanji,* 7:137.

34 Liang Sichang, *Liang Sicheng quanji,* 7:32.

35 The square or squarish plan was very common among extant small-sized buildings dating from the Tang dynasty to the Yuan dynasty. Architecture in premodern China was regulated based strictly on the owner's hierarchy, which is indicated by the number of bays on the facade of a building. If a building was regulated to be a three-bay-wide structure, there was no way the builder could go beyond that on the facade. Therefore, to maximize the depth of the building (perpendicular to the facade) was the only method to acquire more space. This is probably the reason why most small-sized halls are square or nearly square. For discussion on the relation between the hierarchy and the width of the facade, see Zhang Shiqing, "Gudai jianzhu jianjia biaoji de xingshi yu yiyi," 429.

36 The eliminated-column structure was used in the main hall of Fengguo Monastery 奉國寺 (1020), a Liao building located at Yi County, Liaoning province.

37 Concerning the general migration history in premodern China, there are three major waves of southbound migration of the Han-Chinese. The first took place immediately after the Chaos of the Yongjia 永嘉之乱 that was caused by uprisings of the non-Han Chinese people against the Jin dynasty, 307–312 CE; see Ge, Cao, and Wu, *Jianming Zhongguo yiminshi,* 145–214. The second major migration wave of the Han-Chinese people southbound began with the Rebellion of An Lushan (755–763) in the Tang dynasty; see Ge, Cao, and Wu, *Jianming Zhongguo yiminshi,* 243–257. The third and last wave of southbound migration also was caused by warfare among Song, Jin, and Yuan dynasties. Wu Songdi further divided the third migration wave into seven phases. The first four phases, from 1126 to 1224, were caused by the wars between the Jin dynasty and the Southern Song. The fifth phase of migration to the south was instigated by the Mongols' conquest of the Jin dynasty during 1231 and 1234. The last two phases were caused by the Mongols' conquest of the Southern Song from 1235 to 1277. See Wu Songdi, *Beifang yimin yu nan Song shehui bianqian,* 11–36.

38 Wu Songdi, *Beifang yimin yu nan Song shehui bianqian,* 89.

39 Architecture was not the only thing subject to the influence of the immigrations. A more important reason "for treating the arts of the Yuan at the time of unification as a modification of Song cultural inheritance" was the massive movement of peoples from north to south after the Mongol conquest of the Southern Song and the fact that "the immigrants to the south included craftsmen who brought skills and sensibilities that would modify and transform the arts of the Southern Song." See Watt, *The World of Khubilai Khan,* 5–6.

40 As discussed in chapter 1, the simplification of the interface between the beams and columns in the roof framing is also evidence of a shortage of financial resources, which coincidentally provides a solution for later Ming emperors such as Zhu Yuanzhang, who advocated thriftiness and simplicity for his palaces.

41 Smith, "Family, Landsmann, and Status-Group Affinity in Refugee Mobility Strategies," 669–670.
42 For a concise review of the fall of the Southern Song in 1276, see Rossabi, "The Reign of Khubilai Khan," 429–436.
43 Watt, *The World of Khubilai Khan*, 19.
44 Watt, *The World of Khubilai Khan*, 20.
45 A quote from *Yuanshi* 元史 (The History of Yuan) states, "the state troop slaughtered the Prefecture of Xu. Only the craftsmen received exemption." The original text reads: 國兵屠許, 惟工匠得免. See *Yuanshi, juan* 163, p. 3819.
46 Meng Siming, *Yuandai shehui jieji zhidu*, 141–143.
47 Hu Xiaopeng, "Yuandai de xiguan jianghu," 79.
48 Meng Siming, *Yuandai shehui jieji zhidu*, 142.

CHAPTER 3: TIMBER-FRAMED ARCHITECTURE OF THE UPPER YANGZI

1 The main hall of the Monastery of Golden Immortals (Jinxiansi 金仙寺) was discovered in Sichuan in July 2008 and identified as a Yuan building. The extant architecture is in poor condition but bears a lot of inscriptions preserved from the Yuan dynasty. A case study of the main hall of Jinxiansi is not included in this chapter due to the absence of a firsthand survey of the architecture. For more details of the building and its inscriptions, see Lai Xirong, "Sichuan Pengxixian xinfaxian Yuandai jianzhu Jinxiansi," 72–76, and Zhao and Cai, "Sichuan Pengxixian Jinxiansi Zangdian Yuandai tiji ji xiangguan wenti," 88–96.
2 A 7.0 earthquake hit Sichuan province on April 20, 2013, and the epicenter was located in Lushan County. The two Yuan buildings in Lushan were damaged to different extents.
3 Pan Guxi, *Zhongguo gudai jianzhushi*, 4:366–367, 435.
4 See Yao Guangpu, "Qiqushan damiao," 76–80, and Li Xianwen, "Zitong Pantuoshidian," 41–45.
5 See Zhu Xiaonan, "Langzhong Yong'ansi dadian jianzhu shidai ji gouzao tezheng qianxi," 69–71, and Tao Mingkuan, "Sichuan Langzhong Yong'ansi Yuandai dadian jiqi bihua suxiang," 99–102.
6 The Dacheng Kingdom was one of the Sixteen Kingdoms during the Eastern Jin (317–420).
7 Daxiongdian 大雄寶殿 (the Mahāvīra Hall) is a common name for the main hall in a Buddhist monastery. As Lifeng Temple is a Daoist temple, here it is translated as "the main hall" to avoid confusion. Huangniangdian is apparently in memory of Emperor Li Xiong's mother. The history of the temple is recorded in an unpublished document, *Diliupi quanguo zhongdian wenwu baohu danwei shenbao cailiao* 第六批全國重點文物保護單位申報材料 (Application materials for the sixth group of national cultural heritage). It was compiled by the local administration of the Nanbu county.
8 The inscription reads 大元大德十一年太歲丁未正月丙寅 (Dayuan Dade shiyinian taisui dingwei zhengyue bingyin).

9 The original design of the building is quite different from its current condition. A prayer hall was later added and now is attached to the front entrance. Therefore, now people cannot see the entire view of the front elevation.

10 Strictly speaking, this one is in between a railing-architrave (*lan'e* 闌額) and an eave architrave (*yan'e* 簷額), according to the definitions discussed in chapters 1 and 2.

11 For a brief history of the Temple of the Eastern Peak, see Pan Guxi, *Zhongguo gudai jianzhushi,* 4:366.

12 The Nine Pythons Hall was built during the Ming dynasty and was related to a local myth of Sichuan. One legend says that nine girls from Fengdu 豐都, the famous capital of the ghost, located in the current Chongqing Municipality, transformed into nine pythons after death to repay their obligation. Another story connects the nine pythons to a Ming official, Yang Mengying 楊孟瑛, who was a native of Fengdu and was once the governor of Hangzhou. He supervised the construction of Yanggongdi 楊公堤, the Dike of Yang, and saved the West Lake in Hangzhou from drying up. Then he was worshipped posthumously as the God of Nine Pythons (Jiumangshen 九蟒神) in his hometown of Fengdu. A couple of Daoist temples in Fengdu have a hall dedicated to the Nine Pythons, referring either to the nine girls or to the Ming official. In addition, buildings dated to the Qing dynasty, such as the Avalokiteśvara Hall (Guanyindian 觀音殿) and the Vairocana Buddha Hall (Piludian 毗盧殿), clearly are connected to Buddhism.

13 For discussions on the Three Teachings in the Yuan dynasty, see Liu and Berling, "The 'Three Teachings' in the Mongol-Yüan Period," 479–503. For the Three Teachings during the Ming dynasty, see Chen, *Buddhism in China: A Historical Survey,* 445–447.

14 The Taiding stele found in the temple was dated to 1327, and the Chunhua stone tablet was dated to 993.

15 The original text reads: 飛來殿縣西北五里。丘隅環護, 谿澗盤旋。周圍皆湮隰, 獨湧一阜, 其中高朗絕塵, 固天然勝景也。 [One Chinese character cannot be identified] 宇巍巍, 群祠簇湧, 號曰飛來。經始莫能究。但按泰定遺碑內述, 淳化景佑間斷碣略云, 廟址神所自擇。嘗一夕, 有風雷之變。遲明, 小殿歸然。自是民無疾癘, 年谷豐登。邑人因覆以重屋 [One Chinese character cannot be identified] 宇。 [One Chinese character cannot be identified] 飛來非臆說, 而古蹟於邑可知。再攷清誌, 始建於唐, 續鼎於宋, 元之大德復培。於明洪武, 歷久將傾。康熙丁未戊申邑人亟圖救敝而經營之。幸古材貞巨, 但忝換其腐蝕。雖陸離難復, 浸漏無虞矣。 See *Emei xianzhi, juan* 4.

16 Another two stelae produced in the Zhida 至大 reign (1308–1311) of Yuan and Wanli 萬曆 reign (1573–1620) of Ming respectively were once available too. The latter records the restoration activity during the late Ming. Unfortunately, all these stelae and tablets mentioned were demolished in the 1960s during the Cultural Revolution. Only the 1327 stele can be studied partly by its fragments. Now it is only possible to read these inscriptions from rubbings. See Sichuansheng wenwu guanliju, *Sichuan wenwuzhi,* 2:786.

17 Pan Guxi, Zhongguo gudai jianzhushi, 4:366.

18 Pan Guxi, Zhongguo gudai jianzhushi, 4:366.

19 Two other buildings that are famous for coiling dragons along the eave columns are the Sage Mother Hall (Shengmudian 聖母殿, 1023–1032) of the Jin Shrines (Jinci 晉祠) in Taiyuan 太原, Shanxi province; and the Hall of Great Achievement (Dachengdian 大成殿) of the Confucius Temple (dated 1483, repaired 1725) at Qufu 曲阜, Shandong province.

20 *Shengqi* is described in detail in *juan* 5 of the *YZFS*. Also see Liang Sicheng, *Liang Sicheng quanji*, 7:137.

21 This information is found in the inscription on a modern stele outside the building.

22 *Meishan xianzhi, juan* 13.

23 Such diagonal beams also are found in the main hall of Yong'an Monastery and the main hall of Qinglong Monastery. For a study of the development of diagonal beams in Sichuan, see Bo Cheng, "Sichuan Yuandai jianzhu zhong daxiefu jiegou tixi tanxi," 156–158.

24 The original text reads: 永安寺在東九十里唐建宋治平元至正明嘉靖遞有培修. See Xu Jiyong, *Langzhong xianzhi, juan* 2.

25 *Jinshanbei* 禁山碑 is a special type of stele built to warn people against deforestation. On this stele discovered in Yong'an Monastery, a line reads: "Yong'an Monastery was first built in early Tang and was restored in Song, Yuan, Ming, and Qing dynasties, respectively." The original text is 永安寺建於唐初宋元明清均有培修.

26 The original text reads: 本覺院地去閬東六十里許, 先宋僧處林之所創建也。宋英宗治平四年奉敕褒修, 元文宗至順二年式廓增大殿。. . . 我朝洪武敕僧姓李諱永用號君賢者嘗補葺之。. . . . . . 嘉靖丁未歲, 僧號寶峰者夙夜惶惶, 思爲此懼, 乃敬捐衣鉢, 募工匠, 土木金石次第畢舉, 樓閣廊宇, 門殿臺砌, 煥然而更新之. See Zhu Xiaonan, "Langzhong Yong'ansi dadian jianzhu shidai ji gouzao tezheng qianxi," 67.

27 The entire text reads: 大元至順四年太歲癸酉九月壬辰朔二十八日乙未當院至盟比丘寶傳專管修造小師悟一同師第 [Six Chinese characters cannot be identified] 囊資 [One Chinese character cannot be identified] 改鼎新創. See Sichuansheng wenwu guanliju, *Sichuan wenwuzhi,* 2:787.

28 Strictly speaking, this one is in between a railing-architrave (*lan'e* 闌額) and an eave architrave (*yan'e* 簷額), according to the definitions discussed in chapters 1 and 2.

29 Zhu Xiaonan defines the second-tier inclined cantilever as locust head (*shuatou* 耍頭). See Zhu Xiaonan, "Langzhong Yong'ansi dadian jianzhu shidai ji gouzao tezheng qianxi," 68. I believe this member is still an inclined cantilever instead of a locust head because the second-tier inclined cantilever is not parallel to the projecting bracket, but a locust head is.

30 Zhu Xiaonan, "Langzhong Yong'ansi dadian jianzhu shidai ji gouzao tezheng qianxi," 68.

31 It is unknown who this six-armed bodhisattva was. It is probably one of the manifestations of Guanyin.

32 Tao Mingkuan, "Sichuan Langzhong Yong'ansi Yuandai dadian jiqi bihua suxiang," 100.

33 The original text reads: 當院住山修造比丘寶傳, 小師悟真、悟理, 師孫永用、永寶、永堅、永和. . . . . . 以功德莊嚴, 放孜乞智愚方便。粵自癸酉之秋季, 欲修大殿以興工, 供啓愿。誠用求加護。創業未半而上足遷化, 營修以備而慶賀當陳。內外土木之作已周, 塓糚彩畫之功俱畢. . . . . . 至正戊子[Nine Chinese characters cannot be identified].

34 For more information on the Wenchang cult, see Kleeman, *A God's Own Tale: The Book of Transformation of Wenchang, the Divine Lord of Zitong* (1994) and the later section about Pantuoshi Hall.

35 The building actually has two names. One is Wenchangdian (Lord Wenchang Hall), which is inscribed on the horizontal board hanging in the porch of the building.

The other name is Wenchangge 文昌閣 (Lord Wenchang Pavilion), which is inscribed on this stele. For consistency, I will use the first name throughout.

36 The original text reads: 文昌閣始建於唐, 元至正三年重修. See Sichuansheng wenwu guanliju, *Sichuan wenwuzhi*, 2:785.

37 This two-storied base is similar to the base of the main hall of Yong'an Monastery that was built in the same year and is not far away from Wulong Temple. Although the main hall of Yong'an Monastery has many parts that have been altered, the base should be an original piece from the Yuan dynasty.

38 An inscription bearing the date is found on a stone pivot (*menzhen* 門砧) installed on the side of the gate of the monastery.

39 Sichuansheng wenwu guanliju, *Sichuan wenwuzhi*, 2:784.

40 The main hall was restored after the earthquake in 2013. This section is based on its condition before the earthquake.

41 A recent investigation that took place in August 2018 reveals that these words are part of a long prose piece that documents a major restoration/reconstruction of the building in 1443, the eighth year of the Zhengtong period of the Ming dynasty. See Zhao Yuanxiang, "Lushan Qinglongsi dadian jianzhu niandai de xinfaxian," 6.

42 The four inscriptions are Zhiyuan yinian 至元一年 (the first year of the Zhiyuan period, 1336), Zhiyuan liunian 至元六年 (the sixth year of the Zhiyuan period, 1340), Zhizheng shi'ernian renchen 至正十二年壬辰 (the twelfth and Renchen year of the Zhizheng period, 1352), and Zhizheng shisan 至正十三 (the thirteenth year of the Zhizheng period, 1353).

43 The inscriptions are documented in an unpublished local movement document, *Lushan Qinglongsi dadian baohu guihua* 蘆山青龍寺大殿保護規劃 (Preservation plan of the main hall of Qinglong Monastery at Lushan) compiled in February 2007. According to some other inscriptions on the roof tiles, restorations of the main hall took place in both the Ming and Qing dynasties. The latest restoration before the 2013 earthquake was supervised by the Sichuan Cultural Relics Administration in 1990 when the base was reinforced and the timber-framed structure was adjusted.

44 Zhao Yuanxiang, "Lushan Qinglongsi dadian jianzhu niandai de xinfaxian," 6.

45 Jiang Wei (202–264), Zhuge Liang's 諸葛亮 student and successor, was a military officer and later regent of the state of Shu Han during the Three Kingdoms period. His style name is Boyue 伯約, and his honorific title is Marquise Pingxiang 平襄侯.

46 Xu Hongzhong was supposed to be a magistrate of Lushan County during the Shaoxing reign of the Southern Song (1131–1162). In *Lushan xianzhi* 蘆山縣誌 (Gazetteer of Lushan) written in the Qing dynasty, it is pointed out that his family name should be Li 李 instead of Xu. Henceforth I shall use the name Li Hongzhong.

47 The original text reads: 紹興二十三年徐閎中記土人祀姜伯約有廟額曰平襄. See Cao Xuequan, *Shuzhong mingshengji, juan* 14.

48 The cult of Jiang Wei is very popular around Lushan County. It is said that Jiang Wei died on the fifteenth day of the eighth moon, which is Mid-Autumn Day. Therefore, during the Mid-Autumn Festival every year, the local people would set up a stage and colored building models around Pingxiang Pavilion. This became one of the major social events of Lushan.

49 This diagonal beam is something between a slanting cantilever and a two-rafter beam, which also is found in the main hall of Qinglong Monastery as a local feature in Lushan.

50 Pan Guxi, *Zhongguo gudai jianzhushi*, 4:43.

51 The original text reads: 神姓張名亞子居蜀七曲山仕晉戰沒人爲立廟唐宋屢封至英顯王道家謂帝命梓潼掌文昌府事及人間祿籍故元加號爲帝君而天下學校亦有祠祀者. See *Mingshi, juan* 50, *zhi* 25.

52 The Grand Temple today has one building dated to Yuan, ten to Ming, and eight to the Qing dynasty. Most of them are in good condition. See Yao Guangpu, "Qiqushan Damiao," 76–80.

53 Li Xianwen, "Zitong Pantuoshidian jianzhu niandai chutan," 41.

54 The original text reads: 雍正四年冬正殿拜殿鐘樓廟門忠孝樓燬於野燒. See *Chongxiu Zitong xianzhi, juan* 2.

55 A separate "prayer hall" (*baidian* 拜殿) is attached to its front entrance but is not shown in fig. 3.46.

56 Since two eave columns have been removed, there are no capital sets in this building.

57 According to the *YZFS*, a boot-shaped wedge (*xuexie* 鞾楔) is a transitional member that is put into a pile of blocks (*liangzhudou* 連珠鬥) to hold an upward cantilever (*shang'ang* 上昂, a sort of strut). Strictly speaking, the triangular member here in Pantuoshi Hall is not a genuine boot-shaped wedge because there is neither a pile of blocks nor an upward cantilever. Nonetheless, its function is similar to a boot-shaped wedge, which, like a wedge, is to strengthen the diagonal cantilever from inside. The boot-shaped wedge frequently is used in the Yuan buildings in the Lower Yangzi, which will be discussed in chapter 4.

58 The original text reads: 獨柏寺, 縣北五十裡, 唐時建。舊名慧日院。內有佛像高丈餘, [One Chinese character cannot be identified] 巨柏雕成, 飾金, 寺因以名.

59 The original text reads: 永安廟古永安鎮也唐高宗永徽二年守土者以廟請請於朝爲士民水旱疾疫之禱天子是之, 乃奉敕修建今千餘年矣恩敕雖久失落上有紫金梁巍然獨存非吾地之增靈光矣.

60 Information about Yong'an Temple can be found in an unpublished government document, *Sichuansheng wenwu baohu danwei tuijian cailiao* 四川省文物保護單位推薦材料 (Recommendation material for the cultural heritage site of Sichuan Province), compiled by the local administration. The temple is dated to early Ming, although this does not come from any reliable source or even a thorough investigation of the building. Through a personal conversation with the local administrators, the author learned that they prefer the theory that it is a Yuan building.

CHAPTER 4: TIMBER-FRAMED ARCHITECTURE OF THE LOWER YANGZI

1 Lu 路 is an administrative unit of Southern Song that is equivalent to a province.

2 Zhang Yuhuan, *Zhongguo gujianzhu jishushi*, 115–119.

3 Pan Guxi, *Zhongguo gudai jianzhushi*, 4:208–310.

4 See Zhang Shiqing, *Zhongguo Jiangnan Chanzong siyuan jianzhu yanjiu* (2002).

5 Taoxi used to be part of a county called Xuanping 宣平. In 1958, Xuanping county disappeared and was merged with Wuyi county.

6 Chen Congzhou, "Jinhua Tianningsi Yuandai zhengdian," 107.

7 Liang Sicheng mentioned the main hall of Yanfu Monastery in his teaching notes of the 1930s that were published in 1998. See Liang Sicheng, *Zhongguo jianzhushi*, 254–255. Liang surveyed Yanfu Monastery in 1933, but never published any fieldwork research of the monastery.

8 Chen Congzhou, "Zhejiang Wuyixian Yanfusi Yuangou dadian," 32–38.

9 For details of the reparation, see Huang Zi, "Yuandai gucha Yanfusi jiqi dadian de weixiu duice," 413–418.

10 The original text reads: 泰定甲子, 初吉皆山。師德環過余曰, "吾先太祖曰, '公因舊謀新, 四敵是備, 獨正殿巋然, 計可支久, 故不改觀。'" 歲月悠浸, 遽復頹圮, 先師祖梁慨然, 囑永廣孫曰, "殿大役也。舍是不先, 吾則不武。" 用率爾眾, 一乃心力, 廣其故基, 新其遺址。意氣所感, 裡人和甫鄭君亦樂助焉。延佑丁巳, 空翔地湧, 粲然復興, 繼承規禁, 以時會堂。梵唄清樾, 鐃磬間作, 無有高下, 釀爲醇風。方來衲子, 無食息之所者鹹歸焉. See Chen Congzhou, "Zhejiang Wuyixian Yanfusi Yuangou dadian," 32.

11 The original text reads: 延福寺在縣北二十五裡, 晉天福二年僧宗一建。明天順年間, 僧潤清重修。康熙九年, 僧照應重建後殿觀音殿兩廊。雍正八年至乾隆十三年, 僧通茂同徒定明屢次修整大殿, 創興天王寶殿並兩廊廂屋二十一間, 裝塑天王金身四尊。由是獅林大振。舊有六景, 翠屏山、五柳溪、懸磬巖、木魚山、石澗井。道光十八年主持僧漢書重建山門。同治四年主持僧妙顯重修.

12 The original text reads: 距邑二十裡許, 峰環澗繞, 寺立其中。唐天成二年名曰福田, 宋紹熙賜今名。有賜紫宣教太師守一休剏苟完。迨元有堂, 日師及德環等, 繼置田山, 重立碑記。僧宗普惟謙相繼葺理, 其徒文碧潤清耕作惟勤, 積累稍稔。明正統間鄉寇蕘發, 毀宇爲薪。迨靖復業, 文碧等悉意生殖, 諸工旋作, 百廢俱舉, 且購腴田。天順癸未仲春, 潤清丐余志石條, 其續置之業而記之。

13 Chen Congzhou, "Zhejiang Wuyixian Yanfusi Yuangou dadian," 34–35.

14 Chen Congzhou, "Zhejiang Wuyixian Yanfusi Yuangou dadian," 33.

15 The main hall of Yanfu Monastery is not the only example that has a lower eave that was added later. The main hall of Zhenru Monastery, the main hall of Tianning Monastery, and the main hall of Baoguo Monastery, which is dated to Northern Song and located in Ningbo, were all altered in the same way during the Ming and Qing periods. Chen Congzhou believed that this might be a local Ming-Qing tradition of restoration. The lower eaves of the main halls of Zhenru and Tianning Monasteries were removed during the restorations of 1960s and 1980s.

16 According to Chen Congzhong, the structure above the upmost has been altered during the restorations after the Yuan. See Chen Congzhou, "Zhejiang Wuyixian yanfusi Yuangou dadian," 32.

17 Mentioned in chapter 1, Baoguo Monastery 保國寺 is located at Ningbo in Zhejiang province. The main hall of Baoguo Monastery is dated to 1013, the sixth year of Dazhong xiangfu 大中祥符 reign of the Northern Song.

18 Chen Congzhou, "Zhejiang Wuyixian Yanfusi Yuangou dadian," 33.

19 The original text reads: 天寧萬壽禪寺在城西北隅, 舊名大藏院。宋大中祥符間建, 賜號承天。政和更今名。紹興八年以崇奉徽宗, 賜名報恩廣寺, 又改報恩光寺。元延佑間重建, 明正統時修, 復名天寧萬壽寺。舊有石浮圖, 登覽大殿, 後有大悲閣. See Qian Renlong, *Jinhua xianzhi, juan* 5.

20 When Chen Congzhou did his survey in 1954, these Qing buildings were still extant. See Chen Congzhou, "Jinhua Tianning si Yuandai zhengdian," 101.

21 The original text reads: 大元延佑五年歲在戊午六月庚申吉且重建恭祝. See Chen Congzhou, "Jinhua Tianning si Yuandai zhengdian," 101.

22 Zhejiangsheng wenwu kaogusuo wenbaoshi, "Jinhua Tianningsi dadian de gouzao ji weixiu," 176.

23 Zhenru 真如 is the Chinese translation of the Sanskrit word *bhūta-tathātā,* or *tathatā,* meaning "thusness."

24 The original text reads: 真如寺一名萬壽寺, 俗名大寺, 舊在官場。宋嘉定間僧永安以真如院改建。元延祐間僧妙心移建桃樹浦請額改寺。明洪武、弘治間, 僧道馨法雷兩次修建. See Lu Li, *Zhenru lizhi, juan* 1.

25 Liu Dunzhen, "Zhenrusi zhengdian," 91.

26 The original text reads: 峕大元歲次庚申延祐七年癸未季夏月乙巳二十乙日巽時鼎建。

27 For the details of the inscriptions, see Shanghaishi wenwu baoguan weiyuanhui, "Shanghai shijiao Yuandai jianzhu Zhengrusi zhengdian zhong faxian de gongjiang mobi zi," 16–26.

28 Liu Dunzhen, "Zhenrusi zhengdian," 96.

29 In his article, Lu Bingjie compares the main hall of Zhenru Monastery to Japanese architecture of *zenshōyō* 禪宗樣 that are dated to the thirteenth century. Lu suggests that the Shariden 舍利殿 of Engakuji 円覚寺 in Kamakura is the closest example in Japan to the main hall of Zhenru Monastery because of similar building plans and bracket sets. See Lu, "Cong Shanghai Zhenrusi dadian kan Riben Chanzongyang de yuanyuan," 12.

30 Liu Dunzhen, "Zhenrusi zhengdian," 96.

31 Liu Dunzhen, "Zhenrusi zhengdian," 94.

32 The dew plate, *lupan* 露盘, also called *xianglun* 相輪, is a number of tiers of wheel-like elements in the middle part of the pagoda finial.

33 The original text reads: 雲岩禪寺在郭外虎丘, 晉司徒王珣及其弟瑉之別業。鹹和二年捨建。隋仁壽中建塔七成於殿后。初于劍池分爲東西二寺, 後合爲一。宋至道中重建, 郡守魏庠奏, 賜今額。景祐中建禦書閣, 紹興中建藏殿, 尋皆毀於兵。元至元四年重建, 黃溍記。明洪武中火, 永樂初住持法寶重修。宣德中浮圖毀於火。正統間巡撫周忱重建。露盤初上有白鶴數十迴旋塔頂, 久之乃去, 張益有記。又建藏經閣五楹, 供奉敕賜大藏經典, 忱自爲記。崇禎二年冬, 寺復火。巡撫都禦史張國維重建大殿。国朝順治初總兵楊承祖重建天王殿。康熙間, 聖祖仁皇帝南巡, 臨幸賜額。五十三年大殿火, 巡鹽李煦新之。高宗純皇帝南巡, 屢次臨幸, 賜詩章聯額藏香供器。三十年奉皇太后鑾輿臨幸, 頒白金兩次。五十五年僧祖通募修。鹹豐十年毀。同治三年署左軍守備劉啓發捐建石觀音殿, 自爲記。十年郡人陳德基募建天王殿。See Li Mingwan, *Suzhou fuzhi, juan* 42.

34 During the Southern Song and Yuan, the fifteen largest monasteries of Chan Buddhism, mostly in Jiangnan (the Lower Yangzi), were distributed into two grades and each given a rank. The top five were called *wushan* 五山 (five mountains), while the other ten were called *shicha* 十剎 (ten monasteries). The system of *wushan shicha* 五山十剎 symbolized the institutionalization of Chan Buddhism in the Song-Yuan era. See more discussion on the institution of *wushan shicha* in Zhang Shiqing, *Wushan shicha tu yu nan Song Jiangnan Chansi* (2000).

35 The original text reads: 重紀至元之四年, 行宣政院, 以慧燈圓照禪師普明嗣領寺事。至則裝飾佛菩薩阿羅漢金剛神塐, 造文殊普賢觀世音三大士, 繕治舍利之塔、經律論之藏, 範美銅爲钜鐘。視棟宇之摧墮蠹敝者, 或因或革, 石役竝舉。大佛殿、千佛閣、三大士殿、藏院、僧堂、庫司、三門、兩廡、古木、寒泉、劍池、華雨諸亭則仍其舊。祖塔、眾寮並庾庖湢宴休之。平遠堂遊眺之小吳軒山之前爲重門, 則改建使一新。See Huang Jin, "Huqiu Yunyanchansi xingzaoji," in *Huqiu shanzhi* (1676).

36 Another four accounts are also available in *Huqiu shanzhi,* documenting four restoration activities during the Ming dynasty, which are also in accordance with the history of Yunyan Monastery written in *Suzhou fuzhi.*

37 The four heavenly kings (Sanskrit: *caturmahārāja*) of Buddhism were supposed to guard the four cardinal directions of the world. They are collectively named in Chinese as follows: Chiguo tianwang 持國天王 (Sanskrit: Dhṛtarāṣṭra), who guards the east; Zengzhang tianwang 增長天王 (Sanskrit: Virūḍhaka), who guards the south; Guangmu tiianwang 廣目天王 (Sanskrit: Virūpākṣa), who guards the west; and Duowen tianwang 多聞天王 (Sanskrit: Vaiśravaṇa), who guards the north.

38 Xuanyuan is also known as Huangdi 黃帝, the Yellow Emperor. According to early Chinese mythology, he is the common ancestor of all Chinese people, and his full name is Gongsun Xuanyuan 公孫軒轅.

39 The Chinese text reads: 胥王廟即靈順宮在東山楊灣。始建無考。元時有王爛鈔者重建。明末建前殿，祀吳相伍大夫，稱爲胥王廟，陳瑚記。See Jin Youli, *Taihu beikao, juan* 6.

40 The Chinese text reads: 東山靈順宮，祀相國伍員，創自貞觀二年。宋高宗南渡，扈蹕官軍分道經湖，風濤不可航，濤神立應，爲遣官葺治，封員爲王。

41 In the early twentieth century, the local government tried to demolish the temple for political reasons.

42 Chen Congzhou, "Jinhua Tianningsi Yuandai zhengdian," 68.

CHAPTER 5: NON-TIMBER-FRAMED ARCHITECTURE

1 For a concise history of Daoist pilgrimage to Mount Wudang, see Lagerway, "The Pilgrimage to Wu-Tang Shan," 293–332.

2 Xuanwu 玄武 (the Dark Martiality), posthumously known as Xuantian Shangdi 玄天上帝 (Dark Heavenly Upper Emperor) as well as Zhenwu Dadi 真武大帝 (True Warrior Grand Emperor), is one of the highest-ranking and most revered Daoist deities in China. He is venerated as a powerful god, able to control the elements and capable of great magic. He is revered particularly by martial artists. Since the third Ming emperor, Zhu Di 朱棣, claimed that Xuanwu helped him in the war to take over the Ming empire, monasteries were built under Zhu Di's imperial decree in Mount Wudang, where Xuanwu allegedly attained immortality. For a general study of the cult of Xuanwu, see Boltz, *A Survey of Taoist Literature: Tenth to Seventeenth Centuries,* 87–88.

3 *Yuanshi, juan* 21, 456.

4 See a detailed study on the Little Copper Hall in Zhang Jianwei, "Wudangshan Yuandai Xiaotongdian yanjiu," 80–106.

5 For an elaborated research on all metal architecture in ancient China, see Zhang Jianwei, *Zhongguo gudai jinshu jianzhu yanjiu* (2015).

6 According to the Daoist canon *Wudang fudi zongzhenji* 武當福地總真集 (Completed biographies of the Immortals from auspicious Mount Wudang), construction of Zhenqing Palace, also known as Nanyang Palace 南岩宮, started in 1284. See Liu Mingdao, *Wudang fudi zongzhenji, juan* 2, 1. According to *Dayue Taihe shanzhi* 大岳太和山志 (Gazetteer of the Grand Mount Taihe), the project was completed in the ninth month of 1314. See Ren, *Dayue Taihe shanzhi,* 14.

7 The two in the middle are blocked by a horizontal inscribed board.

8 Liu Xujie and Qi Deyao, "Jiangsu Wuxian Jijiansi Yuandai shidianwu," 44. The original text reads: 作石殿三間，就石肖釋迦藥師彌陀像，其菩薩侍衛之神與供養

之具皆石爲之。累石作外門，門上爲重屋，夜眞膏火其中，曰天燈樓。摩崖刻三十五佛名，鑿池左右，立石爲彌勒、彌陀屋焉，署曰 "兜率宮" "極樂園"。前樹梵塔，對峙巍然。他及禪誦之室，庖湢之所，資客之館，咸具如式。

9 It is not so clear whether this floral pattern is lotus, camellia, or peony. Its bud with three arcs is different from the lotus bud surrounding it. It is probably a nonrealistic hybrid form of lotus, camellia, and peony.

10 For a brief description on this coffered ceiling in Jokhang Temple, see Xie, *Zhongguo Zangchuan Fojiao yishu*, 6:9.

11 For a study of Lamaist/Tibetan Buddhism and Buddhist statues of the Yuan dynasty in Hangzhou, see Su Bai, "Yuandai Hangzhou de Zangchuan mijiao jiqi youguan yiji," 55–71, and Paula Swart, "Buddhist Sculptures at Feilai Feng: A Confrontation of Two Traditions," 54–61.

12 Lou Jianlong and Wang Yimin, "Fujian Shunchang Baoshansi dadian," 70.

13 The original text reads: 維大元至正二十三年癸卯歲七月二十八乙未良日己卯時募眾鼎建上祝。

14 Lou Jianlong and Wang Yimin, "Fujian Shunchang Baoshansi dadian," 66.

15 As discussed in chapter 1, according to the *YZFS* and known practice, premodern timber architecture in China is based on a modularized ranking system. The style of the roof also indicates the ranking of a building.

16 Lou Jianlong and Wang Yimin, "Fujian Shunchang Baoshansi dadian," 70.

17 According to Cao Chunping, small temples that are built facing toward a cave in a mountain are all called *yan* in Fujian province. *Yan* literally means rock, but can be translated as "stone temple" in such a context. On Qingyuan Mountain, there are two stone temples. One is the Yuan-era Stone Temple of Amitābha, and the other is called the Stone Temple of Auspicious Statue (Ruixiangyan 瑞像岩), datable to Ming. Although they were built in different times, they actually have a very similar look, which suggests that the Stone Temple of Auspicious Statue was modeled largely on the Stone Temple of Amitābha. Here, I will focus only on the Stone Temple of Amitābha, dated to the Yuan. For a study on both stone temples, see Cao Chunping, "Quanzhou Qingyuanshan Mituoyan yu Ruixiangyan," 93–97.

18 The first day of the second month is called Zhonghejie, Festival of Harmony, when people exchange seeds to pray for a prosperous year. The original text reads: 彌陀岩年深屋弊。金陵僧覺成雲遊來泉，會平章三旦八、御史帖木爾不花、憲史孫三寶、僉事釋迦奴，捐財首倡，化合眾緣，易殿以石，建台塔，改堂宇，再精琢佛像塗金，始末四春。郡士孫世覺舍田充焚修香燈費，以此功德回施眾生，共證菩提者，任役智通 ... 大元至正二十四年甲辰中和日告功立石。

19 This pagoda at Shentong Monastery also is known as Simenta, Four-entry Pagoda. For an illustration, see Fu et al., *Chinese Architecture*, 121.

20 For further study on Shengyousi, see Steinhardt, "China's Earliest Mosques," 339–341.

21 The twin pagodas at Kaiyuansi, one called Renshou Pagoda and the other Zhenguo Pagoda, were built in 1128 and 1238 respectively.

22 Terms of the three generic styles were created by the author.

23 Chou, *Indo-Chinese Relations: A History of Chinese Buddhism*, 183.

24 Atwood, "Validation by Holiness or Sovereignty," 237.

25 Atwood, "Validation by Holiness or Sovereignty," 243.

26 Atwood, "Validation by Holiness or Sovereignty," 242.

27 The Confucians at the first place failed to explain their practices to Chinggis Khan as a form of prayer to Heaven/God/Confucianism. Therefore, they were

not treated as clergy and were excluded from tax exemption. Later, Ögedei Khan was convinced that Confucianism was "a pillar of the state," and then it was added to the other religions. See Atwood, "Validation by Holiness or Sovereignty," 255.

28 Atwood, "Validation by Holiness or Sovereignty," 247.

29 Atwood, "Validation by Holiness or Sovereignty," 251–252.

30 Miaoying Monastery, also known as the White Pagoda Temple (Baitasi 白塔寺), was an imperial-patronized Tibetan Buddhist temple built during the reign of Khubilai Khan. It is famous for the extant White Pagoda that was designed and built by the famous Nepalese architect Araniko. For more information on the White Pagoda and the history of the temple, see Li Qianlang, "Beijing Miaoyingsi Baita," 66–71, and Jing, "The Portraits of Khubilai Khan and Chabi by Anige (1245–1306), a Nepali Artist at the Yuan Court," 40–86.

31 The Kaifeng Synagogue originally was built in 1163 and repaired in 1279 and 1421. It was quite active throughout the Yuan dynasty. The architecture did not physically survive, but extant stele inscriptions document its history. For more information, see Steinhardt, "The Synagogue at Kaifeng," 3–21.

32 The site of Temple of the Cross is located in suburban Beijing, and there are no architectural remains there today. Originally built as a Buddhist temple during the Jin dynasty, it was converted to Nestorianism (an earlier sect of Christianity) a few times during the Yuan dynasty. For more details, see Anami, *Encounters with Ancient Beijing*, 144–145.

33 For more details on the active mosque construction in the Yuan dynasty, see Steinhardt, *China's Early Mosques*, 92–118.

34 Yang's biography was recorded by *Yanggong shendao beiming* 杨公神道碑铭 (Stele inscription for the Spiritual Path along Tomb of Duke Yang), an epigraph in memorial of Yang composed by Yao Sui 姚燧 (1283–1313). The stele is now preserved in the Temple to the Northern Peak (Beiyuemiao 北嶽廟) in Quyang. For more details about Yang's biography and relevant literature, see Cary Liu, "The Yuan Dynasty Capital," 280, and Zhu Qiqian and Kan Duo, "Yuan Dadu gongyuan tukao," 99.

35 Zhu Qiqian and Kan Duo, "Yuan Dadu gongyuan tukao," 99.

36 Zhu Qiqian and Kan Duo, "Yuan Dadu gongyuan tukao," 98.

37 Zhu Qiqian and Kan Duo, "Yuan Dadu gongyuan tukao," 98.

38 The original text reads: 试观其配置, 悉不谬于礼经。即以宫殿额名征之, 亦与汴宫同其泰半。所不同者, 宋世制度简质, 禁中多具山林风味。元宫专尚华缛, 金碧灿烂。. . . 此为华化未彻底之点。See Zhu Qiqian and Kan Duo, "Yuan Dadu gongyuan tukao," 5.

CONCLUSION

1 Watt, "Introduction," 3.

2 Watt, "Introduction," 5.

3 Watt, "Introduction," 3.

4 Watt, "Introduction," 36.

APPENDIX

Unless otherwise noted, all terms used in this book to describe Yuan architecture are the Song dynasty ones used in the *YZFS*.

1 After Qinghua Guo, *Visual Dictionary of Chinese Architecture*, 22.
2 After Qinghua Guo, *Visual Dictionary of Chinese Architecture*, 24.
3 Wu Chengluo, *Zhongguo duliangheng shi*, 242.
4 After Qinghua Guo, *Visual Dictionary of Chinese Architecture*, 32.
5 After Qinghua Guo, *Visual Dictionary of Chinese Architecture*, 41.
6 After Qinghua Guo, *Visual Dictionary of Chinese Architecture*, 50.
7 After Qinghua Guo, *Visual Dictionary of Chinese Architecture*, 79.

BIBLIOGRAPHY

Atwood, Christopher P. "Validation by Holiness or Sovereignty: Religious Toleration as Political Theology in the Mongol World Empire of the Thirteenth Century." *International History Review* 26.2 (2004): 237–256.

Bo Cheng 柏呈. "Sichuan Yuandai jianzhu zhong daxiefu jiegou tixi tanxi" 四川元代建築中大斜栿結構體系探析 (An analysis of big diagonal beams in Yuan architecture in Sichuan). *Sichuan jianzhu* 34.4 (2014): 156–158.

Boltz, Judith. *A Survey of Taoist Literature: Tenth to Seventeenth Centuries.* Berkeley: University of California, Institute of East Asian Studies, 1987.

Cai Xuzhuan 蔡叙專. "Suzhou Jijiansi shiwu" 蘇州寂鑒寺石屋 (The stone house of Jijian Monastery in Suzhou). *Lishi jianzhu* 1 (1959): 132–136.

Cao Chunping 曹春平. "Quanzhou Qingyuanshan Mituoyan yu Ruixiangyan" 泉州清源山彌陀岩與瑞像岩 (The Amitābha Rock and Ruixiang Rock at Qingyuan Mountain, Quanzhou). *Jianzhushi* 19.2 (2003): 93–107.

Cao Xuequan 曹學佺 (1574–1647). *Shuzhong mingshengji* 蜀中名勝記 (Records of places of interest in Sichuan). Beijing: Zhonghua shuju, 1985.

Chai Zejun 柴澤俊. *Fanshi Yanshansi* 繁峙岩山寺 (Yanshan Monastery at Fanshi). Beijing: Wenwu chubanshe, 1990.

——. *Shuozhou Chongfusi* 朔州崇福寺 (Chongfu Monastery at Shuozhou). Beijing: Wenwu chubanshe, 2000.

Chai Zejun 柴澤俊 and Ren Yimin 任毅敏. *Hongdong guangshengsi* 洪洞廣勝寺 (Guangsheng Monastery at Hongdong). Beijing: Wenwu chubanshe, 2006.

Chen Congzhou 陳从周. "Dongting Dongshan de gujianzhu Yangwanmiao zhengdian" 洞庭東山的古建築楊灣廟正殿 (The main hall of Yangwan Temple, ancient architecture of Dongting Dongshan). *Wenwu* 3 (1954): 63–68.

——. "Jinhua Tianningsi Yuandai zhengdian" 金華天寧寺元代正殿 (The Yuan dynasty main hall of Tianning Monastery at Jinhua). *Wenwu* 12 (1954): 101–107.

——. "Luzhi Baoshengsi Tianwangdian" 甪直寶勝寺天王殿 (The Tianwang Hall of Baosheng Monastery at Luzhi). *Wenwu* 8 (1955): 103–110.

——. "Zhejiang gujianzhu diaocha jilue" 浙江古建築調查紀略 (Brief record of the investigation of ancient architecture in Zhejiang). *Wenwu* 7 (1963): 36.

——. "Zhejiang Wuyixian Yanfusi Yuangou dadian" 浙江武義縣延福寺元構大殿 (The Yuan dynasty main hall of Yanfu Monastery, Wuyi County, Zhejiang). *Wenwu* 4 (1966): 32–38.

Chen, Gaohua. *The Capital of the Yuan Dynasty.* Translated by Phoebe Poon. Singapore; Honolulu: Silkroad, 2015.

Chen, Kenneth K. S. *Buddhism in China: A Historical Survey.* Princeton, NJ: Princeton University Press, 1964.

Chen Mingda 陳明達. *Yingzao fashi damuzuo yanjiu* 營造法式大木作研究 (A study of the major carpentry in *Yingzao fashi*). Beijing: Wenwu chubanshe, 1981.

———. "Zhongguo gudai mujiegou jianzhu jishu (nan Song-Ming, Qing)" 中國古代木結構建築技術 (南宋- 明清) (Technology of Chinese ancient timber architecture, from Southern Song to Ming-Qing). In *Chen Mingda gujianzhu yu diaosu shilun* 陳明達古建築與雕塑史論 (Collected essays in ancient architecture and history of sculpture by Chen Mingda), 217–238. Beijing: Wenwu chubanshe, 1998.

Chou, Hsiang-Kuang. *Indo-Chinese Relations: A History of Chinese Buddhism.* Allahabad: Indo-Chinese Literature Publication, 1955.

Dong Li 冬籬. "Shoushan Qianmingsi Yuandai mugou jianzhu" 首山乾明寺元代木構建築 (Yuan dynasty timber architecture in Qianming Monastery at Shoushan). *Kejishi wenji* 2 (1980): 84–91.

Du Xianzhou 杜仙洲. "Yonglegong de jianzhu" 永樂宮的建築 (Architecture of Yongle Palace). *Wenwu* 8 (1963): 3–17.

Ebrey, Patricia Buckley. *The Cambridge Illustrated History of China.* 2nd ed. Cambridge: Cambridge University Press, 2010.

Feng Baiyi 馮百毅. "Huishansi: Yuandai jianzhu yizhen" 會善寺元代建築遺珍 (Yuan architecture of Huishan Monastery). *Zhongguo wenhua yichan* 3 (2009): 51–53.

Feng, Jiren. *Chinese Architecture and Metaphor: Song Culture in the Yingzao fashi Building Manual.* Honolulu: University of Hawai'i Press, 2012.

Ferguson, John C. "Chinese Foot Measure." *Monumenta Serica* 6 (1941): 357–382.

Fu Xinian 傅熹年. *Fu Xinian jianzhushi lunwen ji* 傅熹年建築史論文集 (Collected essays in architectural history by Fu Xinian). Beijing: Wenwu chubanshe, 1998.

———. "Yuan dadu danei gongdian de fuyuan yanjiu" 元大都大內宮殿的復原研究 (A study of the reconstruction of the imperial palaces of Yuan Dadu). In Fu, *Fu Xinian jianzhushi lunwen ji* 傅熹年建築史論文集 (Collected essays in architectural history by Fu Xinian), 326–356. Beijing: Wenwu chubanshe, 1998.

———. *Zhongguo kexue jishu shi. Jianzhu juan* 中國科學技術史建築卷 (History of science and technology in China, volume of architecture). Beijing: Kexue chubanshe, 2008.

Fu Xinian, Guo Daiheng, Liu Xujie, Pan Guxi, Qiao Yun, Sun Dazhang, and Nancy Steinhardt. *Chinese Architecture.* New Haven, CT: Yale University Press, 2002.

Ge Jianxiong 葛劍雄, Cao Shuji 曹樹基, and Wu Songdi 吳松弟. *Jianming Zhongguo yiminshi* 簡明中國移民史 (A concise history of migration in China). Fuzhou: Fujian renmin chubanshe, 1993.

Gugong bowuyuan 故宮博物院, ed. "Emei xianzhi" 峨嵋縣志 (Gazetteer of Emei [completed in 1721]). In *Sichuan fuzhou xianzhi* 四川府州縣志. Haikou: Hainan chubanshe, 2001.

———, ed. "Lushan xianzhi" 蘆山縣志 (Gazetteer of Lushan [completed in 1721]). In *Sichuan fuzhou xianzhi* 四川府州縣志. Haikou: Hainan chubanshe, 2001.

Guo Daiheng 郭黛姮. *Donglai diyishan: Baoguosi* 東來第一山保國寺 (Baoguo Monastery: The first mountain from the east). Beijing: Wenwu chubanshe, 2003.

———. "Shishiji zhi shisanshiji de Zhongguo Fojiao jianzhu" 十世紀至十三世紀的中國佛教建築 (Buddhist architecture in China, tenth to thirteenth centuries). In *Jianzhushi lunwenji di shisi ji* 建築史論文集第14輯 (Collected essays in architectural history, volume 14), edited by Zhang Fuhe, 71–92. Beijing: Qinghua daxue chubanshe, 2001.

———. *Zhongguo gudai jianzhushi* 中國古代建築史 (History of premodern Chinese architecture). Vol. 3, *Song Liao Jin Xixia jianzhu* 宋遼金西夏建築 (Song, Liao, Jin, and Xixia architecture). Beijing: Zhongguo jianzhu gongye chubanshe, 2001.

Guo Huayu 郭華喻. *Mingdai guanshi jianzhu damuzuo* 明代官式建築大木作 (The major carpentry of official architecture of the Ming dynasty). Nanjing: Dongnan daxue chubanshe, 2005.

Guo, Qinghua. *Chinese Architecture and Planning: Ideas, Methods, Techniques.* London: Axel Menges, 2006.

———. *The Structure of Chinese Timber Architecture.* London: Minerva, 1999.

———. *Visual Dictionary of Chinese Architecture.* Victoria, Australia: The Images Publishing Group, 2002.

———. "*Yingzao fashi:* The Twelfth Century Chinese Building Manual." *Architectural History* 41 (1998): 1–13.

Guo Qinglin 郭慶琳. *Meishan xianzhi* 眉山縣志 (Gazetteer of Meishan [completed in 1923]). Taipei: Taiwan xuesheng shuju, 1967.

Harrer, Alexandra. "Fan-Shaped Bracket Sets and Their Application in Religious Timber Architecture of Shanxi Province." PhD diss., University of Pennsylvania, 2010.

———. "Where Did the Wood Go? Rethinking the Problematic Role of Wood in Wood-Like Mimicry." *Frontiers of History in China* 10.2 (2015): 188–221.

He Xiuling 何修齡. "Hanchengxian suojian de Yuandai jianzhu jiqi jiben tezheng" 韓城縣所見的元代建築及其基本特徵 (Yuan architecture and its basic characteristics at Hancheng County). *Wenwu* 11 (1957): 54–58.

Hu Xiaopeng 胡小鵬. "Yuandai de xiguan jianghu" 元代的系官匠戶 (The official craftsmen of the Yuan dyansty). *Xibei shida xuebao (shehui kexue ban)* 40.2 (2003): 77–83.

Huang Jin 黃溍. "Huqiu Yunyan chansi xingzaoji" 虎丘雲岩禪寺興造記 (Records of the construction of Yunyan Chan Monastery at Tiger Hill). In *Huqiu shanzhi* 虎丘山志 (Gazetteer of Tiger Hill [completed in 1676]), edited by Huang Yujian 黃輿堅 (1620–1701).

Huang Zi 黃滋. "Yuandai gucha Yanfusi jiqi dadian de weixiu duice" 元代古
剎延福寺及其大殿的維修對策 (Conservation strategy for the main hall of
Yanfu Monastery of the Yuan dynasty). In *Zhongguo wenwu baohu jishu xiehui
dierjie xueshu nianhui lunwenji* 中國文物保護技術協會第二屆學術年會論文
集 (Conference proceedings of the Second Annual Conference of Conservation Technology in China). Xi'an, July 2002.

Hubeisheng bowuguan 湖北省博物館. *Wudangshan* 武當山 (Wudang Mountain).
Beijing: Wenwu chubanshe, 1991.

Ito Chuta 伊東忠太. *Shina kenchiku shi* 支那建築史 (Architectural history of
China). Tokyo: Yuzankaku, 1931.

Jin Youli 金友理 (18th century). *Taihu beikao* 太湖備考 (References to Lake Taihu
[completed in the 18th century]). Nanjing: Jaingsu guji chubanshe, 1998.

Jing, Anning. "The Portraits of Khubilai Khan and Chabi by Anige (1245–1306), a
Nepali Artist at the Yuan Court." *Artibus Asiae* 54.1/2 (1994): 40–86.

Kleeman, Terry F. *A God's Own Tale: The Book of Transformation of Wenchang, the
Divine Lord of Zitong.* Albany: SUNY Press, 1994.

Kohn, Livia. "A Home for the Immortals: The Layout and Development of Medieval Daoist Monasteries." *Acta orientalia* 53 (2000): 79–106.

Lagerway, John. "The Pilgrimage to Wu-Tang Shan." In *Pilgrims and Sacred Sites
in China,* edited by Susan Naquin and Chun-fang Yu, 293–332. Berkeley: University of California Press, 1992.

Lai Xirong 賴西蓉. "Sichuan Pengxixian xinfaxian Yuandai jianzhu Jinxiansi" 四川
蓬溪縣新發現元代建築金仙寺 (The newly discovered Yuan architecture of
Jinxian Monastery at Pengxi County, Sichuan). *Sichuan wenwu* 5 (2012): 72–76.

Langlois, John D., Jr., ed. *China under Mongol Rule.* Princeton, NJ: Princeton University Press, 1981.

Lee, Sherman E. *Chinese Art under the Mongols: The Yuan Dynasty (1279–1368).* Cleveland, OH: Cleveland Museum of Art, 1968.

Li Jiannong 李劍農. *Song Yuan Ming jingji shigao* 宋元明經濟史稿 (The economic
history of Song, Yuan, and Ming). Beijing: Sanlian shudian, 1957.

Li Jie 李誡 (1035–1110). *Yingzao fashi* 營造法式 (Building standards). Nanjing:
Jiangnan tushuguan, 1925; reprint, Beijing: Zhongguo shudian, 2006.

Li Jinglin 李景林. "Yuandai de gongjiang" 元代的工匠 (Craftsmen of the Yuan
dynasty). *Yuanshi ji beifang minzushi yanjiu jikan* 5 (1981): 36–47.

Li Mingwan 李銘皖. *Suzhou fuzhi* 蘇州府志 (Gazetteer of the Prefecture of
Suzhou [completed in 1877]. Nanjing: Jiangsu guji chubanshe, 1991.

Li Qianlang 李乾朗. "Beijing Miaoyingsi baita" 北京妙應寺白塔 (The white
pagoda of Miaoying Monastery in Beijing). *Zijincheng* 10 (2009): 66–71.

Li Xianwen 李顯文. "Emei Dongyuemiao Feilaidian he Xiangdian jinxing luojia
weixiu" 峨嵋東嶽廟飛來殿和香殿進行落架維修 (The reparation of Feilai
Hall and the Incense Hall of the Temple of the Eastern Peak at Emei). *Sichuan
wenwu* 3 (1984): 92.

———. "Zitong Pantuoshidian jianzhu niandai chutan" 梓潼盤陀石殿建築年代初探 (A study of the date of Pantuoshi Hall at Zitong). *Sichuan wenwu* 1 (1984): 41–45.

Liang, Sicheng. *Chinese Architecture: A Pictorial History*. Cambridge, MA: MIT Press, 1984.

———. *Liang Sicheng quanji* 梁思成全集 (Complete collection of Liang Sicheng). Vol. 6, *Qingshi yingzao zeli* 清式營造則例 (*Yingzao zeli* of the Qing style), edited by Guo Daiheng. Beijing: Zhongguo jianzhu gongye chubanshe, 2001.

———. *Liang Sicheng quanji* 梁思成全集 (Complete collection of Liang Sicheng). Vol. 7, *Yingzao fashi zhushi* 營造法式註釋 (Annotation of *Yingzao fashi*), edited by Xu Bo'an 徐伯安 and Wang Guixiang 王貴祥. Beijing: Zhongguo jianzhu gongye chubanshe, 2001.

Ling Zhenrong 凌振榮. "Nantong Tianningsi Daxiongzhidian weixiu jilu" 南通天寧寺大雄之殿維修記錄 (Documentation of the reparation of the Daxiong hall of Tianning Monastery at Nantong). *Dongnan wenhua* (1996), 126–129.

Liu, Cary. "The Yuan Dynasty Capital, Ta-Tu: Imperial Building Program and Bureaucracy." *T'oung Pao* 78.4/5 (1992): 264–301.

Liu Dunzhen 劉敦楨. "Suzhou gujianzhu diaochaji" 蘇州古建築調查記 (Investigation of ancient architecture in Suzhou). *Zhongguo yingzao xueshe huikan* 6.3 (1936): 17–68.

———. "Zhenrusi zhengdian" 真如寺正殿 (The main hall of Zhenru Monastery). *Wenwu* 8 (1951): 91–97.

———. *Zhongguo gudai jianzhushi* 中國古代建築史 (A history of Chinese premodern architecture). Beijing: Zhongguo jianzhu gongye chubanshe, 1984.

Liu, James T. C. *Reform in Sung China: Wang An-Shih (1021-1086) and His New Policies*. Cambridge, MA: Harvard University Press, 1950.

Liu Lin'an 劉臨安. "Puzhaosi Yuandai jianzhu bowuguan" 普照寺元代建筑博物馆 (Puzhao Monastery, a museum of Yuan architecture). In *Zhongguo gujianzhu wenhua zhilü* 中国古建筑文化之旅 (A journey of ancient architectural culture of China), 60–63. Beijing: Zhishi chanquan chubanshe, 2004.

Liu Mingdao 劉明道 (Yuan). *Wudang fudi zongzhenji* 武當福地總真集 (A collection of records of Mount Wudang as a paradise). Nanjing: Jiangsu guji chubanshe, 2000.

Liu Rui 劉瑞. "Shaanxi Yuandai jianzhu damuzuo yanjiu" 陝西元代建築大木作研究 (A study of the major carpentry of Yuan architecture in Shaanxi). Master's thesis, Xi'an University of Architecture and Technology, 2009.

Liu, Ts'un-yan, and Judith Berling. "The 'Three Teachings' in the Mongol-Yüan Period." In *Yuan Thought: Chinese Thought and Religion under the Mongols*, edited by Hok-Lam Chan and William Theodore De Bary. New York: Columbia Univesity Press, 1982.

Liu Xixiang 劉習祥. "Henan Bo'aixian faxian Yuandai jianzhu Tangdidian" 河南博愛縣發現元代建築湯帝殿 (Yuan architecture Tangdi Hall discovered at Bo'ai County, Henan). *Wenwu* 8 (1980): 93–96.

Liu Xujie 劉敘杰 and Qi Deyao 戚德耀. "Jiangsu Wuxian Jijiansi Yuandai shidianwu" 江蘇吳縣寂鑒寺元代石殿屋 (Jijian Monastery, a Yuan dynasty stone house at Wu County, Suzhou). In *Kejishi wenji*,1:44–47. Shanghai: Shanghai kexue jishu chubanshe, 1979.

Lou Jianlong 樓建龍 and Wang Yimin 王益民. "Fujian Shunchang Baoshansi dadian" 福建順昌寶山寺大殿 (The main hall of Baoshan Monastery at Shunchang, Fujian). *Wenwu*, no. 9 (2009): 65–72.

Lu Bingjie 路秉杰. "Cong Shanghai Zhenrusi dadian kan Riben Chanzongyang de yuanyuan" 從上海真如寺大殿看日本禪宗樣的淵源 (Origin of the Japanese Zen Buddhist style in the main hall of Zhenru Monastery in Shanghai). *Tongji daxue xuebao (shehui kexue ban)* 7.2 (1996): 7–13.

Lu Li 陸立. *Zhenru lizhi* 真如里志 (Gazetteer of Zhenru [completed in 1768]). In *Shanghai xiangzhen jiuzhi congshu* 上海鄉鎮舊志叢書 (A collection of old gazetteers of Shanghai), edited by Shanghai shi difangzhi bangongshi 上海市地方志辦公室 (Office of local gazetteers of Shanghai). Shanghai: Shanghai shehui kexue chubanshe, 2003.

Meng Siming 蒙思明. *Yuandai shehui jieji zhidu* 元代社會階級制度 (Social hierarchy in the Yuan society). Shanghai: Shanghai renmin chubanshe, 2006.

Miller, Tracy. *The Divine Nature of Power: Chinese Ritual Architecture at the Sacred Site of Jinci.* Cambridge, MA: Harvard University Press, 2007.

Needham, Joseph, Ling Wang, and Gwei-djen Lu. *Science and Civilisation in China.* Vol. 4, pt. 3. Cambridge: Cambridge University Press, 1971.

Nielsen, Bent. *A Companion to Yi Jing Numerology and Cosmology.* London: Routledge, 2015.

Pan Guxi 潘谷西. *Zhongguo gudai jianzhushi* 中國古代建築史 (History of premodern Chinese architecture). Vol. 4, *Yuan Ming jianzhu* 元明建築 (Yuan and Ming architecture). Beijing: Zhongguo jianzhu gongye chubanshe, 2001.

Pan Guxi 潘谷西 and He Jianzhong 何建中. *Yingzao fashi jiedu* 營造法式解讀 (Interpretation of the Yingzao *fashi*). Nanjing: Dongnan daxue chubanshe, 2005.

Pan Qing 潘清. *Yuandai jiangnan minzu chongzu yu wenhua jiaorong* 元代江南民族重組與文化交融 (Ethnic reorganization and interaction in Jiangnan during the Yuan dynasty). Nanjing: Fenghuang chubanshe, 2006.

Pi Shutang 皮樹棠 and Pi Xirui 皮錫瑞. *Xuanping xianzhi* 宣平縣志 (Gazetteer of Xuanping County [completed in 1878]). Taipei: Chengwen chubanshe, 1976.

Qian Renlong 錢人龍. *Jinhua xianzhi* 金華縣志 (Gazetteer of Jinhua [completed in 1894]). In *Zhongguo difangzhi jicheng* 中國地方志集成 (Collection of local gazetteers in China). Nanjing: Jiangsu guji chubanshe, 1992.

Qu Yuxuan 屈宇轩. "Song Jin jianzhu yingzao jishu dui houshi de yingxiang—yi Jindongnan Yuandai jianzhu weili" 宋金建築營造技術對後世的影響—以晉

東南元代建築爲例 (The influence of Song-Jin architecture and its technology—taking Yuan architecture in southeast Shanxi as an example). Master's thesis, Taiyuan University of Technology, 2014.

Ren Ziyuan 任自垣. *Dayue taihe shanzhi* 大嶽太和山志 (Gazetteer of the Grand Taihe Mountain [completed in 1431]). In *Mingdai Wudangshan zhi erzhong* 明代武當山志二種 (Two Ming dynasty gazetteers of Wudang Mountain), edited by Yang Lizhi 楊立志. Wuhan: Hubei renmin chubanshe, 1999.

Rossabi, Morris. "The Reign of Khubilai Khan." In *The Cambridge History of China: Alien Regimes and Border States, 907-1378,* edited by Frank Herbert and Denis Twitchett, 414–489. Cambridge: Cambridge University Press, 1994.

Ruitenbeek, Klaas. *Carpentry and Building in Late Imperial China: A Study of the Fifteenth Century Carpentry's Manual Lubanjing.* Leiden: Brill, 1993.

———. "Foreword." *Philadelphia Museum of Art Bulletin* 92.389/390 (2004): 7–9.

Shanghaishi wenwu baoguan weiyuanhui 上海市文物保管委員會. "Shanghai shijiao Yuandai jianzhu Zhenrusi zhengdian zhong faxian de gongjiang mobizi" 上海市郊元代建築真如寺正殿中發現的工匠墨筆字 (Ink inscriptions by craftsmen discovered in the main hall of Zhenru Monastery, Yuan architecture in suburban Shanghai). *Wenwu* 3 (1966): 16–26.

Shi Weimin 史衛民. *Yuanchao shehui shenghuoshi* 元朝社會生活史 (The history of society and life in the Yuan dynasty). Beijing: Zhongguo shehui kexue chubanshe, 1996.

Sichuansheng wenwu guanliju 四川省文物管理局. *Sichuan Wenwuzhi* 四川文物誌 (Gazetteer of Sichuan cultural relics). Chengdu: Bashu shushe, 2005.

Sichuansheng wenwu kaogu yanjiuyuan 四川省文物考古研究院. *Huaying Anbing mu* 華鎣安丙墓 (The An Bing tomb at Huaying). Beijing: Wenwu chubanshe, 2006.

Smith, Paul. "Family, Landsmann, and Status-Group Affinity in Refugee Mobility Strategies: The Mongol Invasions and the Diaspora of Sichuanese Elites, 1230–1330." *Harvard Journal of Asiatic Studies* 52.2 (1992): 665–708.

Song Lian 宋濂 (1310–1381). *Yuanshi* 元史 (History of Yuan). Beijing: Zhonghua shuju, 1977.

Soper, Alexander. *The Evolution of Buddhist Architecture in Japan.* New York: Hacker Art Books, 1978.

———. "Japanese Evidence for the History of the Architecture and Iconography of Chinese Buddhism." *Monumenta Serica* 4 (1939–1940): 638–678.

Steinhardt, Nancy. "The Architecture of Living and Dying." In *The World of Khubilai Khan: Chinese Art in the Yuan Dynasty,* edited by James Watt, 65–73. New York: Metropolitan Museum, 2010.

———. *China's Early Mosques.* Edinburgh: Edinburgh University Press, 2015.

———. "Chinese Architectural History in the Twenty-first Century." *Journal of the Society of Architectural Historians* 73.1 (2014): 45–68.

——. *Chinese Architecture in an Age of Turmoil, 200-600.* Honolulu: University of Hawai'i Press, 2014.

——. "Imperial Architecture along the Mongolian Road to Dadu." *Ars Orientalis* 18 (1990): 177–189.

——. "A Jin Hall at Jingtusi: Architecture in Search of Identity." *Ars Orientalis* 33 (2003): 77–119.

——. *Liao Architecture.* Honolulu: University of Hawai'i Press, 1997.

——. "The Plan of Khubilai Khan's Imperial City." *Artibus Asiae* 44.2/3 (1983): 137–158.

——. "Shishi, a Stone Structure Associated with Abaoji in Zuzhou." *Asia Major* 19.1–2 (2007): 241–266.

——. "Standard Architecture in a Multi-centered, Multi-cultural Age." In *China in a Multi-centered Age,* edited by Hung Wu, 38–69. Beijing: Center of the Art of East Asia, University of Chicago, 2013.

——. "The Synagogue at Kaifeng : Sino-Judaic Architecture of the Diaspora." In *The Jews of China: Vol. 1: Historical and Comparative Perspectives,* edited by Goldstein and Schwartz, 3–21. Abingdon: Routledge, 1990.

——. "The Temple to the North Peak in Quyang." *Artibus Asiae* 58.1/2 (1998): 69–90.

——. "Towards the Definition of a Yuan Dynasty Hall." *Journal of the Society of Architectural Historians* 47.1 (1988): 57–73.

Su Bai 宿白. "Yuandai Hangzhou de Zangchuan mijiao jiqi youguan yiji" 元代杭州的藏傳密教及其有關遺跡 (Tibetan Buddhism in Hangzhou during the Yuan dynasty and related historical remains). *Wenwu,* no. 10 (1990): 55–71.

Sun, Zhixin Jason. "Dadu: Great Capital of the Yuan Dynasty." In *The World of Khubilai Khan: Chinese Art in the Yuan Dynasty,* edited by James Watt, 41–64. New York: Metropolitan Museum of Art, 2010.

Sunanqu wenwu guanli weiyuanhui 蘇南區文物管理委員會. "Wuxian Luzhi Baoshengsi diaocha baogao" 吳縣用直鎮保聖寺調查報告 (Investigation report on Baosheng Monastery at Luzhi, Wu County). *Wenwu* 7 (1950): 15–16.

Swart, Paula. "Buddhist Sculptures at Feilai Feng: A Confrontation of Two Traditions." *Orientations* 12 (1987): 54–61.

Tao Baocheng 陶保成. "Xuanyuangong zhengdian de buluojia kexue baohu" 軒轅宮正殿的不落架科學保護 (Non-dissembling conservation of the main hall of Xuanyuan Palace). *Dongnan wenhua* 7 (2001): 95–96.

Tao Mingkuan 陶鳴寬. "Sichuan Langzhong Yong'ansi Yuandai dadian jiqi bihua suxiang" 四川閬中永安寺元代大殿及其壁畫塑像 (The Yuan dynasty main hall and its murals and sculptures in Yong'an Monastery, Langzhong, Sichuan). *Wenwu* 12 (1955): 99–102.

Tomoyasu, Iiyama. "Maintaining Gods in Medieval China: Temple Worship and Local Governance in North China under the Jin and Yuan." *Journal of Song-Yuan Studies* 40 (2010): 71–102.

Unknown. "Zhejiang lianxu faxian gudai mugou jianzhu" 浙江連續發現古代木構建築 (Consecutive discoveries of ancient timber architecture in Zhejiang). *Wenwu* 3 (1955): 59.

Wang Biwen 王璧文. "Yuan Dadu siguan miaoyu jianzhi yangebiao" 元大都寺觀廟宇建置沿革表 (Chronicle of temples and monasteries constructions in Yuan Dadu). *Zhongguo yingzao xueshe huikan* 6.4 (1937): 130–161.

Wang Hui 王恢. *Zhongguo lishi dili tiyao* 中國歷史地理提要 (Summary of Chinese historical geography). Taipei: Xuesheng shuju, 1980.

Wang Qiheng 王其亨. "Jin ke *Chong jiaozheng dili xinshu* suo yin Song *Yingzao fashi* zouyi" 金刻《重校正地理新書》所引宋《營造法式》芻議 (Quotations of the Song dynasty *Yingzao fashi* in the Jin print of *Chong jiaozheng dili xinshu*). In *Ningbo Baoguosi dadian jiancheng yiqian zhounian xueshu yantaohui ji zhongguo jianzhu shixue fenhui 2013 nianhui lunwenji* 寧波保國寺大殿建成1000週年學術研討會暨中國建築史學分會2013年會論文集 (Conference proceedings of the Symposium for the Millennial Anniversity of the Main Hall of Baoguo Monatery in Ningbo), 1–9. Ningbo, 2013.

Wang Shiren 王世仁. "Yonglegong de Yuandai jianzhu he bihua" 永樂宮的元代建築和壁畫 (Yuan architecture and murals in Yongle Palace). *Wenwu* 9 (1956): 32–40.

Wang Yuan 王媛 and Lu Bingjie 路秉杰. "Zhongguo de fodian jianzhu yu foxiang" 中國的佛殿建築與佛像 (Chinese Buddhist architecture and sculptures). *Tongji Daxue xuebao* 1 (1998): 89–93.

Wang Ziqi 王子奇. "Shanxi Dingxiang Guanwangmiao kaocha zhaji" 山西定襄關王廟考察札記 (A survey of the Guanwang Temple at Dingxiang, Shanxi). *Shanxi Datong daxue xuebao* 23.4 (2009): 23–30.

Watt, James C. Y. "Introduction." In *The World of Khubilai Khan: Chinese Art in the Yuan Dynasty,* edited by James Watt, 1–40. New York: Metropolitan Museum of Art, 2010.

Wright, Arthur F. *Buddhism in Chinese History.* Stanford, CA: Stanford University Press, 1959.

———. *Studies in Chinese Buddhism.* Chicago: University of Chicago Press, 1990.

Wu Chengluo 吳承洛. *Zhongguo duliangheng shi* 中國度量衡史 (History of Chinese weights and measures). Shanghai: Shanghai shudian, 1984.

Wu Songdi 吳松弟. *Beifang yimin yu Nansong shehui bianqian* 北方移民與南宋社會變遷 (Immigrants from the north and changes in the Southern Song society). Taipei: Wenjin chubanshe, 1993.

Xie Jisheng 謝繼勝. *Zhongguo Zangchuan fojiao yishu* 中國藏傳佛教藝術 (Tibetan Buddhist Art of China). Vol. 6, *Mudiao* 木雕 (Wooden carving). Beijing: Beijing meishu sheying chubanshe, 2006.

Xu Jiyong 徐繼鏞. *Langzhong xianzhi* 閬中縣志 (Gazetteer of Langzhong [completed in 1851]). Xu Jiyong, 1851. Print.

Xu Yitao 徐怡濤. "Gongyuan qi zhi shisi shiji Zhongguo fubigong xingzhi liubian yanjiu" 公元七至十四世紀中國扶壁栱形制流變研究 (A study of the transformation of the buttress-bracket from the seventh to the fourteenth centuries in China). *Gugong bowuyuan yuankan* 5 (2005): 85–101.

Yang Jiayou 楊嘉祐. "Shanghai diqu gujianzhu" 上海地區古建築 (Ancient architecture in Shanghai). *Jianzhu xuebao* 7 (1981): 46–49.

Yang Zirong 楊子榮. "Lun Shanxi Yuandai yiqian mugou jianzhu de baohu" 論山西元代以前木構建築的保護 (Conservation of pre-Yuan timber architecture in Shanxi). *Wenwu jikan* 1 (1994): 62–67.

Yao Guangpu 姚光普. "Qiqushan Damiao" 七曲山大廟 (The Grand Temple at Qiqu Mountain). *Sichuan wenwu* 5 (1991): 76–80.

Zhang Guoxiong 張國雄. "Zhongguo lishishang yimin de zhuyao liuxiang he fenqi" 中國歷史上移民的主要流向和分期 (Major directions and phases of migrations in Chinese history). *Beijing daxue xuebao* 2 (1996): 98–107.

Zhang Jianwei 張劍葳. "A Study of the Three Buddhist Copper Hall Projects, 1602–1607." *Frontiers of History in China* 10.2 (2015): 289–322.

——. "Wudangshan Yuandai Xiaotongdian Yanjiu" 武當山元代小銅殿研究 (A study of the Yuan dynasty little copper hall on Mount Wudang). *Jianzhushi* 27 (2010): 80–106.

——. *Zhongguo gudai jinshu jianzhu yanjiu* 中國古代金屬建築研究 (Chinese ancient metal architecture). Nanjing: Dongnan daxue chubanshe, 2015.

Zhang Shiqing 張十慶. "Gudai jianzhu jianjia biaoji de xingshi yu yiyi" 古代建築間架表記的形式與意義 (Form and meaning of using framework in ancient architecture). In *Zhang Shiqing Dongya jianzhu jishushi wenji* 張十慶東亞建築技術史文集 (Collected essays of the history of architectural technology in East Asia by Zhang Shiqing), edited by Zhang Shiqing, 413–435. Shenyang: Liaoning meishu chubanshe, 2013.

——. "Jiangnan diantang jianjia xingzhi de diyu tese" 江南殿堂間架形制的地域特色 (Local characteristics of mansion-style frameworks in Jiangnan). *Jianzhushi lunwenji* 19 (2003): 47–62.

——. "Luzhi Baoshengsi dadian fuyuan tantao" 甪直保寶聖寺大殿復原探討 (A discussion on the restoration of the main hall of Baosheng Monastery at Luzhi). *Wenwu* 11 (2005): 75–87.

——. "Nanfang shang'ang yu tiaowo zuofa tanxi" 南方上昂與挑斡做法探析 (Analysis of upward cantilever and *tiaowo* in the south). *Jianzhushi lunwenji* 16 (2006): 31–45.

——. "Song Yuan Jiangnan siyuan jianzhu de chidu yu guimo" 宋元江南寺院建築的尺度與規模 (Dimension and scale of Song-Yuan monastic architecture in Jiangnan). *Huazhong jianzhu* 3 and 4 (2002): 99–100, 96–99.

——. "Tang Yingshanling dizhai jinxian tiaowen bianxi yu shidu" 唐營繕令第宅禁限條文辨析與釋讀 (Analyze and interpret the entry about residential regulations in Tang *Yingshanling*). In *Zhongguo jianzhu shilun huikan* 中國建築史論匯刊 (Journal of Chinese Architecture History). Vol. 3, edited by Wang Guixiang 王貴祥, 142–163. Beijing: Qinghua daxue chubanshe, 2010.

———. *Wushan Shichatu yu Nan Song Jiangnan Chansi* 五山十剎圖與南宋江南禪寺 (The "Five Mountains and Ten Monasteries" chart and Southern Song Chan Buddhist monasteries in Jiangnan). Nanjing: Dongnan daxue chubanshe, 2000.

———. "Yingzao fashi de jishu yuanliu jiqi yu jiangnan jianzhu de guanlian tanxi" 營造法式的技術源流及其與江南建築的關聯探析 (The technology origin of the *Yingzao fashi* and its relation to Jiangnan architecture). *Jianzhushi lunwenji* 17 (2003): 1–11.

———. *Zhongguo Jiangnan Chanzong siyuan jianzhu yanjiu* 中國江南禪宗寺院建築研究 (Architecture of Chan Buddhist monasteries in Jiangnan, China). Wuhan: Hubei jiaoyu chubanshe, 2002.

Zhang Tingyu 張廷玉 (1672–1755). *Mingshi* 明史 (History of Ming). Beijing: Zhonghua shuju, 1974.

Zhang Xianghai 張香海. *Chongxiu Zitong xianzhi* 重修梓潼县志 (Gazetteer of Zitong, rewritten [completed in 1858]). Nanjing: Jiangsu guji chubanshe, 1992.

Zhang Yuhuan 張馭寰. "Dui Hancheng Yuwangmiao Yuandai jianzhu de taolun" 對韓城禹王廟元代建築的討論 (A discussion on the Yuan architecture of Yuwang Temple at Hancheng). In *Zhang Yuhuan wenji* 張馭寰文集 (Collected essays by Zhang Yuhuan), edited by Zhang Yuhuan, 71–72. Beijing: Zhongguo wenshi chubanshe, 2008.

———. "Shanxi Yuandai diantang de damu jiegou" 山西元代殿堂的大木結構 (The major carpentery structure of Yuan halls in Shanxi). In *Kejishi wenji* 科技史文集 (Collected essays of history of science), 2:71–106. Shanghai: Kexue jishu chubanshe, 1979.

Zhao Xiangdong 趙向東. "Chengqi bianyi shilun Yuan gou zhong fanying de bufen xingzhi shanbian tezheng" 承啓變異試論元構中反映的部分形制嬗變特徵 (Inheritance and variation: Analysis of evolutionary characteristics of Chinese ancient architecture through Yuan architecture). *Xinjianzhu* 2 (2013): 124–128.

Zhao Yiyuan 趙義元. "Qiantan Mianyang mugou gujianzhu ji xiangguan wenti" 淺談綿陽木構古建築及相關問題 (Ancient timber architecture at Mianyang and related issues). *Sichuan wenwu* 6 (2000): 55–60.

Zhao Yuanxiang 趙元祥. "Lushan Qinglongsi dadian jianzhu niandai de xinfaxian" 蘆山青龍寺大殿建築年代的新發現 (A new discovery of the date of the main hall of Qinglong Monastery in Lushan). *Zhongguo wenwubao*, October 12, 2018, 6.

Zhao Yuanxiang 趙元祥 and Cai Yukun 蔡宇琨. "Sichuan Pengxixian Jinxiansi Zangdian Yuandai tiji ji xiangguan wenti" 四川蓬溪縣金仙寺藏殿元代題記及相關問題 (Yuan dynasty inscriptions and related issues in the sutra hall of Jinxian Monastery at Pengxi County, Sichuan). *Sichuan wenwu* 5 (2014): 88–96.

Zhejiangsheng wenwu kaogusuo wenbaoshi 浙江省文物考古所文保室. "Jinhua Tianningsi dadian de gouzao ji weixiu" 金華天寧寺大殿的構造及維修

(The structure and reparation of the main hall of Tianning Monastery at Jinhua). *Zhejiangsheng wenwu kaogusuo xuekan* (1981): 176–183.

Zhongguo guojia wenwuju 中國國家文物局. "Diqipi quanguo zhongdian wenwu baohu danwei mingdan" 第七批全國重點文物保護單位名單 (The seventh list of national cultural heritage sites). 2013. http://www.sach.gov.cn./col /col1650/index.html (accessed October 7, 2018).

Zhu Guangya 朱光亞. "Zhongguo gudai mujiegou puxi zaiyanjiu" 中國古代木結構譜系再研究 (Revisit the genealogy of ancient timber structure in China). In *Jianzhu lishi yu lilun yanjiu wenji 1997-2007* 建築歷史與理論研究文集 (Collected essays on architectural history and theory), edited by Liu Xianjue 劉先覺 and Zhang Shiqing 張十慶, 150–158. Beijing: Zhongguo jianzhu gongye chubanshe, 2007.

Zhu Qiqian 朱啓鈐 and Kan Duo 闞铎. "Yuan Dadu gongyuan tukao" 元大都宮苑圖考 (An illustrated study of the palaces and gardens in Yuan Dadu). *Zhongguo yingzao xueshe huikan* 1.2 (1930): 1–125.

Zhu Xiaonan 朱小南. "Langzhong Yong'ansi dadian jianzhu shidai ji gouzao tezheng qianxi" 閬中永安寺大殿建築時代及構造特徵淺析 (Analysis of the date and structure of the main hall of Yong'an Monastery at Langzhong). *Sichuan wenwu* 1 (1991): 69–71.

Zhu Xie 朱偰. *Yuan Dadu gongdian tukao* 元大都宮殿圖考 (An illustrated study of the palaces in Yuan Dadu). Beijing: Beijing guji chubanshe, 1990.

Zuo, Lala. "Build for the Living: Stone Buildings of the Yuan Dynasty." *Frontiers of History in China* 10.2 (2015): 264–288.

INDEX

Page numbers in boldface type refer to illustrations.

Feng, Jiren, 3, 183n2

Fengguo Monastery (Yi County, Liaoning), 186n27, 190n36

Foguang Monastery (Mount Wutai, Shanxi), 5, **6–7**, 185n25, 189n16

forking-hand (*chashou*) struts, 11, **78**, 79, 172

Fu Xinian, xiv, 8, 33

Gaozong, Emperor (Song), 141

Grand Temple (Qiqushan damiao; Mount Qiqu, Sichuan), 69, 105, 106, 195n52. *See also* Pantuoshi Hall

Great East Hall (Foguang Monastery; Mount Wutai, Shanxi), 6, **7**, 185n25, 189n16

Great Wenchuan earthquake (2008), xiii

Guangji Monastery (Wutai, Shanxi), 29, **30**, 189n12

Guangsheng Monastery (Hongdong County, Shanxi), xv, 28, **29–32**, 188n5, 188n11

Guangxiao Monastery (Guangzhou, Guangdong), 185n7

Guanwang Temple (Dingxiang, Shanxi), **19**, 187n66

Hall of Great Achievement (Confucius Temple; Qufu, Shandong), 192n19

Heavenly Kings, 198n37; halls of (*Tianwangdian*), 53, 120, 126, 135; statues of, 137. *See also* Yunyan Monastery

hidden roof (*noyane*), **131–132**, 134

Hualin Monastery (Fuzhou, Fujian), 8, 185n7

Huang Jin, 135, 136

Huangniangdian (Lifeng Temple; Nanbu, Sichuan), 191n7

Huangqian Hall (Temple of Heaven, Beijing), **21**

huatouzi (two-scroll bracket arm), 108, 109, 127

Huizong, Emperor (Northern Song), 3, 65

Huo Prefecture Municipal Hall (Huo County, Shanxi), **33**, 189n18

Islam, 162, 165

Islamic architecture, 162, 163, 164, 165

Japanese architecture, 118, **131–132**, 134, 183n10, 197n29

Jiang Wei, 101, 194n45, 194n48

Jiangzhou, Grand Hall of (Shanxi), 22, 31

Jidu Temple (Jiyuan County, Henan), 16

Jieyi Temple, Transit Hall of (Shanxi), 22

Jijian Monastery (Suzhou, Jiangsu), 152–157

Jin architecture, xiv, xv, 1, 6–9; bracket sets in, 30, 44; Buddha halls in, 6–7; columns in, **5**, 12, 27, 189n13; and northern architecture, 27, 28, 64, 167; oblique arms in, 24, 65, 187n71; roof framing in, 32, 33; and Song architecture, 8–9, 168; in Upper Yangzi, 117; and *Yingzao fashi*, 8–9

Jin (Jurchen) dynasty, 2, 64–65; Mongol destruction of, 67; and southbound migration, 65, 190n37

Jingkang Period, Disorders of, 65

Jinhua xianzhi (Gazetteer of Jinhua County), 125–126

Jin Shrine (Taiyuan, Shanxi), 5, 185n21, 192n19

Jokhang Temple (Dazhaosi; Lhasa, Tibet), **155–156**, 157

Judaism, 165

Kaifeng Synagogue (Kaifeng, Henan), 165, 200n31

Kaiyuan Monastery (Quanzhou, Fujian): pagodas of, 162, **163**, 199n21

Kaogongji (Records of examination of craftsmen), xiii

Khitan (Liao) dynasty, 3. *See also* Liao architecture

Khubilai Khan, xiv, xv, 25, 66, 165, 166, 167

101, 105, 113, 116, 192n12; and Yuan architecture, xvi, 11, 167, 169

Ming dynasty: Beijing in, 9, 169; repairs and restorations in, 87, 96, 102, 106, 120, 121, 148, 158

Mingshi (History of the Ming; Zhang Tingyu), 25–26, 105

Mingyingwang Hall (Shuishen Temple, Guangsheng Monastery), **29**, **31–32**, 188n11

modular units (*cai, fen, zhi*), xiii, xvi, 7–8, 11, 18, 27, 187n63; in Lower Yangzi, 53–54, 122, 130, 134; in non-timber-framed buildings, 160–161, 163; in regional comparisons, 62; in Upper Yangzi, 39–40, 73, 79, 80, 88, 108

Monastery of Golden Immortals (Jinxiansi; Pengxi, Sichuan), 191n1

Mongols, 65, 166, 169; and Japanese architecture, 184n10; and southbound migration, 190nn37–39; and Tibetan Buddhism, 157, 164–165. *See also* Yuan dynasty

Moni Hall (Longxing Monastery; Zhengding, Hebei), **4**, **23**, 24, 185n19

Mosque of the Companions (Shengyou Mosque; Quanzhou, Fujian), 162, 165

Mount Wudang (Hubei), 146–147

Mujing (Timberwork manual; Yu Hao), 4

municipal halls, 28, 31, **33**, 189n18

Nanjing, 9, 25, 169

Nanyang Palace (Zhenqing Palace; Mount Wudang, Hubei), 198n6

Nine Pythons Hall (Temple of the Eastern Peak; Emei, Sichuan), **75**, 192n12

Niuwang Temple (Linfen, Shanxi), 22, 31, **33**

non-timber-framed construction, 145, 146–166, **plate 4**; cave-temple style of, 163–164; and tombs, 146; types of, 163–166. *See also* metal construction; stone construction

Northern and Southern dynasties, 33

northern architecture, 27, 28–36, **plate 1**; architraves in, 15–17, 19, 21, 32, 33, 34; big-architrave style in, 28, 31, 32–34, **33**, 167; bracket sets in, 21–24, 30, **31**; comparisons to, 62–64; influence of, 69, 80–81, 90, 96, 99, 117; and Jin dynasty, 2, 8, 167; and Mongol invasions, 65; and Song architecture, 24, 25

Northern Song architecture, 18, 24, 25, 126, 156, 160, 185n7; influence of, 117, 167, 168; and Jin architecture, 8–9; and *Yingzao fashi*, 3–4

Northern Song dynasty, xiv, 2–3, 25, 147, 166, 168; and Jin dynasty, 64–65

oblique-arms (*xiegong*), **23**; in Jin architecture, 24, 65, 187n71; in Ming architecture, 23, 187n70; in non-timber-framed buildings, 150, 151; in northern architecture, 30, **31**; regional comparisons of, 63, 64; in Upper Yangzi, 44, 52, 80, **84**, 85, 92–95, **94**, 98, 101, 114, 117

official-style architecture (*guanshi jianzhu*), xiii, 10–11, 20, 21, 24–25, 186n45; vs. non-official, 11, 168–169, 187n70. See also *Yingzao fashi*

Ögedei Khan, 165, 200n27

pagodas, 146, 153, 156, 161, 162, 164–166, 199n19

paintings, 4, 67, 90–91, 188n4, 188n11

palatial style (*diangeshi*), 7, 12, 14, 173, 185n20, 186n27; in Lower Yangzi, 57, 134; in Upper Yangzi, 46, 48, 52, 73, **74**

Pan Guxi, xv, 9–10, 11, 16, 27, 69, 189n13

Pantuoshi Hall (Grand Temple, Mount Qiqu), 22, 39–42, 51, 105–109, 189n24, 195n57, **plate 2**; bracket sets in, **40**, **44–46**, 107–109, **108–109**, 189n25; and Lord Wenchang Hall, 105; plan of, 37,

38, 106, **107**; roof framing of, 47, 50, 108, **109**

Pingxiang Pavilion (Lushan, Sichuan), 69, 101–105, **102**, **104**, **plate 2**; bracket sets in, **39–42**, 44, **45**, 103–105, **103**; plan of, 37, **38**, **103**; and Qinglong Monastery, 102, 105; roof framing of, 50

plans, architectural, 2, 188n10; in Lower Yangzi, 53, **121**, 130, **131**, **136–137**, 141, **142**; in Ming and Yuan architecture, 13; in non-official architecture, 11; in non-timber-framed buildings, **148**, **154**, 158; in northern architecture, 29; regional comparisons of, 62; and social status, 190n35; in Song architecture, 4; in Upper Yangzi, 37–38, 70, 74, 76, **77**, **82**, **86–87**, **92**, **96**, 97, **103**, 106, **107**, 110, **113**

post-and-tie construction style (*chuandou*), 149, 159, 173

press-projection (*yatiao*), 30, **31**, 48, 63, 64, 181

purlins (*tuan*): buffalo-spine (*niujituan*), 177; lower (*xiapingtuan*), 44, 46, 79, 80, 83, **84**, **90**, 93, 108–111, 116, **122–123**, 127, **128–129**, 132, **144**, 145, 171, 179, 180; middle (*zhongpingtuan*), 79, 90, **95**, **100**, **123**, 128, **129**, 145, 179, 182; ridge (*jituan*), 8, 73, 79, 90, 95, 124, 129, 132, **139**, 145, 149, 158, 172, 175, 177; upper (*shangpingtuan*), 73, **100**, **123**, 124, 129, 178, 182

Qianlong, Emperor (Qing), 135

Qing architecture, xiv, 1, 10, 105, 106, 145, 192n12

Qing dynasty, 9; repairs and restorations in, 87, 96, 101, 113, 121, 158

Qinglong Monastery (Jishan, Shanxi), Middle Hall of, 22

Qinglong Monastery (Lushan, Sichuan), main hall of, 22, 69, 96–101, **97**, 193n23, 194n49, **plate 2**; bracket sets in,

38–42, **44–45**, 97, **98–99**, 101; and Lord Wenchang Hall, 94, 101; and Pingxiang Pavilion, 102, 105; plan of, 37, **38**, **96**; restorations of, 96, 194n43; roof framing of, **46**, 50, 51, **100**; and Yong'an Temple, 101; and Zhenqing Palace, 151

Qingmeng Daoist Temple (Gaoping, Shanxi), **31**

Qinzong, Emperor (Northern Song), 65

Qutan Monastery (Qinghai), 9

regional architecture, xiv, xvi, xvii, 21–22, 27–68; bracket sets in, 22–23, 27; vs. central authority, 28, 68; comparisons of, 62–65; influence of, 24–25, 167; pre-Yuan traditions of, 67–68, 168–169; and *Yingzao fashi*, 27–28, 62–64, 66. *See also* Lower Yangzi (Jiangnan) region; northern architecture; official-style architecture; Upper Yangzi region

Renshou Pagoda (Kaiyuan Monastery; Quanzhou, Fujian), 199n21

roof framing, 2, 167; column-and-beam style (*zhuliangshi*) of, xv, 7, 12, 46; and costs, 190n40; in Lower Yangzi, 57–61, **58–60**, 131–132, 140, 144–145; in Ming architecture, 11–12; in non-timber-framed buildings, 148–149, 152, 153, 158–160; in northern architecture, 28, 31–36; regional comparisons of, 62, 63–64; in Song architecture, 4, 7–8, 25; in Song-Ming architecture, 14–21; in Upper Yangzi, **46–52**, 73, 82–85, 89–90, 95, **97–100**, **108–111**, 114, 116

Ruitenbeek, Klaas, 10

SACH (Guojia wenwuju; State Administration of Cultural Heritage), 2, 102, 110, 111

Sage Mother Hall (Shengmudian, Jin Shrine; Taiyuan, Shanxi), **5**, 185n21, 192n19

Sanqing Hall (Qingmeng Daoist Temple; Gaoping, Shanxi), **31**

Sanqing Hall (Xuanmiao Daoist Temple; Suzhou, Jiangsu), 185n7

Sanqing Hall (Yongle Palace, Shanxi), 22

Sanqing Hall (Yuanmiao Daoist Temple; Putian, Fujian), 185n7

Sansheng Monastery, 22

Semu people, 165

Shangdang Gate (Changzhi, Shanxi), 16

Shangdu (Xanadu), xiv

Shanghai, xvi, 27, **plates 3, 4.** *See also* Zhenru Monastery

Shengji Hall (Confucius Temple; Qufu, Shandong), 10

Shengyou Mosque (Mosque of the Companions; Quanzhou, Fujian), 162, 165

Shentong Monastery (Shandong), 162, 199n19

Shenwumen (Spiritual and Martial Gate; Forbidden City, Beijing), 9

Shenzong, Emperor (Song), 3

Shi Kexin, 153

Shousheng Monastery (Xinjiang, Shanxi), 32, **33**, 36, 189n23

Shuishen Temple (Guangsheng Monastery; Hongdong, Shanxi), **29**, **31–32**, 188n5, 188n11

Shuzhong mingshengji (Records of places of interest in Sichuan; Cao Xuequan), 101

Sichuan, 2, 20, 27, 69, 188n2, **plates 1, 4**; architraves in, 19, 21; bracket sets in, 23, 88; earthquake in, xiii; Mongol invasions of, 66. *See also* Upper Yangzi region; *particular structures*

Sichuan Cultural Relics Administration (Sichuan wenwuju), 69

Smith, Paul, 66

social status, xiii, 7–8, 10, 11, 135, 159, 183n2, 186nn45–46, 190n35

Song architecture, xiv, xv, 2–9, 185n7; architraves in, 14–20, 21; bracket sets in, 14, 21–24, 25, 44; and Buddha halls, 6–7; columns in, 2, 5, 13, 20–21, 27, 60, 189n13; extant examples of, 2–3, 15; and Japanese architecture, 183n10; and Jin architecture, 8–9, 168; in Lower Yangzi, 24–25, 57, 60, 118, 167; and Ming architecture, 11, 12, 21–24, 34; in non-timber-framed buildings, 18, 156, 160, 161, 164; and northern architecture, 24, 25, 34, 64; revival of, 24–26; roof framing in, 4, 7–8, 14–21, 25, 32; in Upper Yangzi, 77, 80, 101, 109, 117, 126; and *Yingzao fashi*, 2–8; and Yuan architecture, xvi, 1, 65, 66–67, 167. *See also* Northern Song architecture; Northern Song dynasty; Southern Song dynasty

Song system (*Songzhi*), 25–26

Southern Song dynasty, 2, 5, 118, 168; conquest of, 25, 65, 66, 67, 157; ranking of monasteries in, 135, 159; repairs and restorations in, 87, 130, 153; and southbound migration, 190nn37–39; and *Yingzao fashi*, 4, 13

South Jixiang (Auspicious) Monastery (Linchuan, Shanxi), 24, 187n71

statues: Buddhist, 6–7, 53, 90–91, 96, 109, 122, 131, 136, 137, 153, 154, 161; Daoist, 70, 106, 148; of folk deities, 80, 82

Steinhardt, Nancy, xiii–xiv, xv

stone construction, xvi, **18**, 146, 150–166, 168; and stonemasons, 165–166

Stone Temple of Amitābha (Qingyuan Mountain; Quanzhou, Fujian), 161–163, **162**, 199n17, **plate 4**; history of, 161–162

Stone Temple of Auspicious Statue (Qingyuan Mountain; Quanzhou, Fujian), 199n17

Sui dynasty, 135

Suzhou fuzhi (Gazetteer of Suzhou prefecture), 134, 197n36

diversity in, xiv, xvii, 1, 25; religious diversity in, 164–166. *See also* Mongols

Yuanshi tianzun shuo beifang zhenwumiaojing (Sublime scripture of the Primeval Lord of Heaven explaining the Northern True Warrior), 147

Yunyan Monastery (Suzhou, Jiangsu), **plate 3**; history of, 134–136; pagodas at, 134, 156; reconstructions of, 135, 136, 197n36

Yunyan Monastery Second Gatehouse (Suzhou, Jiangsu), 53–61, **61**, 134–140, **137**, **140**; bracket sets in, **55–56**, 137–139, **138**; plan of, **54**, **137**; roof framing in, **58–59**, **139**; and Temple of Western Paradise, 153; and Tianning Monastery, 140; and Xuanyuan Palace, 138, 144, 145; and Yanfu Monastery, 124, 140

Zhang Shiqing, 118, 186n27, 186n45

Zhang Tingjie, 153

Zhang Tingyu, 25

Zhang Yiyou, 135

Zhang Yu, 153

Zhang Yuhuan, xv, 15, 16, 189n13, 189n23; on conventional style, **34–35**; on northern architecture, 28, 31, 32

Zhenguo Pagoda (Kaiyuan Monastery; Quanzhou, Fujian), **163**, 199n21

Zhenqing Palace (Mount Wudang, Hubei), **150–151**, 163, 164, 166, **plate 4**; and Baoshan Monastery, 157, 158, 160; and Qinglong Monastery, 151; and Zhenru Monastery, 152

Zhenru lizhi (Gazetteer of Zhenru), 130

Zhenru Monastery (Shanghai), main hall of, 13, 53, 118, 130–134, **131**, 145, 190n30, 196n15, **plate 3**; bracket sets in, 132, **133–134**; history of, 130; and Japanese architecture, 197n29; restorations of, 134; roof framing of, 57–61, **58**, **61**; and Tianning Monastery, 131; and Xuanyuan Palace, 142; and Yanfu Monastery, 131; and Zhenqing Palace, 152

Zhezong, Emperor (Song), 3

Zhihua Monastery (Bejing), 9

Zhongguo gudai jianzhushi (History of ancient Chinese architecture), 118

Zhongguo gujianzhu jishushi (History and development of ancient Chinese architectural technology), 118

Zhongguo Jiangnan Chanzong siyuan jianzhu (Architecture of Chan Buddhist monasteries in Jiangnan, China; Zhang Zhiqing), 118

Zhongguo Yingzao Xueshe (Society for Research in Chinese Architecture), 28, 118, 188n6

Zhou Chen, 135

Zhou dynasty, 10

Zhu Di (Ming emperor), 198n2

Zhu Qiqian, 166, 188n6

Zhu Xiaonan, 193n29

Zhu Yuanzhang (Ming emperor), 9, 26, 190n40

Zhuanyun Hall (Mount Wudang, Hubei), 148

Zhuge Liang, 194n45

Zixiao Palace (Mount Wudang, Hubei), main hall of, 9

ABOUT THE AUTHOR

Lala Zuo is assistant professor of Chinese at the United States Naval Academy. She has published a number of articles in both English and Chinese that reflect her interests in Chinese architecture, heritage preservation, and teaching Chinese architecture in North America.